CW00458042

Roy Greenslade was a Fleet Street editor and, for 28
years, worked as media commentator for *The Guardian*.
He is a former Professor of Journalism at City, University
of London. This is his fourth book. He divides his time
between Ireland (Donegal) and England (Brighton).

Other books by Roy Greenslade:
Goodbye to the Working Class (1976)
Maxwell's Fall (1992)
Press Gang (2003)

THE PEER, THE PRIESTS AND THE PRESS

A Story of the Demise of Irish Landlordism

Roy Greenslade

Beyond the Pale Books

First published November 2023

BTP Books Ltd
Teach Basil
2 Hannahstown Hill
Belfast BT17 0LT

www.beyondthepalebooks.com

978-1-914318-25-2 Pb

Printed by Walsh Colour Print
Castleisland, County Kerry

Front cover image taken by Derry photographer James Glass c. 1889. It
was one of 24 in an album of pictures commissioned by the defence team
of Fr McFadden and a few of his parishioners, on trial for the killing of
Detective Inspector Martin. This was the first occasion that photographic
evidence had ever been presented in an Irish court.
With permission of National Museums NI ©

The author and publishers have made all reasonable efforts to contact
copyright holders for permission. We apologise for any omissions or
errors in the credits given and will make any necessary corrections in any
future editions.

Table of Contents

Dedication

For Noreen, the Kelly boys and the Taylor girls

Preface

This began as a biography and developed into almost, but not quite, a double biography. The main subject, a 19th century Irish landlord, probably never met the secondary subject, an Irish journalist who played such an important walk-on role in his life. But they knew of each other once their otherwise parallel lives overlapped. Better to call it a collision because they were on either side of the deep fault lines that divided Irish society: religion, nationality, class. This is not, however, a simplistic story of an evil landlord and a crusading journalist. Their personal stories are replete with contradictions, as is the period in which they lived and died.

Consider first the portrait of Lord George Augusta Hill in his British cavalry uniform, a handsome head of dark wavy hair, side-whiskered, otherwise smooth of face. He stares blankly and obliquely out of the frame. Serious without being solemn, the faintest hint of a smile suggests he is holding his natural affability in check. Despite the shining breastplate, there is no sign of a military bearing. Instead, looking far younger in his portrait than his thirty years, the enduring image it presents is one of innocence.[1]

Fast forward a couple of decades and a celebrated writer drew a word picture of Lord George as a 'handsome, grave-smiling man of 50 or more; thick grizzled hair, elegant club nose, low cooing voice, military composure and absence of loquacity; a man you love at first sight'.[2] Move on further into old age and a young lad thought him 'a charming man and an Irish (sic) gentleman of the old school'.[3] Another admirer considered him to be 'a very pattern of gentleness and courtesy, short, white-haired and white-bearded'.[4] Perhaps the most perceptive comment of all came from someone who knew him only by reputation: 'He seems to have been

---

1 Portrait by Alfred Edward Chalon. A lithograph of the image was made by Richard James Lane (National Portrait Gallery ref D22025).
2 Carlyle (1882): 230.
3 Bayne (2016): 12.
4 Gwynn (1903): 142.

a most extraordinary character & a strong disciple of the 19th century school of Romanticists'.[5]

His forty-year record as an Irish landlord was lauded. Prime minister Robert Peel commended his works, calling him 'a public benefactor to his country'.[6] Other politicians acclaimed him for his reforming zeal, as did fellow landlords, and a host of travellers from abroad. Journalists queued up to write about the famous 'improving landlord' of Donegal. Not every journalist, however. Amid the deferential chorus of praise, a newspaper editor referred to Hill as 'a pretentious philanthrope ... a special blessing on two legs, sent by Providence for the comfort of the neglected Celts of the wilds of Donegal'.[7] He was not singing solo. Other detractors considered the 'wretched nobleman' far too ready to blow his own trumpet.[8] It sounded 'very hollow', remarked one.[9] A priest, one of many who took a similar line, contended that Lord George headed 'a syndicate of landlords ... to subjugate the people'.[10] That view has since found support among some modern historians. 'He was full of good intentions', wrote one commentator, but 'he bribed and bullied his tenants ... his arrogance was breathtaking'.[11]

This book is an attempt to discover the truth about Lord George. Who was he? And why, when he was so celebrated during his lifetime, was he virtually forgotten by the time of his death? Perhaps his fate was foretold by the artist. Take a second look at the picture. Here, surely, is a dreamer rather than a soldier. He lacks a warrior's belligerent manner. His face retreats inside the regimental livery. He does not appear cut out for the army, choosing only to wear its boots while seeking to discover a purpose to his life. As the fifth son of a marquess, he has no clear role. He must strike out and find one. As a member of the Protestant Ascendancy, his decision to become a landlord was both unsurprising and surprising. The former because he was following the path carved out by his ancestors. The latter because landlordism in Ireland was mired in controversy and there was no pressure on him to take such a fateful step.

Now consider a very different man: Denis Holland. Born a quarter of a century after Lord George, he was a journalist. There is no portrait.

---

5 Davis (2021a): 10 Brendan Bonar letter, Sept 1969.
6 Hansard, 27 April 1846, col 1128.
7 Holland (1858): 59.
8 Ó Gallchobhair (1962): 24.
9 Mac Cnáimhsi (1970): 187.
10 McFadden (1889): 14.
11 Percival (1995): 51, 53.

We must rely instead on a single description: 'about 5 foot 7 inches tall, with a rich brown beard, a high, unwrinkled forehead, a clear, bluish eye, an upright gait and the most perfect gentlemanly manner'.[12] We can add to that picture of him through his own words. Hundreds of thousands of them. Often passionate, sometimes contentious, always readable. A Catholic raised in Cork, he delivered his first polemics on behalf of the temperance movement, gradually giving way to an intense commitment to Irish nationalism. He learned his trade while working for publishers who shared neither his politics nor his religion. By the age of just twenty-four, he had proved to be such a reliable and capable reporter that he was trusted with an editor's chair.

But Holland did not want to work for others. He required the kind of press freedom only attainable by newspaper ownership. Neutrality was not for him. As proprietor-editor, he could pursue the journalism of attachment, journalism with an agenda, journalism that made a difference. He did not, however, believe journalism alone could solve every problem. For him, there were times when he considered that the pen, mighty as it sometimes was in his hands, was not mightier than the sword. He dared to defend the sword-bearers.

Holland was also to become Hill's nemesis. Both men believed they knew what would be of greatest benefit for the poorest people of 19th century Ireland. The noble lord put his faith in his own ability to transform Irish peasant society. The humble writer believed it was landlordism which denied people the chance to transform themselves. In 1857, their opposing cures for society's ills led to a clash that was, in microcosm, the struggle fought on a broader scale across the country for the future of every Irish man and woman. Hill vs Holland, landlord vs journalist, unionist vs nationalist, conservative vs radical, autocrat vs democrat, capitalist vs republican, Anglo-Irish Ascendancy vs indigenous middle class, Protestant vs Catholic, coloniser vs the colonised. Binary differences are entertaining, if shallow. We need context and detail to make sense of their stories.

I am connected in separate ways to these men's lives. In 1989, I came to live in Donegal, my wife's birthplace. When we bought our house in Ramelton, we had no idea it had been Lord George Hill's residence for the last thirty-five years of his life. Indeed, we had never

---

12 Clarke (1873).

heard of him, and it was several months before we discovered he had been owner of thousands of acres in nearby Gweedore. Although we were intrigued by the history, our attention at the time was much more on the present because of the ongoing conflict raging across the border. 'The Troubles', the euphemistic term for the confrontation between Britain and the nationalist people of Ireland's northern six counties, were all-consuming.

The more we learned about Lord George, the more fascinated we became. There was such a divergence of opinion about him. At one extreme, he was regarded as the kindest of landlords, a paragon. At the other, a devious manipulator, a wolf in sheep's clothing. What was not at issue was that he was the central figure in a parliamentary inquiry into the treatment, or mistreatment, of tenants by Donegal landlords. This controversy, which revolved around tenant rights, was one of the factors that culminated in the formation of the Irish National Land League, an organisation dedicated to the abolition of landlordism. The League 'reinforced the politicisation of rural Catholic nationalist Ireland' and helped to foster opposition to 'Englishness and – implicitly – Protestantism'.[13]

The rise of nationalism engendered the revolt within Ireland against British/English imperialism and resulted in the country's partition. Therefore, it is not fanciful to make a link between 'the Troubles' and Lord George. His life merits a closer study than it has had previously because it is easy to criticise landlordism by referring to the legion of absentee, rack-renting, profiteering landlords who evicted thousands of poverty-stricken people from their homes and refused to help their tenants during the Great Hunger. Far greater understanding of landlordism's deficiencies, and the reason for its eventual collapse, can be gleaned from choosing to focus on a man who was regarded as the very model of the breed.

There are only passing mentions of Lord George in Irish history books, although longer passages exist in a sprinkling of academic articles. Partial, often inaccurate, versions of his life and times can be found online. Little in our house, beyond his name on the deeds, was of much help. Research, however, proved wonderfully productive, not least when I came across Hill's most vituperative critic, Denis Holland. His trade, like mine, was journalism. However, very little of his journalistic output resembled my own. His advantage was to work in an era when profit had yet to become

---

13 Foster (1988): 415.

the major motive for publishing a newspaper. Even so, he was to discover that there is a price to pay for unbridled opinion.

Newspaper content in the mid-19th century has a resonance with what was published in the newspapers I worked for in the final decades of the following century in the sense that the choice of editorial material was anything but random. It was selected (or unselected) in order to make a point, to influence (or reinforce) the cultural, social, political and economic views of its readers. This is also a story about the growing power of the press.

Lord George's celebrity was not a matter of chance. In the special circumstances of the relationship between Britain and Ireland in the Victorian era, there was a reason for the prominence given to him in the newspapers of his time. It served the purposes of the overwhelming majority of proprietors and editors who supported the rule of an English-based political elite over an increasingly rebellious Irish population. Naturally, many Irish newspapers controlled by the Protestant Ascendancy, or in thrall to it, adopted a similar stance. Even the majority of the anti-English, anti-landlord, nationalist press tended to avoid attacking Lord George. Not so Denis Holland. He may have overstated his case. He may not have accurately forecast the future. But there cannot be any doubt that he, rather than Lord George, indicated the direction Ireland would eventually take.

Acknowledgements

I have several people to thank for their help and advice. Martin Davis, archivist of the Sandys family of Ombersley Court, Worcestershire, was extremely cooperative and unsparing in his attention to detail. Sophia Hillan, author of *May, Lou & Cass: Jane Austen's nieces in Ireland*, was hugely supportive, as was Professor Breandán Mac Suibhne, whose work and knowledge on 19th century Donegal is unsurpassed.

I must thank Cathal Póirtéir, author of *An Tiarna George Hill agus Pobal Ghaoth Dobhair* (published by Cló Iar-Chonnacht); Falcarragh-based historian and teacher, Dr Seosamh Ó Ceallaigh; two Gweedore-based historians, Mícheál Ó Domhnaill and Vincent Breslin; and former An Chúirt owner Patricia Doherty.

I also want to thank Lord George's great great granddaughter, Jean Chippindale, for providing the letter written by his youngest son; Barry Hillier of Holyhead for information on Denis Holland's son, Gerald; Mike Maguire of Limerick City and County Council; Patrick Maume, contributor to the Dictionary of Irish Biography; Niamh Brennan, the Donegal County Council archivist; and the staffs of the National Library of Ireland, PRONI, the British Library, the London Library and Letterkenny Library, especially Gavin Burke.

Much praise to Karen Ievers for discovering Lord George's album of photographs, and thanks to Donegal County Council for permission to use them. Thank you too to Clare McCahill for photographing the portrait of Lord George in the hallway of Ballyarr.

Finally, I want to record my heartfelt thanks to my wife, Noreen, for her practical help in terms of research; for her emotional support during moments of discouragement; and for her love, which sustained me over the years it took to bring the book to fruition. It was, after all, her Donegal ancestors, in Falcarragh and Carrigart, who faced the reality of landlordism.

Dramatis Personae

The Hill family

Lord George Augusta Hill (1801-1879), fifth son of the 2nd Marquess of Downshire, godson of King George III, soldier, MP and, from 1836, owner of 23,000 acres in Donegal.

Arthur Hill, 2nd Marquess of Downshire (1753-1801), father of Lord George, owner of more than 70,000 acres in County Down, centred on Hillsborough Castle, with further land holdings in Counties Wicklow and Offaly, plus property in England, including Hertford Castle.

Dowager Marchioness of Downshire, the former Mary Sandys (1764-1836) and, from 1802, 1st Baroness Sandys. Lord George's mother. Close friend of the Prince Regent before he became George IV. Wealthy in her own right as inheritor of large estates in Worcestershire and Berkshire.

Arthur Blundell Sandys Trumbull Hill, 3rd Marquess of Downshire, (1788-1845), Lord George's eldest brother.

Lieutenant-General Arthur Moyses William Hill (1792-1860). From 1936, 2nd Baron Sandys. Lord George's brother, known as Atty. Career soldier.

Lord Arthur Marcus Cecil Hill (1793-1863). From 1860, 3rd Baron Sandys. Lord George's brother, known as Marcus. Diplomat and politician.

Lord Arthur Augustus Edwin Hill (1800-31), Lord George's sickly brother and close companion until his early death.

Ladies Charlotte Hill (1794-1821) and Mary Hill (1796-1830), Lord George's beloved sisters, ladies-in-waiting to their mother.

The Austen-Knights

Cassandra Jane Knight (1806–1842), first wife of Lord George. Youngest daughter of Edward Knight, brother of the novelist Jane Austen.

Louisa Knight (1804–1889), Cassandra Jane's sister and god-daughter of Jane Austen. Second wife of Lord George.

Fanny Austen Knight (1793-1882), from 1820, Lady Knatchbull. Eldest sister of Cassandra Jane and Louisa. Said to be Jane Austen's favourite niece.

Marianne Knight (1801-96), older sister of Cassandra Jane and Louisa. Companion to Louisa after Lord George's death and buried beside her.

Lord George's children

Norah Mary Elizabeth Hill (1835-1920), married Captain Somerset Richard Hamilton Augusta Ward, son of Viscount Bangor.

Captain Arthur Blundell George Sandys Hill (1837-1923), soldier, inheritor of his father's Gweedore and Ballyarr estates.

Augustus Charles Edward Hill (1839-1908), civil servant, investor.

Cassandra Jane Louisa Hill (1842-1901), friend of Charlotte Grace O'Brien, daughter of the Young Irelander, William Smith O'Brien.

George Marcus Wandsbeck Hill (1849-1911), unmarried, lawyer.

Lord George's associates

James Dombrain (1794-1871), British naval officer, founder of the Irish coastguard service, Donegal land-owner, philanthropist, introduced Lord George to Donegal.

John Pitt Kennedy (1796-1879), agricultural reformer.

Francis Forster (1799-1858), Hill's land agent and owner of an estate in Burtonport.

Visitors to Lord George's hotel

Thomas Carlyle (1795-1881), British historian and philosopher.

William Allingham (1824-89), poet and diarist born in Ballyshannon, County Donegal.

John Mitchel (1815-75), Irish nationalist, Young Irelander, sentenced to transportation.

The Donegal landlords

Wybrants Olphert (1811-92), owner of 18,133 acres centred on Falcarragh.

John Obins Woodhouse (1804-69), owner of around 1,000 acres in Donegal plus several islands. Estate adjacent to Hill's holding.

William Sydney Clements (1806-1878), 3rd Earl of Leitrim, owner of estates in counties Donegal, Leitrim, Galway and Kildare.

Francis Conyngham (1797-1876), 2nd Marquess Conyngham, owner of 122,300 acres adjacent to Hill's estate, plus extensive holdings in counties Clare and Meath, plus land in England.

Rev Alexander Nixon (1804-82), owner of 3,212 acres near Falcarragh, victim of attempted assassination.

John George Adair (1823-85), owner of 11,600 acres in Donegal, responsible for a mass eviction at Derryveagh.

The journalists

Denis Holland (1826-72), born and raised in Cork, journalist, orator, editor *The Ulsterman*, *The Irishman*.

John Francis Maguire (1815-72), founder of *The Cork Examiner*, employer of Holland, member of Commons inquiry into Gweedore disturbances.

James MacKnight (1801-76), editor *Londonderry Standard*, tenant right campaigner.

Francis Dalzell Finlay (1793-1857), founder of the *Northern Whig*, employer of Holland.

Alexander M. Sullivan (1829-84), Irish nationalist, editor of *The Nation*, Holland's opponent.

James Williams (dates unknown), influential reporter for the *Dublin Evening Post*.

Robert Arthur Wilson (c.1820-75), editor *Belfast Morning News*. Born in Falcarragh.

Holland's political associates

William Sharman Crawford (1780-1861), radical Protestant landlord and Liberal MP, campaigner for tenant right.

Charles Russell (1832-1900), later Baron Russell of Killowen, Lord Chief Justice of England.

Thomas Neilson Underwood (1830-76), tenant right campaigner, co-founder of the National Brotherhood of St Patrick.

The priests

John Doherty (1819-1881), parish priest of Gweedore until transferred to Carrigart. Hill regarded him as 'obnoxious'.

James McFadden (1842-1917), parish priest of Gweedore, arrested after the murder of a police officer.

LAND CONFLICT IN IRELAND

1641	Irish rebellion, a Catholic uprising against British rule, also directed at Protestant English and Scottish settlers. At the time, some 60 per cent of land in Ireland is owned by Catholics.
1649-53	Oliver Cromwell, in setting the seal on Britain's colonisation of Ireland, confiscates vast swathes of land and hands it to his Protestant supporters.
1689-90	British Protestant king William III defeats deposed British Catholic king James II in an Irish war. More land is confiscated from Catholics.
1780	By this date, it is estimated that 5,000 Protestant landlords (the Anglo-Irish) own more than 95 per cent of all of Ireland's productive land.
1838	Lord George Hill begins to acquire land in Gweedore.
1843-5	Devon Commission. Inquiry into land occupation finds that tenant leases are unfairly weighted in favour of landowners. Nevertheless, the report underpins landlord property rights by rejecting tenants' demands for the 3Fs: fair rent, fixity of tenure, free sale.
1847	Tenant Right League formed in Ulster to check the power of landlords and advance the rights of tenant farmers. Movement gathered pace during the Great Famine (1845-49) and especially afterwards.
1849	Encumbered Estates Court facilitates sale of estates by landlords who had become indebted due to the famine, but does not recognise tenant rights. Superseded in 1858 by the Landed Estates Court, which enables sale of more than 10,000 estates by 1880.
1856	Lord George Hill's tenants oppose his introduction of sheep-farming on his Gweedore estate and complain about raised rents.
1858	House of Commons inquiry into claims of destitution among tenants in Donegal.
1870	Estimated that 50 per cent of Irish land is now owned by just 750 families while only 3 per cent of Irish farmers own their own land. Landlord and Tenant (Ireland) Act strengthens tenant's rights for the first time.
1879	Lord George dies. His son, Captain Arthur Hill, inherits his Donegal estate.
1879-81	Land League, led by Charles Stewart Parnell and Michael Davitt, unites reformist and revolutionary wings of tenant rights movements. Its central aim is to secure Irish land for Irish people.
1881	The Land Law (Ireland) Act was regarded as a victory for the Land League. From it stemmed the Irish Land Commission, which established and fixed fair rents through the Land Court. Over the course of a century the commission was the body responsible for redistributing farmland.
1884	Hill's Gweedore tenants apply for rent reductions, successfully, to the Land Court.

A TIMELINE

1885	Ashbourne Land Act allows tenants to borrow the full amount of the purchase price for their holdings, to be repaid at 4 per cent over 49 years. Up to 1888, some 25,400 tenants, many in Ulster, take advantage of the law.
1886-91	Plan of Campaign. After the suppression of the Land League, Parnell had founded the Irish National League in 1882. Its most successful initiative was the Plan, which involved tenants withholding rent from landlords unwilling to accept reduced rents. Recalcitrant landlords were often boycotted; some were subject to intimidation.
1887	The Coercion Act. In response to the Plan, the government enacted the Criminal Law and Procedure (Ireland) Act in order to prevent boycotting, intimidation, unlawful assembly and supposed conspiracies over the non-payment of rents. Similar acts followed, leading to the imprisonment of hundreds of politicians and activists.
1888	Land Law (Ireland) Act provides a larger pot of money to enable more acquisitions but is unpopular with tenants because of its complicated legal clauses.
1891	Congested District Board created to assist poverty-stricken areas in the west of Ireland. Given the power to purchase and resell land, its main aim is to convert uneconomic holdings (usually held in rundale) into viable economic units.
1892	The Land Registry is established to record property transactions and registers of legal title.
1894	Hill places the Gweedore estates in the hands of the court, effectively ending his ownership.
1896	An amended Land Law (Ireland) Act increases the amount available for purchase and removes clauses which had made the original Act unattractive. Land Courts empowered to sell 1,500 bankrupt estates to tenants. A total of 47,000 holdings are bought between 1891 and 1896.
1898	Landlords finally lose control of local authorities. Under the Local Government (Ireland) Act, people are allowed to vote for their political representatives.
1903	Land Purchase Act, the result of a conference the year before under the auspices of the Chief Secretary for Ireland, George Wyndham. It introduces a much more attractive scheme to enable tenants to purchase land in which the government agreed to pay the difference between the price offered by tenants and that demanded by landlords. Many millions of acres are acquired by tenants.
1909	A second Land Purchase Act allows for the Land Commission to compulsorily purchase land from owners on behalf of tenants.

AUSTEN KNIGHT FAMILY

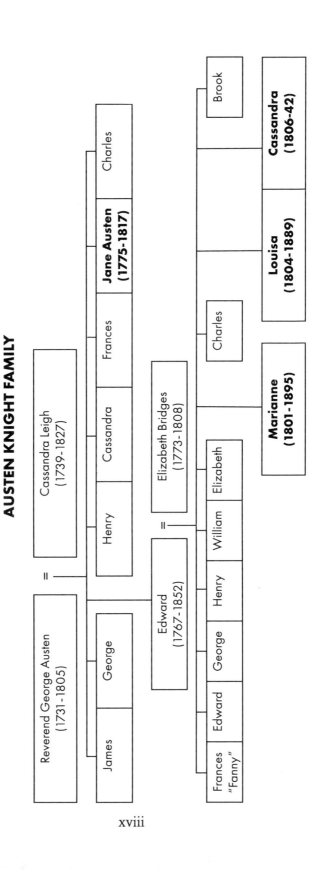

HILL FAMILY

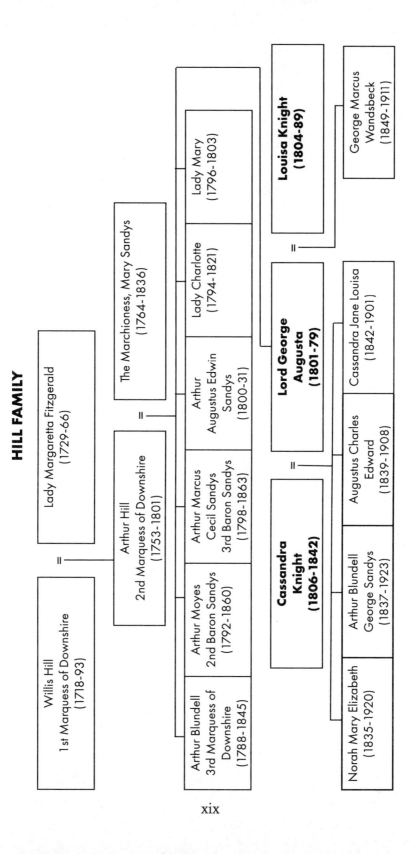

1

BY GOD AND BY SWORD

*The moment the very name of Ireland is mentioned, the English seem to bid
adieu to common feeling, common prudence, and to common sense, and to
act with the barbarity of tyrants, and the fatuity of idiots* – Sydney Smith[1]

For almost twenty years, Lord George Augusta Hill, godson to a British
king and a British princess, was widely regarded as one of Ireland's most
compassionate landlords. The fifth son of a marquess and one of England's
richest women, former soldier, former Dublin Castle minion, former darling
of high society balls, was feted in newspapers, praised in parliament and
admired across the world for the way he ran his estates. Soon after his 1838
purchase of land in west Donegal, he was being celebrated as a visionary
agricultural reformer. Unlike so many Irish landlords, known for their gross
mistreatment of tenants, he enjoyed a reputation for tolerance.

Reputation, however, was not necessarily matched by reality. By
December 1857, Lord George was struggling to maintain his image
as a kindly landlord. He was under attack from a group of priests who
believed him guilty of misrepresenting the conditions under which their
parishioners existed. In a world where his class controlled the majority
of the mainstream press, he could well have survived the onslaught. But,
just as he was celebrating his fifty-sixth birthday, a journalist arrived
in Donegal to investigate whether there was any truth to the priestly
complaints about the parlous state of Lord George's tenantry. Denis
Holland, thirty-one-year-old proprietor and editor of a Belfast newspaper,
was building a reputation of his own as a champion of Ulster's tenantry.
He was not in the least inhibited by the noble lord's fame and status.

These two men had reached this point of conflict from very different routes.
Given the twenty-five year difference in their ages, we must wait to explore

---

1 *Two Letters on the Subject of Catholics*, Letter II: 23 (London: J Budd, 1807).

1

Holland's background. First then, let's meet Lord George Hill. Born in England to a family whose wealth and titles derived from large land-holdings in Ireland, he was therefore a member of a fraction of the British elite known as both the Anglo-Irish and the Protestant Ascendancy. Most of this minority had secured their estates during Britain's centuries-long colonisation of its neighbouring island. At the time of Hill's birth, Ireland had just become a constituent part of a concocted new confederacy known as the United Kingdom. His family may have affected to call themselves Irish, but they were as English as any of their landed counterparts in Worcestershire, Berkshire or Devon, the county from which the founder of their dynasty sprang.

He was Moyses Hill, a soldier – in prosaic modern parlance, a chancer – who arrived in Ireland during Elizabeth I's reign to join military campaigns against the Gaelic chieftains, Hugh O'Neill and Hugh O'Donnell. His reward in 1592 was a regal grant of land near Larne, County Antrim. How odd then that an historian should observe that, unlike most of the 18th century aristocracy, 'the wealth of the Hill family was not founded on confiscation'.[2] This fiction conveniently overlooks the fact that it was conquest which enabled an English queen to make him a gift of land in another country. Elizabeth's successor, James I, a Scottish-cum-English king, then granted Moyses additional Irish land, in Carrickfergus. But he wanted still more. The soldier of fortune pressured a rebellious Gaelic nobleman, Con O'Neill, into selling him land in County Down which stretched from the Ards peninsula to modern-day Lisburn.[3] By the time of his death in 1630, Sir Moyses owned a substantial swathe of land in the province of Ulster, some 2,000 acres in Antrim and 40,000 acres in Down.

There is no need to detain ourselves with the details of a 200-year story of successive descendants of Moyses progressively enlarging their estates through land speculation, political opportunism, consanguineous marriage and slices of good luck except to note that, running in parallel with their acquisition of land, was their rising social status. Rung by rung up the aristocratic ladder, through knighthood, viscountcy and earldom, picking up both Irish and British titles, the Hill family reached the apex in 1789 with a marquisate, just one rank below a dukedom.

This was the singular achievement of Lord George's grandfather, Wills Hill, who was by far the most politically engaged, and upwardly mobile, member

---

2 Green (1949): 1.

3 Cregan (1963); Greer (2019). O'Neill signed over most of his lands after two Scots, Hugh Montgomery and James Hamilton, helped him escape from Castlereagh Castle.

of the dynasty. Despite securing ministerial office in four governments, he was not highly regarded. A Whig colleague, Horace Walpole, thought him 'a tragic scaramouche' (a clown), 'arbitrary, ignorant, and inconsiderate', and possessing 'more pomp than solidity'.[4] The king was none too complimentary about his faithful servant, observing that he 'did not know a man of less judgement'. No matter. Wills kept his eye on the prize and the king elevated him.[5]

As Marquess of Downshire, he chose a motto for his coat of arms that overtly referred to the Elizabethan conquest which had enabled his ancestor, Moyses, to seize his chance: *Per Deum Et Ferrum Obtinui* [By God and By Sword I have obtained]. He was acknowledging that his family's wealth and position had derived from the combination of his Protestant form of worship and force of arms. This was the reality that the English state, through propaganda, the passage of time and the exercise of political and military power, sought to gloss over.

It was never entirely concealed. Despite internal Protestant tensions between Episcopalians and Presbyterians – and notable exceptions, such as the United Irishmen insurrection at the end of the 18th century – the descendants of the people planted from Scotland and England under James I largely accepted the primacy of the landowning English aristocracy. By contrast, those descended from the dispossessed, native, Catholic Irish, were always aware that their lands had been misappropriated. They understood they had been colonised. And they remained suspicious of, and occasionally hostile to, the colonial elite of the ascendancy.

Among that class there was a persistent struggle to gain more land and to secure greater political advantage at Westminster. One of the biggest clashes, which had a direct influence on Lord George's prospects, was between Wills Hill and Robert Stewart, owner of land in Down, as well as Derry and Donegal. In the 1790 general election, twenty-one-year-old Robert Stewart (later Lord Castlereagh) stood for one of the two County Down seats controlled by Wills, whose son, Arthur, was also a candidate. The Stewarts were so determined to win that they invested the extraordinary sum of £60,000 to secure the votes of freeholders. In order to defend his interests, Wills spent a reputed £30,000.

The contest was bitterly fought. At one point, Stewart accused Arthur of being 'an absentee, a whoremaster, a pimp and an adulterer'.[6] Six

4 Steuart (1910): 34, 126, 169.
5 ODNB; Maguire (1972): 6; Pares (1953): 171n. Wills was regarded as a 'conspicuously successful courtier' and 'the most convinced "King's Friend"'.
6 Hyde (1933): 56.

months after the poll, which saw both Stewart and Arthur returned as MPs, the Marquess suffered a stroke, eventually dying, aged 75, in 1793. His legacy was the refurbished and magnificent Hillsborough Castle and a mountain of debt, totalling £69,600.[7] It would appear that some of Wills's clownish characteristics were inherited by Arthur once he became the second Marquess of Downshire.

As was common among the ascendancy, Arthur was educated in England and spent most of his time there, enjoying a cosseted life. He secured a parliamentary seat, as a Tory, for a rotten borough in Cornwall and, from 1776, represented Down until inheriting his title. Along the way, he picked up several civil and military appointments in England and Ireland: lieutenant-colonel of the Hertfordshire Militia; colonel of the Downshire Militia; governor of County Down and later the county's High Sheriff. He was also appointed to the Privy Council of Ireland and, in 1786, was given the plum sinecure position of register of the court of chancery, worth more than £1,500 a year.

Regarded as brave for having risked his life to save prisoners from a jail in Downpatrick during a fire, he was credited some years later with running spies in an intelligence operation to thwart the United Irishmen.[8] This, despite his first cousin, Lord Edward FitzGerald, son of the Duke of Leinster, being a United Irish leader.[9] Arguably, Arthur's most dazzling feat was his choice of bride. He made what was regarded as 'a brilliant marriage' to Mary Sandys, a wealthy heiress who brought with her both English and Irish estates inherited from a great-aunt.[10] In Ireland, there was Edenderry in King's County (now Offaly), with 14,000 acres, and Dundrum in County Down with 5,000 acres. The main English property, 'the jewel' of her inheritance, was Easthampstead Park in Berkshire, perfectly situated for 'access to parliament in London and royalty at Windsor'.[11] In addition, she brought funds: '£60,000 in ready money and £3,000 a year'.[12]

Arthur's father thought twenty-one-year-old Mary 'a genteel, agreeable little girl, not a beauty but as nearly being so as a wise man would choose his wife to be, of a cheerful, sweet disposition', adding cannily: 'Her fortune is

---

7 Approximately £10.3 million today.

8 Davis (2020b): 34; McCall (1881) 54-5; NAI, Rebellion Papers: 620/28/295.

9 Tillyard (1997), Woods (2011).

10 She was Mary Bertie, Duchess of Ancaster and Kesteven, Mistress of the Robes to Queen Charlotte, wife of George III.

11 Malcomson (1982): 105.

12 Ibid. 134. £3,000 would be approximately £270,000 today.

more than he wants or wished for, though it will do him no harm'.[13] Mary's cash enabled Arthur to purchase control of more constituencies in the Irish parliament, giving him command of nine seats. Although described as 'the most powerful political magnate in late 18th century Ireland', his record suggests otherwise.[14] He spoke only twice at Westminster, and his attempt to exercise his so-called power to oppose the 1801 Act of Union met with a spectacular lack of success. Winning few allies to his cause, he enraged a host of political colleagues and the king. Aware his opposition would be costly, he told his wife: 'I expect all the virulence that can be used against me'.[15] He expected correctly. He was stripped of every honour and effectively ostracised from society.[16] Arthur's desire to maintain a separation between Ireland and England indicates the dichotomy of being Anglo-Irish. Without wishing to overstate the effect of this duality, it rendered him and his ascendancy peers as neither quite English enough to be acceptable to the aristocracy in England nor Irish enough to be embraced by the native Irish.[17]

The Act of Union abolished the Irish parliament, which meant the loss of seven seats controlled by Downshire. Although the government paid £52,500 in compensation, it made little difference to his mountain of debt and did nothing to assuage his loss of status. 'The indignities he had suffered pressed heavily on him and rapidly undermined a naturally robust constitution', observed one historian.[18] This euphemism for what appears to have been a mental breakdown culminated in Arthur's death – probably by his own hand – aged 48, on 7 September 1801. The family chose to ascribe his death to 'a severe attack of the gout in the stomach'.[19]

Arthur's death occurred when Mary was six months' pregnant with the couple's seventh child. She had previously given birth to four sons, all confusingly named Arthur, and two daughters. Her new baby boy was born on 9 December at Mary's favourite English house, in Roehampton. He escaped the Arthur moniker because the widowed marchioness shrewdly took advantage of her royal connections to choose his name. Her father had been equerry to George III's uncle, which meant she grew up as part of the extended royal circle. A near

13 Ibid. 134; Davis (2020b): 30.
14 Malcomson (1981) :102.
15 Ibid.
16 Ibid. 106.
17 Ibid. 118.
18 McCall, op. cit. 59.
19 *Morning Post*, 15 Sept 1801.

contemporary of the king's eldest son (later, the Prince Regent), they were childhood playmates.

After her husband's death, the king showed compassion for what were euphemistically described as Mary's 'severe domestic troubles'.[20] So, the king and his daughter, Princess Augusta, stood as godparents to her newly-born son, presenting him with a gift of a large silver-gilt inkstand, with royal arms and inscription.[21] The now dowager marchioness acknowledged the honour by giving him their names: George Augusta.[22] Within a couple of months, the king also granted the marchioness a title in her own right, making her Baroness Sandys of Ombersley, and adding a special 'remainder' which ensured that her younger sons and their successors would inherit the title and thus perpetuate her name. It meant that in 1806, on the death of her late uncle's widow, Mary became the owner of the magnificent Ombersley Court in Worcestershire and its surrounding 5,000-acre estate. From this point on, she signed herself as Mary Downshire Sandys and was known within the family by the acronym MDS.

For the next thirty-five years, the 'genteel, agreeable' Mary Sandys with 'a cheerful, sweet disposition' became the dominating, sometimes domineering, force in the fortunes of the family she had married into. Although she was chatelaine of Hillsborough, she spent most of her time in England, as courtier to the Prince of Wales and confidante to his 'wife', Mrs Maria Fitzherbert.[23] An influential Whig hostess, with houses in Mayfair and Roehampton, the marchioness took care to groom her children in the ways and manners of the court. Her most pressing problem was money.[24] Even so, she spent lavishly in order to pursue her political battle with the Stewarts, whom she blamed for the death of her husband. At the 1805 Westminster election, she funded a candidate in Down with the express purpose of unseating Lord Castlereagh.[25]

Ahead of the poll, she travelled to Hillsborough, accompanied by her eldest son, Arthur, the 16-year-old third Marquess of Downshire. Her arrival was hymned in poetry.[26] She toured the county, visiting farmhouses

---

20 *Morning Post*, 26 Dec 1801.

21 Davis (2021a): 19.

22 Inevitably, Augusta was regularly and wrongly changed to Augustus.

23 It was a morganatic marriage. Although legally valid, it debarred her from acceding to the prince's rank. Mrs Fitzherbert was unacceptable to the Crown on three counts: she was a divorcée; she was of lesser rank; and she was a Roman Catholic.

24 Maguire (1972): 91.

25 Creevey (2018): 43, 62-3.

26 John Stewart, Genevieve, of the spirit of the Drave, London: 1810.

and beseeching wives to encourage their husbands to vote for her man.[27] She succeeded so well that Castlereagh stepped aside when his defeat became inevitable, grumbling about the 'defective' poll register and the Downshire family's 'undue influence'.[28]

While young Arthur was studying at Eton and Oxford, Mary assumed total control of the family's business, overseeing the management of the estates. 'The little marchioness', as the petite lady was condescendingly (perhaps admiringly) known, gained popularity for acts of charity towards her tenants. In 1804, she also illustrated a liberal attitude towards those of a different faith by granting land, and donating £50, for the building of a Roman Catholic chapel. She was constant in her commitment to Catholic emancipation.

The dowager marchioness watched carefully, sometimes intrusively, over the progress of her children as they moved into adult life. Lord Arthur Moyses – known to family and friends as Atty – chose an army career; Lord (Arthur) Marcus preferred diplomacy and politics; Lord (Arthur) Augustus was bound for the church, although ill-health prevented it; her two daughters, Charlotte and Mary, became her *de facto* ladies-in-waiting; and then there was Lord George. After his birth, the marchioness received an optimistic, morale-boosting letter from a friend, Lady Elizabeth Palk: 'I think he will do well for a thousand reasons ... I think your very great personal watchfulness ... is the principal thing under Heaven that will contribute to his Preservation & besides that I always consider Children who come into the World under his peculiar Circumstances as more especially protected by Divine Providence'.[29]

Known by the family in infancy as Jennah and then as Georgy, Hill was doted on by his sisters, who were seven and nine when he was born. They recorded his progress in jointly-written journals that provide a revealing glimpse of a rarified aristocratic world of ease and elegance, a seemingly endless round of balls at grand houses, card parties, concerts, long lunches, visits to the opera, and regular travels, both abroad and within Britain, especially to Brighton where the Prince Regent held court.[30] Mary, although at the epicentre of the elite of elites, did not overlook her maternal obligations.

She had her youngest son schooled at home in his early years, either in London – at the family's elegant house in Hanover Square, Mayfair – or in her favoured residence, a mansion in Roehampton that became known

---

27 ODNB.
28 *Morning Chronicle*, 17 Aug 1805; *London Courier & Evening Gazette*, 17 Aug 1805.
29 Davis (2020b): 100.
30 Ibid.

as Downshire House. George had lessons in German, singing, dancing, plus the playing of piano, guitar, flute and harp.[31] At twelve, he joined his older brothers, Marcus and Augustus, in Eversholt, Bedfordshire, some 40 miles outside London, to be taught by the Rev. James Reed. Evidently, he liked his time there 'very much'.[32]

Georgy, as was entirely natural, was inculcated with the norms of aristocratic society, and was sealed off from London's teeming population, having no contact – aside from domestic servants – with the overwhelming majority of the inhabitants, whether they be workers, paupers, vagrants or the emerging business class. During the Regency period, the contrast between 'so much wealth and so much poverty' surprised the American ambassador.[33] Despite the 'violent state convulsion'[34] wrought by the industrial revolution and the advent of a monied *nouveau riche* there remained a strict division between classes.

In what was regarded as 'an aristocratic age', the landowning classes were largely untouched by the new spirit of commerce.[35] The privileges they had enjoyed for so long appeared, at least to them, to be eternal. They also controlled the country's politics, dominating both houses of parliament. The House of Commons was not at all common with 500 seats controlled by either the nobility or gentry.[36] The majority held fast to a belief, espoused during the Commons debates on the protective corn laws, that agriculture was the basis of national prosperity. A modern reader of parliamentary reports in the early 1800s would find it difficult to distinguish the difference between Whigs and Tories.

Unsurprisingly, young Hill's friends were drawn entirely from within his own milieu – his sisters sent him 'to see his friend Caulfeild' (James, eldest son of the Earl and Countess of Charlemont)[37] and sometimes he went 'to Bingham' (the future third Earl of Lucan).[38] His regular journeys

---

31 His main tutor was Samuel Christopher Bettans, possibly of Swiss origin. He later married Mary Fernan, Queen Victoria's dressmaker.
32 Davis, Goseys, Vol 2: 10. Reed, a former master at Eton and one of the king's chaplains, had been given the position as rector of Eversholt in 1809 by the marchioness, it being in the Downshire family's gift. (*St James's Chronicle*, 14 November 1809). Reed was to remain close to the Hill boys, bequeathing them money on his death.
33 Richard Rush, cited by Mortimer (2020): 88.
34 Southey (1807): 73.
35 Pares (1953): 35.
36 Cf. Croker (1967): 370-1.
37 Davis, Goseys Vol 1: 12.
38 Ibid. Vol 1: 4.

between Mayfair and Roehampton were made in the comfort of the family's barouche, a large carriage drawn by two horses that separated him from *hoi polloi*. When attending his mother's parties, Hill endeared himself to the titled guests and was encouraged to do so. During one At Home in Hanover Square, twelve-year-old 'Georgy's waltzing was universally admired'.[39] He liked to perform. After dinner one evening, his sisters urged him to 'sing his droll songs to Lord Hutchinson [later, second Earl of Donoughmore]'.[40] Royalty did not disconcert him. He was regarded as something of a character, a child who was not overlooked. The Duke of Gloucester, the king's nephew, made a point of asking after him.[41] Less welcome was a visitor with a request to take Georgy to a fireworks party. The marchioness refused even to see the caller, Lady Caroline Lamb, who was fresh from being spurned by Lord Byron. The marchioness remarked that Lady Caroline should be shut up and she herself would deserve to be shut up should she have entrusted her with her son.[42]

George, like Marcus and Augustus, was encouraged to ride from an early age. By the time he was fifteen, his skills impressed his eldest brother who observed that 'George will make a hard rider'.[43] Like Mary and Charlotte, he also developed a passion for music.[44] During his time at Eversholt, there were two pointers toward his later life. He showed a liking for country living and demonstrated a flair for trade. He made 5 shillings in profit by selling two pigs for 27 shillings, and 'with the money bought another pig which he is fattening and intends to sell to the butcher'. His sisters remarked admiringly: '*Il fait très bien ses affaires*' [He does his business very well]. But young Hill was no pushover. When Lord Ossory suggested his bailiff might give him an order for peas if he was prepared to collect them by riding his donkey from Eversholt to Ossory's family seat in Ampthill, a distance of some four miles, he refused. 'Georgy says he does not think it is worth his while to go so far for so little', noted his sisters, adding: 'Georgy is an universal favourite making himself useful as well as agreeable'.[45]

His farming enterprise aside, it is unclear whether his academic studies with the Rev. Reed went well. Like two of his older brothers, he did

39 Davis (2020b): 9.
40 Davis, Goseys, Vol 4: 38.
41 Ibid. 35.
42 Davis (2020b): 15.
43 Davis (2021a): 3.
44 Davis (2020a): 32.
45 Davis (2020b): 101. John Fitzpatrick, second Earl of Upper Ossory.

not go on to university. As the fifth son of a marquess, there was no definite role for Lord George. Primogeniture's iron rule is that only the first-born son gets to inherit, so the younger sons and daughters of landowners, regardless of their titles, must remain landless and, if not exactly penniless, then anything but wealthy. It meant that, for a nobleman like Hill, his rank gave him three career choices: politics, the church, or the armed forces. Like brother Atty, he chose the last.

Ahead of joining up, a month before his seventeenth birthday, in 1818, Hill set off on a European tour with his brother, Augustus, who was sixteen months' older than him and perpetually ill, requiring continual medical care. They spent time in France, Belgium, Holland and Germany. Their mother obliged them to study mathematics, Latin and German, along with several artistic pursuits. Hill's daily regime involved three hour-long classes every morning, beginning with dancing, followed by drawing and fencing. In the afternoon, after two hours of German, he spent an hour learning the flute.[46] In the late summer, they were joined by their mother and sisters, who arrived at Spa in Belgium to take the waters.[47] The following month, the family travelled together to Paris,[48] where the Dowager, who was on good terms with Louis XVIII, introduced her children to the French court. While there, they met Louis's brother, Charles, the future king.

Although Hill's major role was to act as companion to the sickly Augustus, it did not stop him from enjoying a social life, evidently 'becoming the life and soul of every party'.[49] Among his dancing partners were the Ladies Harriet and Emily Trench, daughters of the second Earl of Clancarty, owner of a vast Irish estate in east Galway and Roscommon.[50] He told of dancing '6 quadrilles & 7 waltzes' and reported that Lady Emily sent '2 great bits of gingerbread this morning'. He was aware that this news would be welcomed by his sisters who loved dancing and gossip in equal measure. By contrast, he knew to calm the concerns of their earnest eldest brother, the third Marquess of Downshire, who worried about his younger siblings' safety. So Hill, when setting out on a journey from Brussels, urged

---

46 Davis (2021a): 3. PRONI, Downshire Papers, D/3880 'Continental disbursements on account of Lords Augustus and George Hill', 21 Nov 1818-10 Dec 1819.
47 Davis (2020b): 92.
48 *Saunders's News-Letter*, 2 Sept 1818.
49 Davis (2021a): 3.
50 Casey (2015). Some 50 years later, George's son, Arthur, married their cousin, Helen. See chapter 13.

his sisters to pass on a message: 'Tell D, I take my pistols with me'.[51]

During Hill's absence from England, the post-Waterloo economic depression was marked by a period of social unrest. England and Ireland were still suffering from the after-effects of the agricultural disaster caused by the so-called Year Without a Summer in 1816.[52] The dawning of the industrial revolution was also provoking turbulence. In the north west, the Luddites were destroying machinery they viewed as a threat to their jobs. Radical action was on the rise. In 1819, magistrates in Manchester ordered cavalry to disperse a crowd of some 60,000 people at a rally to protest about falling living standards. As a result, eleven people died and 400 were wounded in what became known as the Peterloo massacre. More positively, there were signs of humanitarian progress with increasing opposition to slavery, a growing revulsion towards hanging and a recognition of the need for prison reform. None of this drama affected Hill's life as a young soldier.

He was five months into his seventeenth year, in May 1819, when his mother paid the expensive fee necessary to purchase him a commission in one of the best regiments. He became a cornet, the lowest grade of commissioned officer, in the Royal Horse Guards (the Blues).[53] Maybe just before, or possibly around the same time, he also had a spell at the Royal Military Academy in Woolwich.[54] Soldiering for Hill was devoid of excitement because post-Napoleonic life for household cavalry regiments was relaxed. They avoided service in India, the only arena likely to require fighting. Instead, their major function was to accompany the new king – the Prince Regent became George IV on 29 January 1820 – at ceremonial events.

By this time, Hill must have grasped that his mother's enthusiasm for partying bordered on the obsessive. Newspapers which recorded the movements and entertainments of 'the fashionables' were replete with mentions of Mary attending this 'splendid ball' and that 'brilliant dinner' at the Pavilion in Brighton.[55] It was rare in the dowager marchioness's London household for weeks to pass without a dinner party 'involving a sprinkling of diplomats and perhaps a royal duke or two'.[56] In an age

---

51 Davis (2021a): 4.
52 A world-wide extreme weather event caused by a volcanic eruption in the Dutch East Indies (now Indonesia).
53 *National Archives*, Folio 105/WO 25/783/52. According to one newspaper report, George was just fifteen when he joined the Blues (*London Gazette*, 20 May 1817).
54 Hillan (2011): 77.
55 Creevey, op. cit. 49; *Belfast Commercial Chronicle*, 4 Dec 1805.
56 Davis (2020a): 13.

of excess, she was excessive. At 'a most splendid entertainment' in the Pavilion attended by 'the *Elegantes*', the marchioness's appearance was singled out for mention: 'dressed in white satin, tastefully embellished with diamonds to an immense amount'.[57] Her wealth and position was the subject of wonder. According to a report in 1806, she may 'now be considered one of the richest, as she was before, one of the most distinguished ornaments of her sex in the Empire'.[58] She was also considered to be 'the belle of fashionable society'.[59]

With a handsome jointure of £5,000 a year, and a penchant for spending more, she entertained on a lavish scale. She threw parties that attracted the *haut ton*. The Duke of Wellington, who was related to the Hills through his grandfather, was a regular guest.[60] Mary's sister-in-law, the Marchioness of Salisbury, was often invited despite being a prominent *Tory* hostess. Political rivalry did not seem to affect their friendship. At one of Mary's parties in 1814, in honour of the King of Prussia (Frederick William III), one of the main attractions for her children was the attendance of 71-year-old Field Marshal Blücher. They called him '*mon brave Maréchal*' and delighted in counting his medals. 'We dragged him in triumph to the refreshment room, and drank a glass of wine with him, which he tossed off with good grace', reported the girls. 'Georgy wanted to give him more.' The Duke of Gloucester, the king's nephew, was intrigued by hearing Charlotte speak French to Georgy and asked why. 'Told him we had been accustomed to speak [it] among ourselves.'[61]

The marchioness's dizzying round of glittering functions in London was matched by the daily round of engagements during her regular visits to Brighton, where she spent many nights attending parties at what Thomas Creevey's wife, Eleanor, called 'the wicked Pavilion'.[62] She recorded one of the Prince Regent's pranks in which the marchioness played a walk-on role. In order to show off his marksmanship with an air-gun, he shot at a target he had set up inside one of the palace's larger rooms. Mrs Creevey reported: 'He did it very skilfully and wanted all the ladies to attempt it. The girls and I excused ourselves on account of our short sight, but Lady

---

57 *Belfast Commercial Chronicle*, 4 Dec 1805.

58 *British Press*, 19 Nov 1806.

59 *St James's Chronicle*, 28 April 1832.

60 Wellington's grandfather was Arthur Hill-Trevor, whose elder brother, Trevor Hill, was the father of Wills Hill, first Marquess of Downshire.

61 Davis, Goseys, Vol 4: 35-6.

62 Creevey, op. cit. 65.

Downshire hit a fiddler in the dining room'.[63] In the years up to 1811, the marchioness and the prince were fast friends. In 1807, she entertained him and his brother, the Duke of Sussex, at Ombersley Court. For one dinner, attended by 300 people sitting in tented booths, a large oxen was roasted, 30 plum puddings were baked and a local inn supplied 50 dozen bottles of 'strong beer'.[64] The following year, the prince and the duke returned to Ombersley for another stay.[65]

But the dowager marchioness's relationship with the prince, and her enjoyment at attending and throwing parties, should not obscure her serious side. In a note to her sons, she advised them to pay careful attention to the politics of the day, urging them to examine 'as impartially as you can' the 'great parliamentary questions'. Read the newspapers, she told them, and search for 'discussions which relate to the principles of the Constitution' while paying attention to both current politics and 'the history of former administrations', most particularly 'the period which gave rise to the Whigs and Tories'.[66] For several years, her commitment to the Whig agenda and her principled belief in the need for Catholic emancipation were in accord with the views of the Prince Regent. Unlike her, he changed his mind.

Once the prince turned his back on Mrs Fitzherbert in 1808, in favour of the Marchioness of Hertford, he gradually withdrew his support from the Whigs and his sympathy for Catholic relief. It caused a breach with the marchioness, prompting the sisters to remark disparagingly about the 'very fat and old' prince who was 'so fond of us three or four years ago and used to call us his children'.[67] The frost continued until June 1819 when the Prince deigned to speak to the marchioness and her daughters at a party in the Spanish embassy.[68] Once the prince ascended the throne the following year, the thaw continued, if slowly and intermittently.

In August 1820, Lord George secured promotion by purchasing the rank of lieutenant.[69] Soon after, he and Augustus visited one of George III's daughters, Princess Elizabeth, Landgravine of Hesse-Homburg, in Germany. She wrote to the marchioness to say she 'thought them delightful, both very pleasing, one extremely interesting from ill-health but better, the other enchanted me

63 Ibid. 66; Davis (2020b): 61.
64 Davis (2020b): 63; *Morning Chronicle*, 28 Sept 1807.
65 *Worcester Journal*, 29 Sept 1808.
66 Davis (2020b): 41.
67 Davis, Goseys, Vol 4: 27.
68 Davis (2020b): 67.
69 *The Star*, 7 August 1820.

from his likeness to his father whose attachment to my adored father and all of us I can never forget'.[70] That supposed likeness was caught when Hill posed for Alfred Edward Chalon, the Swiss-born artist who was on his way to becoming one of London society's foremost portrait painters. Looking rather splendid in the regiment's distinctive uniform, the young officer, staring to one side and sporting a set of straggly side whiskers, cuts a handsome figure.[71]

What is not revealed is his slightness of build. It would appear that Hill, like his brother Marcus, was on the short side. No matter. He exhibited more than a degree of self-confidence, even to the point of indulging in some good-natured boasting. He bragged to his sisters that 'the Prince of Orange told me that I was a very aspiring young man because I was so smart'.[72] He was widely regarded as a 'dashing' cavalry officer and was able to enjoy a busy social life in London. Among the balls he is thought to have attended was one in January 1821 in Brussels thrown by Fanny, Lady Knatchbull. Newly married to Sir Edward Knatchbull MP, she was the daughter of Edward Knight, brother of the celebrated novelist, Jane Austen, who had died almost four years before. The fact that Hill was known to Fanny Knight was to have far-reaching consequences.

Hill's light-hearted outlook in these years is gleaned from letters to his sisters. By far the most revealing vignette was provided by Augustus when sharing accommodation with his brother in Brussels. He told his sisters: 'I assure you G. wants something to sober him, he is such a rake! & if you do not come soon, & keep him in order his dissipated habits will be confirmed'.[73] Augustus may well have been exaggerating, but it does appear that Hill was enjoying himself to the full. He told his sisters: 'My hair is beautiful all up in front like hay cocks, short behind & full of bears grease quite the thing'.[74] Eight months' later, in September 1821, tragedy extinguished the comedy. Sister Charlotte died, aged just 27, probably from tuberculosis.

Lolotte, as she was known in the family, became ill in Germany while accompanying her mother and sister, Mary, on a visit to Princess Elizabeth in Homburg. Like her sickly brother, Augustus, she had been under the care of Sir Henry Halford, president of the Royal College of Physicians and one of the king's doctors. The death plunged the family into gloom

---

70 Davis (2020b): 70.
71 A lithograph of the image, made by Richard James Lane, dated c1825-30, is in the National Portrait Gallery, ref D22025.
72 Davis (2021a): 3.
73 Letter from Augustus to his sisters, 23 Jan 1821, Omb, AFSH: 3.
74 Davis (2021a): 3.

and proved to be the precursor to the marchioness's decision to rent out the house in Hanover Square, choosing instead to live at Roehampton.[75]

The cultured, bookish Augustus accepted medical advice and decamped to Naples, where he was joined by George until he was required by his regiment to return to London. The following year, Hill continued to pursue the life of a playboy soldier with some enthusiasm, attending balls and parties along with regular visits to Brighton. He sometimes acted alongside his brother Atty in amateur theatricals.[76] He also found time to travel. At the end of the year, when he came of age, he finally had money of his own to spend. The twenty-one-year-old soldier was given £5,000 by his brother, the marquess, a settlement which necessitated an order by the court of chancery.[77]

In the spring of 1823, Hill was among 'many of the leading fashionables' at the Dowager Marchioness of Lansdowne's assembly; dancing at Lady Ravensworth's ball in Portland Place; and joining his mother, 'and her fair daughter', at the Brighton races attended by the king.[78] The following year, at an Almack's summer ball, he was picked out as one of the 'most distinguished dancers' in company with Lady Maria Clements, daughter of the second Earl of Leitrim.[79] At another ball, he was identified as a 'principal dancer', this time in the company of Lady Mary Berkeley (daughter of the fifth Earl of Berkeley).[80]

A privileged young man, he appears to have been engaged enthusiastically in the inconsequential pastimes of his class. Although economic and political change was under way in late Georgian society, it had no discernible effect on the nobility's life of leisure, as exemplified by a dissolute king and his brothers. So, Lord George, scion of a wealthy, titled family, was merely doing what was expected of him. However, the contented pattern of his life was disrupted by two unrelated incidents in the summer of 1826.

First, in what seems to have been a well-intentioned if mistaken jumping of the gun, Hill was proposed as a parliamentary candidate for the seat of Carrickfergus, the Ulster town where the Downshires owned substantial tracts of land. The nomination was aimed at unseating Sir

---

75 Her first tenant was Earl Grey, a future prime minister, and the second, from 1830, was Prince Talleyrand, when he became French ambassador.

76 Omb, Arthur: 49.

77 The Star, 16 Dec 1822. £5,000 would be £445,000 today.

78 Morning Post, 21 March 1823; Morning Post, 14 May 1823; Sussex Advertiser, 16 June 1823.

79 Morning Post, 23 July 1824. See Chapter 14.

80 Morning Post, 22 July 1825.

Arthur Chichester on the grounds that 'the men of Carrickfergus had not been treated with respect or deference' by him.[81] As one approving report noted: 'Should Lord George Hill be put into Parliament the ranks of the supporters of Roman Catholic Emancipation will receive an auxiliary'.[82] But Hill knew nothing of the nomination and swiftly withdrew, allowing Chichester to be returned as MP. In spite of his lordship's embarrassed surprise at his nomination, it proved to be something of a trial run.

The second incident was also a little embarrassing. In summer 1825, Hill had transferred from the Blues to the 8th King's Royal Irish Hussars, attaining the rank of captain.[83] It was in his new role that he found himself appearing with another officer before magistrates at Canterbury's Guildhall. They were summoned after an affray in which it was said that a group of Hussars had been involved in an argument and 'knocked down' several people. As a result, 'two or three respectable inhabitants of that quarter' were 'much hurt'.[84] In response, 'some of the lower class inhabitants', wielding large sticks, attacked the soldiers as they made their back to their barracks.

Despite a suggestion that Hill was among the offenders, it was more likely that, as a duty officer, he was required to answer for his rowdy troops. He was bound over to keep the peace.[85] Hill was also accused of assaulting a police constable.[86] Nothing came of that charge and the affair had no impact on his reputation. Later that year, he attended the king's levée in recognition of his promotion to captain.[87]

At the beginning of 1827, the Irish Hussars were assigned a four-year posting to Ireland. But Hill, due to an unspecified injury to his arm, was late in joining them. The delay proved fortuitous. At some time between March and May, he was introduced to a modest and attractive nineteen-year-old woman called Cassandra Knight, sister to Lady Knatchbull, and niece of the late celebrated novelist, Jane Austen.

---

81 *Belfast Commercial Chronicle*, 17 June 1826.

82 *The Globe*, 20 June 1826.

83 *Southern Reporter & Cork Commercial Courier*, 30 June 1825; *Enniskillen Chronicle & Erne Packet*, 7 July 1825.

84 'Affrays with the military', *Kent Herald*, 28 June 1826; 'Riots with the military', *Kentish Weekly Post*, 30 June 1826; *The Globe*, 7 July 1826.

85 *The Star*, 1 July 1826.

86 *Kentish Weekly Post*, 11 July 1826; *The Representative*, 15 July 1826.

87 *Morning Chronicle*, 28 Nov 1826.

2

MAMA KNOWS BEST

It is a truth universally acknowledged, that a single man in possession of a good fortune, must be in want of a wife – Jane Austen[1]

In Lord George Hill's era, as with Jane Austen's the generation before, it was a truth also universally acknowledged that a single man without a fortune was not much of a marriage prospect. That was especially true if that single man was a minor sprig of the aristocracy. At 25, with an impeccable pedigree, royal connections and a title, Hill may well have been regarded by people outside his class as a catch. He was good-looking, multi-lingual, musical and renowned for his dancing abilities. But, within his class, he lacked what really counted: money. There was no estate, no grand house and no likelihood of obtaining either. At some future stage, on the death of his mother, he could expect to inherit, if not a fortune, then a comfortable settlement. Comfortable, however, was not a sought-after commodity. His lack of funds undoubtedly compromised his eligibility.

Monetary calculations were openly made in Georgian society where marriages rarely, if ever, occurred without reference to a person's financial worth. Making 'a good match' – both the cliché and euphemism of the era – was all about ensuring enhanced income. From Hill's perspective, which means his mother's perspective, he was therefore expected to parlay his status (his title and proximity to royalty) to his economic advantage. In the marchioness's view, he should have been able to find a woman – a woman from within his own class – who would not only be willing to overlook his lack of wealth but also to provide a decent dowry. Surely, the fifth son of a marquess could find the fifth daughter of a wealthy earl or viscount?

---

1 *Pride and Prejudice* (1813).

Hill mixed in circles where there were plenty of opportunities to meet potential brides. His social life revolved around balls and dinner parties where he danced with the daughters of dukes, marquesses, earls, viscounts, barons, and baronets. Yet there was no hint of an aristocratic romance. Instead, within months of meeting a woman drawn from an inferior class, the landed gentry, he proposed marriage. Given the conventionality of his life thus far, we perceive a character trait that sets him somewhat apart. He did not feel it necessary to do what was expected of him.

Hill may have been introduced to Cassandra Jane Knight when his regiment was quartered near Canterbury in the summer of 1826.[2] The city was some eight miles from the Knight family's large estate, Godmersham Park. Another possible link was Cassandra's eldest sister, Fanny, Lady Knatchbull, who had once invited George to a ball.[3] Cassandra and Fanny were the daughters of Edward Austen Knight, brother of the novelist Jane Austen.[4] It was Fanny who was on hand at the beginning of the couple's romance, recording that Lord George 'accompanied Cass, Lou and me' on a shopping expedition.[5] A week later, by chance or design, Fanny attended an 'assembly' at the London home of Hill's aunt, the Dowager Marchioness of Salisbury. Among the guests was Hill's mother.[6] Seven further meetings in June between George and Cass, were witnessed by Fanny. They included shopping trips, a night at the opera, and a walk in Kensington Gardens. After a visit on 25 June, when Hill dined at Fanny's house, he finally felt well enough to join his regiment in Ireland. Despite spending the summer apart from Cass, his mind was made up. He proposed by letter.[7]

Cass's father, unlike Hill's mother, agreed to the match. Before the end of the month, he informed Fanny 'of Lady Downshire's disapprobation' of the marriage 'on acct. of not money enough'.[8] In a succinct, cold-hearted

---

2 Davis (2021a): 6. That was the memory, some seventy years after the event, of Cassandra's niece, Fanny Margaretta Rice, the Dowager Countess of Winchilsea.

3 Letter to his sisters, 18 Jan 1821, Davis (2021a): 9. Fanny was married to Sir Edward Knatchbull, Tory MP for Kent, a noted opponent of Catholic emancipation (*Morning Chronicle*, 12 Jan 1821). Richard Lalor Sheil regarded him as 'a proud, obstinate, dogged sort of squire, with an infinite notion of his own importance' (*New Monthly Magazine*, 1828 ii: 479).

4 Knight, born Austen, changed his surname after being adopted by wealthy childless relatives.

5 FCK, 8 May 1827, Knatchbull archive, cited by Hillan: 74. Lou was Cassandra's sister, Louisa.

6 *Morning Post*, 18 May 1827.

7 Hillan (2011): 75.

8 Ibid. FCK, 27 Aug 1827, Pocket Books, CKS Knatchbull archive, U951/F24/24.

comment, the marchioness dismissed Cass: 'No money – all charms'.[9]
Fanny later wrote: 'Ld G. Hill paid [Cass] great attention in London &
proposed to her in August, but they could not make money enough and it
all went off'.[10] Without money, Hill could not be master of his own fate and
was obliged to accept his mother's decision. As his brother, Marcus, noted
to a friend: 'Our fortunes as younger brothers are anything but liberal'.[11]

Hill knuckled down to his military duties and continued to enjoy a
convivial social life, given that his 'peacekeeping duties' in the north of
Ireland were less than arduous. In February 1828, Captain Lord George
Hill was appointed as one of the six aides-de-camp to the incoming Lord
Lieutenant of Ireland, the Marquess of Anglesey.[12] A month before, his
cousin, the Duke of Wellington, became prime minister in what proved
to be a momentous year for Ireland. For five years, Daniel O'Connell
had been leading a campaign for Catholic emancipation in which he had
mobilised hundreds of thousands of the poor while uniting a large section
of the burgeoning Catholic middle class. His increasing success unnerved
the British authorities and split the Commons, with the Whigs broadly in
favour of emancipation and the Tories broadly against it. Matters came
to a head when O'Connell was elected to parliament. As a Catholic, he
could not swear the oath of supremacy which acknowledged George IV
to be supreme governor of the established Protestant church. Wellington,
although a Tory, was born in Dublin and was more aware than most of
his fellow party members of the public mood in Ireland. Emancipation,
which he considered inevitable, was essential to avert civil unrest. But
he also knew the king had to be handled delicately and would require
months of persuasion to agree to the necessary legislation.

Hill's employer, Anglesey, who had substantial land holdings in
counties Down and Louth, also favoured emancipation and did not
attempt to hide his support for Catholics. So, he was relaxed about
his son, William, attending a Catholic Association meeting in Dublin,
accompanied by Hill, to hear O'Connell speak.[13] Witnessed 'vehemently'
applauding the speeches, their attendance caused 'a great sensation',

9 Captain John Hart to Viscountess Forbes, 17 September 1834. PRONI Granard Papers,
Register of Irish Archives, K/3/1. Cf. Malcomson, Pursuit: 174.
10 Hillan (2011): 76. FCK, 31 December 1827. Pocket Books, CKS, Knatchbull
archive, U951/F24/24.
11 Davis (2020a): 62.
12 *Dublin Evening Post*, 19 Feb 1828; *Morning Post*, 23 Feb 1828.
13 *Tipperary Free Press*, 23 April 1828.

upsetting Orangemen and alarming some of Wellington's ministers.[14] This was the first public hint of Hill's sympathy for Catholics, which echoed the opinion of his mother and eldest brother, the Marquess of Downshire. Devout Protestants they may have been, but they believed Catholics should share the same civil rights, including the right to sit in parliament. That meeting apart, Hill's ADC duties were largely trivial: he was little more than a glorified party organiser.

His participation in such events was noted in obsequious newspaper reports, which Hill would have taken for granted. Within England, he was the beneficiary of the kind of fawning press coverage that the nobility and aristocracy accepted as entirely natural to their station. The innocuous pursuits of lords and ladies were amplified beyond their significance. Inconsequential details of their travels, their parties and their dress were given disproportionate prominence in reports notable for their magniloquence. To modern eyes, although the content and style appears risible, there is some similarity with the way film and TV celebrities are reported today. The coverage of the aristocracy served a purpose by reinforcing their status and underlining the notion that a hierarchical society was the natural order of things. Its effect was to encourage deference from 'us' and a sense of entitlement by 'them'.

The Irish press, split by religious affiliation, was a little different. The Protestant Ascendancy newspapers in Dublin – notably the *Evening Mail*, its weekly counterpart, *The Warder*, and the *Evening Packet* – tended to mimic the English papers in terms of content and style. This was also true of another of the best-read titles, the 'Castle Catholic' *Evening Post*. Even in the news columns of the nationalist pro-O'Connell press it was possible to find uncritical reports about the insignificant activities of the aristocracy, including the landlord class. Anglesey's known sympathy for Catholic emancipation ensured that he received almost no criticism. But Wellington, and the king, were unimpressed with Anglesey's sympathies, and he was recalled, a decision which infuriated Hill.[15] He said nothing in public and remained at the Castle to await the next incumbent, the Duke of Northumberland. Soon after his arrival, Wellington finally succeeded in guiding the Catholic Relief Bill through parliament. Emancipation had arrived.

There was a sting in its tail: it disenfranchised the so-called forty-shilling freeholders, both Catholics and Protestants, who rented or

---

14 *The Atlas*, 27 April 1828; *Dublin Evening Post*, 22 April 1828.

15 PRONI, Downshire mss D671/C/348/4, 5.

owned land worth at least £2. It raised the new minimum requirement for voters to £10. O'Connell accepted the change in the belief that the forty-shilling freeholders were unable to vote independently from the wishes of their landlords.[16] That loss of voting rights rankled with many of O'Connell's nationalist supporters as he turned his attention to a new campaign: the repeal of the Union. It found no favour with Hill and his brother, Downshire. Having supported emancipation, they felt they had done enough for Ireland's Catholics. For them, in company with almost the entire Irish landlord class, repeal was out of the question. Their father may have been against the Union, but some thirty years on from its establishment, they were now firmly in favour of it.

Hill moved on to become aide-de-camp to Sir John Byng, commander of forces in Ireland.[17] His duties were not arduous and he was able to combine them with an active social life in England.[18] He attended George IV's final 'grand ball' at St James's Palace, although the obese king was anything but grand.[19] It may have acted as a reminder to Hill of his own passing years. As he turned twenty-eight, what could he celebrate? Although he was hardly alone among his peers in living a largely superficial life, he must have been aware he had achieved nothing of genuine value. His army rank of captain, after twelve years in the military, was relatively insignificant. As an ADC, he was little more than a personal servant. He had a modest income. His marriage ambitions had been frustrated. Compared to two of his elder brothers, he was marking time. The industrious Downshire was overseeing the advance of his plans to reform his Ulster estates. Atty, a lieutenant-colonel in the Scots Greys, had been a Whig MP for County Down since 1817.[20]

The new year signalled a new, and probably unwelcome, change of direction for Hill. Before he confronted it there was a very different sort of challenge. Along with officers from his regiment, he took leading roles in two light-hearted drama productions to raise money for charity. In front of a 'fashionable audience' at Dublin's Adelphi Theatre, he appeared in

16 Beckett (1966): 301.
17 *Belfast News-Letter*, 16 April 1830; *The Times*, 19 June 1828; *London Gazette*, 11 Oct 1831.
18 PRONI Downshire Papers D/671/C/348/2. *Belfast News-Letter*, 14 July 1829; *Drogheda Journal*, 22 July 1829; *London Courier*, 11 Nov 1829; *The Times*, 12 Nov 1829; *Dublin Morning Register*, 14 April 1829.
19 *The Globe*, 26 May 1829; *Chester Chronicle*, 19 June 1829. According to the artist Sir David Wilkie, the king resembled 'a great sausage stuffed into the covering' and was perpetually drugged on laudanum. Smith (1999): 266, 269.
20 Davis (2020c): 38.

a one-act burlesque musical *Bombastes Furioso*.[21] In the 'whimsical, farcical, operatical, tragical burletta', he played the king of Utopia, Artaxominous, and was required to wear a flowing powdered wig, rolled silk stockings and high-heeled shoes. One of his lines must have struck a chord: 'I'll seek the maid I love, though in my way a dozen generals stood in fierce array!' How could he not have reflected that in his way to the maid he loved, Cassandra, stood just one general – his mother?

His round of parties was interrupted by news of a family tragedy. His sister, Mary, died aged 33.[22] Hill and his brothers – Downshire, Atty and Marcus – were chief mourners at her funeral on the Downshire family's Berkshire estate, Easthampstead Park.[23] Augustus, who was to die the following year, was too frail to travel from Italy. Another death very soon after was to have a profound influence on George's life. Throughout the spring, it had been obvious that George IV was dying and Downshire, at his mother's behest, began to groom his youngest brother for an entirely new role, that of politician. When the king died in June 1830, as tradition demanded, parliament was dissolved. Hill was immediately named as the Whig candidate for the seat of Carrickfergus. His first step was to obtain a promotion within the Hussars and his second was to transfer voluntarily to the half pay list, the system which enabled officers to join what was, in effect, the army's reserve force.[24] From this point on, having bid farewell to soldiering, he would be known formally as Major Lord George Hill.

Hill had never betrayed an enthusiasm for politics. Political indifference was hardly a bar to becoming an MP among his class in the Georgian era where it was viewed, at best, as a sort of aristocratic public duty and, at worst, as little more than a rite of passage. Parliament was, for many members, no more than a club. A Westminster seat offered status but no income: MPs were not paid a salary. Getting elected often proved to be expensive, given that votes were, in effect, purchased.

In Ireland, especially in eastern Ulster, parliamentary contests were fought between rival land-owners vying for local power and control. By far the most prominent were the three marquisates of Downshire (Hills), Londonderry (Stewarts) and Donegall (Chichesters). Downshire,

---

21 *Dublin Morning Register; Freeman's Journal*, 25 Feb 1830.
22 *Morning Post*, 28 May 1830. To follow the progress of Mary's life prior to her death, see *The Star*, 16 Dec 1829; *Morning Post*, 19 Dec 1829; *Sussex Advertiser*, 21 Dec 1829; *Morning Post*, 12 Jan 1830; *Morning Post*, 8 March 1830.
23 *Brighton Gazette*, 10 June 1830; *Newry Telegraph*, 11 June 1830.
24 *The Times*, 7 July 1830.

imitating his mother, the dowager marchioness, and clearly with her support, decided to oust the Chichesters from Carrickfergus. Despite it running counter to his financial strategy to avoid spending money on politics, Downshire had been planning to regain control of the district for some years.[25] It appears he was upset by Chichester's part in the formation of a Brunswick Club, one of the militant Protestant societies which campaigned against Catholic emancipation.[26] Downshire was confident that he would prevail with brother George as his candidate. But it did not go smoothly.

Chichester was less than pleased at the need to fight for a seat he regarded as his own by right of his family connections and his standing within the town. In previous elections, he had been returned unopposed. As a Tory, he also resented opposition from a Whig. Once again, the Downshires found themselves engaged in a bitter and costly fight in which it is hard not to see Hill as something of a pawn. Did he want to be an MP? One advantage he enjoyed was that the Chichesters were regarded as 'exceedingly unpopular'.[27] According to a Dublin newspaper, Hill's candidacy was regarded as affording 'no small satisfaction to the many electors [of Carrickfergus] who have long wished for a day of reckoning with their noble mayor, the Marquis of Donegall'.[28]

Hill cannot be faulted for his response to the call. He threw himself into the fight with enthusiasm. In his opening address to electors, he embraced the fact that he his name had been put forward previously, stating that he had been 'invited' for a second time 'by a numerous and respectable body' of the Carrickfergus constituency. Pointing to his family's long connection with the borough, he accepted that he had no 'personal services' on which to base his claim for the seat, pledging instead his 'sincere and ardent desire to discharge the duties of the trust you are inclined to repose in me'.[29] A narrow majority was so inclined in spite of 'a good deal of altercation among the friends of the respective parties'.[30]

Chichester stood down, but not in good grace. He accused Hill of bribery by indulging in 'the most corrupt and unwarrantable practices'. Downshire responded by standing Marcus as a back-up candidate should

25 PRONI, Downshire mss C/2/240/1, C/2/372.
26 *Belfast News-Letter*, 7 Oct 1828.
27 *Newry Telegraph*, 23 July 1830.
28 *The Pilot*, 23 July 1830.
29 *Newry Telegraph*, 23 July 1830.
30 *Saint James's Chronicle*, 10 Aug 1830; *Belfast News-Letter*, 6 Aug 1830.

George face legal charges. The brothers succeeded easily, together obtaining 552 of the 796 votes cast and giving George a majority of 113 over Marcus. It was, said the *Newry Telegraph*, 'the triumph of the popular candidate'.[31] The Chichesters immediately petitioned parliament to declare George's election null and void on the grounds that his victory had been 'procured by undue, illegal and unconstitutional and unjust means'. He had secured votes, they alleged, by 'offering gifts, rewards, promises and agreements', and was therefore guilty of bribery and corruption. The Commons decided to investigate.

Downshire, although irritated by the complaint, was delighted with George's victory, saying it 'exceeded my expectations'. The cost, which included the acquisition of a small estate at Carrickfergus, also exceeded his expectations. He had to provide his brother with £300 a year in order to comply with the necessary property qualification. Downshire noted that these costs would 'retard the repayment of the debt of which I never lose sight'.[32] More legal expenses were incurred during the parliamentary inquiry, which dragged on for months. Downshire astutely hired the staunchly Protestant ultra-Tory Sir Robert Inglis to present George's case. His central contention was that the Chichester petition, made in the names of 30 electors, was fraudulent. A Commons select committee appointed in December 1830 found that 14 signatures had indeed been forged, including one belonging to a dead man.[33]

Finally, in February 1831, Hill joined his brother Atty in the House of Commons. That may not be literally true, because there is no record of the pair attending together. Hill did not re-order his life around Westminster. Soon after the Carrickfergus poll, he was on duty in Limerick as Sir John Byng's ADC.[34] Afterwards, he was a guest at many parties.[35] His two overtly political acts, aside from his general support for Earl Grey's coalition government, revealed his antipathy to O'Connell's campaign for the repeal of the Union and his initial ambivalence about radical electoral reform. In company with

31 *Newry Telegraph*, 13 Aug 1830. Figures reported elsewhere differed, but with the same outcome: George, 301; Marcus, 236; Adair, 207. *London Evening Standard*, 13 Aug 1830.
32 Maguire (1972): 95. Downshire mss C/2/442/1 and C/5/413.
33 *Saint James's Chronicle*, 8 Feb 1831. Downshire mss C/1/653A and C/2/447/1. No action was taken against the fraudsters: *The Times*, 25 Feb 1831; *Belfast News-Letter*, 1 March 1831.
34 *Freeman's Journal*, 21 Sept 1830.
35 *Dublin Morning Register*, 20 Oct 1830; *Morning Post*, 1 Dec 1830; *Freeman's Journal*, 17 Jan 1831; *Dublin Evening Mail*, 28 Jan 1831; *Freeman's Journal*, 11 Feb 1831.

numerous aristocrats and MPs, he signed 'the Leinster Declaration of the Friends of the Union', a statement reflecting 'anxiety' about repeal which declared it to be 'impracticable' and 'injurious to the prosperity of Ireland'.[36] Although he refused to present a Carrickfergus petition for parliamentary reform, he did vote for the second reading of the Reform Bill, which was carried by a single vote.[37] In that sense, he could be said to have played a crucial role in the bill's passage. He also voted against a subsequent wrecking amendment, which, when passed, caused the dissolution of parliament.[38]

At the resulting general election, Hill was returned unopposed – the Chichesters having stood aside – in what was a landslide result for pro-reform candidates.[39] His brother, Atty, was also elected without opposition in Down, but his reformist-minded commanding officer, Sir John Byng, failed to win a seat in Derry.[40] Hill's support for Byng, in company with another of the general's aides-de-camp, proved controversial. It forced Byng to issue a defensive statement in which he described Hill as 'my personal friend' who had received 'no order to rally round me'.[41] Byng soon stood down as commander of forces in Ireland, which cost Hill his ADC post.[42] Although he is not recorded as having made any parliamentary speeches, Hill appears to have been more assiduous in attending the Commons than either of his MP brothers, Atty and Marcus. He attended several key debates and voted for the English poor laws to be extended to Ireland, a motion that was narrowly defeated.[43]

While the London parliament's attention was devoted to the question of electoral reform, there was growing alarm in Dublin about the failure of the potato crop, due to blight, in three counties on Ireland's west coast. The Marquess of Anglesey, having been restored to the post of Lord Lieutenant of Ireland, received reports from landlords, magistrates and clergy about the consequent distress. Deprived of their staple diet, some 200,000 people in Galway, Mayo and Donegal were said to be destitute

---

36 *Newry Telegraph*, 26 Nov 1830; *Dublin Evening Post*, 18 Dec 1830.

37 *Belfast Guardian*, 4 Feb 1831; *The Times*, 28 Feb 1831; *Public Ledger and Daily Advertiser*, 21 June 1831.

38 *Belfast News-Letter*, 29 April, 6 May 1831.

39 *Belfast News-Letter*, 29 April, 6 May 1831; *London Courier*, 8 May 1831.

40 *Londonderry Sentinel*, 21 May 1831.

41 *Dublin Morning Register*, 18, 20 May 1831; *Cork Constitution*, 23 June 1831.

42 Byng was later elected as Whig MP for Poole, *London Gazette*, 11 Oct 1831.

43 *Hansard*, 29 Aug 1831 https://api.parliament.uk/historic-Hansard/commons/1831/aug/29/poor-laws-ireland.

and had been forced to resort to begging. Anglesey was asked to provide aid. One of the people he relied on for information was James Dombrain, Inspector General, and founder, of the Irish Coast Guard.

Dombrain, an English former Royal Navy officer, was well regarded by the authorities in Dublin and London. He was praised as 'a gentleman, whose discrimination and accuracy of judgment are only surpassed by his high character and benevolence' for his actions on behalf of the poor people of Donegal.[44] Newspapers in England and Ireland carried extracts of his disturbing report. 'The people are dying', he wrote. 'Having lived for time on the common sea-weed, they have been suddenly been afflicted with swellings all over their bodies; it has the appearance of dropsy, but attacks all parts; they are sinking under it.' He took steps to help: 'I am still pouring in the food. I have ordered nine cargoes of potatoes'.[45] It earned Dombrain an encomium as 'the well-known active and prudent Distributor of the Relief collected for the Sufferers by famine'.[46]

Dombrain was soon recruited as the 'accredited agent' of the Relief Association for the Suffering Peasantry in the West of Ireland.[47] The charity was set up by a committee of clergymen and MPs led by the Archbishop of Tuam and an Irish peer, Viscount Lorton, which raised money to import Indian corn (maize). Lord George Hill was listed among the donors, making an initial contribution of £2.10s to the fund.[48] The modesty of his donation, especially when compared to the £50 sent by his brother, Downshire, indicated his comparatively straitened financial circumstances. Hill could not fail to have noticed the praise heaped on Dombrain from the so-called 'principal inhabitants' of Donegal for his 'rescue of hundreds from starvation'.[49] It was the beginning of what was to become a close friendship between the two men.

In July 1831, George's 31-year-old brother, Augustus, died at their mother's house in Roehampton after 'a long and lingering illness', which he reportedly 'bore with Christian meekness and resignation'.[50] The family, having previously lost Charlotte and Mary, cleaved together. It wasn't until the late autumn that they resumed their social life with George,

---

44 *London Evening Standard*, 9 June 1831.
45 *Morning Post*, 27 May 1831; *London Courier and Evening Gazette*, 31 May 1831.
46 *Leicester Chronicle*, 4 June 1831.
47 *Saint James's Chronicle*, 18 June 1831.
48 *Dublin Mercantile Advertiser*, 13 June 1831.
49 *Dublin Evening Packet & Correspondent*, 27 Dec 1831.
50 *Morning Post*, 12 July 1831.

Atty and Marcus joining their mother in 'a splendid suite of apartments' at Brighton's Royal York Hotel.[51] Their closeness to royalty surfaced once more when they enjoyed what newspapers called 'the honour of dining with their Majesties' at the Pavilion.[52] Hill spent Christmas at Hillsborough where there was 'a succession of splendid entertainments' crowned by 'a sumptuous ball' attended by a variety of marriageable young aristocratic women.[53] None tempted him.

On his return to London he chaired a meeting of pro-reform Irish MPs who wanted to restore the franchise to forty-shilling freeholders.[54] He also took part in discussions about the controversy over the payment of tithes by the economically hard-pressed Catholic peasantry. They were obliged, by a law passed in 1823, to pay what amounted to a tax in order to fund the upkeep of the established (Protestant) Church of Ireland. From late 1830 onwards, groups of people refused to pay, the beginning of what would later be called a 'war'. The rebels received only slight support from O'Connell, who regarded repeal of the Union as of paramount importance. But his largely assumed support was a major reason for the movement's growing success. Although opposed to the occasional outbreaks of brutality perpetrated by the secret societies known as Whiteboys or Ribbonmen, he showed more sympathy for those whose peaceful protests resulted in violence.[55]

Hill would have been aware of such incidents before the tithe vote in March 1832. It followed the recommendations of a Commons committee set up to consider how to react to the rebellion against payment. O'Connell lampooned the committee's call for the tithes to be enforced in exchange for the amelioration of Catholic grievances as a wishy-washy compromise. Hill was one of the Irish members who voted, with the majority, in favour of that decision. A larger number of Irish MPs were among the minority, seeing no reason to do anything other than enforce payments.[56] While his vote identified Hill as being on the liberal wing of the Whigs, he failed to recognise that the compromise would not satisfy the majority of Irish Catholics. He appeared unaware of the depth of feeling within Ireland against

---

51 *Morning Post*, 28 Nov, 6 Dec 1831; *Sussex Advertiser*, 5 Dec 1831.
52 *The Sun*, 5 Dec 1831; *Sussex Advertiser*, 12 Dec 1831.
53 *Dublin Observer*, 8 Jan 1832.
54 *Freeman's Journal*, 1 March 1832.
55 O'Donoghue (1966).
56 *Dublin Morning Register*, 12 March 1832.

tithes and, in company with the overwhelming majority of MPs, he underestimated O'Connell's political intuition. The committee's strategy to end the rebellion proved hopelessly inadequate.

Later that month, Hill's liberal credibility, in an Irish context, was further enhanced when he attended the St Patrick's dinner in London, a charity event organised to raise money for the destitute children of Irish expatriates. Newspapers were critical of the poor attendance by Irish MPs.[57] *The Evening Mail*, which called the absences 'shameful', praised Hill for being among 'the three honourable exceptions'.[58]

Hill's political career was over almost before it began. His brother, Downshire, decided not to fund him to stand in the post-Reform Act general election called in December 1832. Hill understood Downshire's reasoning. In spite of his considerable income, he thought he and his wife were lacking sufficient funds to live as well as others of their rank.[59] Lord George issued a statement offering ill health as a reason for his withdrawal.[60] It did not prevent him from accepting the 'honour' of being 'at the royal table', along with Marcus, in the Pavilion at Brighton in early December.[61] Nor did it stop him later that month from campaigning on Marcus's behalf in Newry against Dennis Maguire, a Catholic who advocated repeal.[62] It proved to be a rowdy affair during which Marcus considered Hill to have been 'of the greatest use'.[63] During the poll, a pro-Maguire mob attacked Marcus's supporters, one of whom was stabbed to death.[64] Hill and Atty celebrated Marcus's victory at a New Year's Day celebration. In proposing a toast to the army and navy, George attempted a joke: 'Though there are several gentlemen present connected with the service, major to me in years, I alone it appears am Major in rank'.[65] It is not recorded whether anyone laughed.

---

57 *The Sun*, 19 March 1832.

58 *Evening Mail*, 19 March 1832. The others being Richard Lalor Sheil and Colonel Henry White (later Baron Annaly), owner of a large estate on the outskirts of Dublin.

59 Letter to Thomas Handley: 'Lady Downshire & I ... have been much remarked upon as living in a much less becoming manner than the cravings of many, and the Habits of the World, sanction as a right and as a custom.' Davis (2021a): 4-5.

60 *Morning Post*, 25 Dec 1832. The seat was taken by Conway Richard Dobbs, a Tory landowner, supported by Lord Downshire.

61 *The Times*, 3 Dec 1832; London Courier, 3 Dec 1832.

62 *Newry Commercial Telegraph*, 4 Jan 1833.

63 Davis, *Letters*:118.

64 *Belfast News-Letter*, 28 Dec 1832.

65 Davis (2020a): 120.

Hill's loss of his seat illustrated, yet again, that without money he could not be his own master. His fate was in the hands of his mother – who had ruled against his chosen marriage partner – and his eldest brother, who had thrust him into parliament and, within two years, had hoisted him out of it. What then was George to do? The immediate answer was to accept an offer from his former employer, the Marquess of Anglesey, to become comptroller of his household.[66] This puffed-up title was an imitation of the similar position within the monarch's household, signifying that the Lord Lieutenant in Dublin Castle was a proxy for the British king. The appointment prompted Hill's brother, Downshire, to remark: 'I am sure the Lord Lieutenant is happy to have you back in his family. Who is there who could do him so much service and be more agreeable to him? It also serves him *dans la politique*.'[67]

In his largely ceremonial role, Hill's main duty was to act as a public companion to Anglesey. On one excursion to Dublin's Adelphi Theatre, he also participated in the entertainment on behalf of his patron before an invited audience. He stepped on stage to repeat his portrayal of the king of Utopia in the musical farce, *Bombastes Furioso*. According to *The Observer*, 'the exquisite humour' of Hill and his co-star had 'convulsed the house with laughter'.[68]

Anglesey was no longer the darling of the Irish press. Owners and editors of both Protestant and Catholic titles were temporarily united in their opposition to restrictions on their freedom as they campaigned against newspaper stamp duty while fighting off a succession of legal actions, either for contempt of court or libel.[69] Several proprietors were jailed.[70] Anglesey was accused of leading 'the most tyrannical' government England had forced on Ireland.[71] There was little surprise when he was recalled in the autumn of 1833 to be replaced as Lord Lieutenant by the Marquess of Wellesley, elder brother of the Duke of Wellington, and therefore Hill's cousin. He was happy to keep George in place.[72] Wellesley, aware of the political difficulties facing the man who

66 *The Globe*, 26 Feb 1833.
67 Davis (2021a): 5.
68 *Dublin Morning Register*, 14 March 1833; *The Observer*, 24 March 1833.
69 Inglis (1950); *Irish Monthly Magazine*, Nov 1832; *The Comet*, 2 Dec 1832.
70 *Morning Register*, 28 April 1832, 19 July 1832; *Dublin Evening Mail*, 23 Nov 1832; *The Pilot*, 12 June 1833.
71 *Irish Monthly Magazine*, Nov 1832.
72 *Dublin Morning Register*, 24 Sept 1833. Maguire (1972): 11.

had appointed him, the Whig prime minister, Earl Grey, wanted a loyal friend at Dublin Castle. He also knew of his cousin's popularity. Hill was hymned by one newspaper for having 'endeared him[self] to all classes of persons' by 'his mild, affable, and efficient conduct'.[73] This short, favourable description of Hill's personality was the first to be published.

Soon after, a previously unknown aspect of Hill's interests came to light. A lengthy letter to a newspaper referred to him as 'a zealous investigator of Irish literature'.[74] The writer told how Hill had spent part of July in Denmark to discover whether there was any truth to rumours of there being Irish manuscripts in the royal archives in Copenhagen. He was able to confirm the existence in the library of two sets of vellum documents, one containing a copy of the ancient Celtic Brehon Laws and the other, a collection of Gaelic poetry. George copied out an extract of the Brehon manuscript, which was translated by the letter-writer, Owen Connellan, who gloried in the title given to him by George IV, 'Irish Historiographer to his Majesty'.[75] Connellan went on to publish the first English translation of the *Annals of the Four Masters*, the chronicles of Irish medieval history compiled by monks in Donegal. He also produced a book of Irish grammar.[76]

This revelation of Hill's scholarly pursuits was a counterweight to what can be gleaned from newspaper reports about his public roles. He had made little mark as an MP. Instead, he was routinely portrayed either as soldier or as an official aide to senior military and political figures. In addition, there were the frequent reports of him attending royal and high society events. But the Connellan letter offered a glimpse of a different Lord George. Behind the scenes, without attracting any publicity, he had been quietly engaged in an intellectual vocation. It was the first clue to his intense interest in the history, archaeology, culture and language of Ireland. Eventually, his collection of manuscripts and antiquities would be deposited in the country's National Library.[77] He was also among the founders of the Dublin Shakespeare Club,

---

73 *Cork Constitution*, 21 Sept 1833.

74 *Waterford Chronicle*, 2 Nov 1833. Hill was 'an avid collector of Irish language manuscripts', Blaney (1996): 165.

75 Connellan's account of Hill's mission is supported by Reuben John Bryce. Letter to *Belfast News-Letter*, 12 April 1879.

76 *Dublin Weekly Nation*, 9 March, 23 Nov 1844. Connellan dedicated an 1844 edition of his *A Practical Grammar of the Irish Language* to 'Lord George Augusta Hill, MRIA ... as a mark of my respect for your Lordship's acquirements as an Irish scholar'.

77 Hillan (2011): 91. Cf Manuscripts Reading Room, National Library of Ireland MS G.1.121.

becoming its inaugural vice president, and soon after joined the Royal Irish Academy's committee of antiquities.[78] Nevertheless, parties continued to dominate the public's knowledge of Hill.[79]

He remained close to his brother, Downshire, whose politics had moved steadily to the right. At a public dinner held to mark the coming of age of his eldest son, the Earl of Hillsborough, the band struck up, to the tune of Lillibullero, *The Protestant Boys*. The song called on 'loyal Protestants now to unite' to show the support of the 'Orange and Blue' for 'our king'. Downshire, noted a journalist who covered the event, 'may be a Whig, but the simple truth is, that he is as near a Tory as a Whig can be'.[80] Lord George's own political views were opaque. He observed his employer, Lord Wellesley, struggling to reconcile his need to support the government with his dislike of moves to introduce yet another Irish coercion act in order to deal with the militant opposition to tithes. For his troubles, Wellesley found himself criticised by both sides.[81]

Given the delicacy of his employer's situation, it might have been expected that Hill would remain constantly at his side. Yet, for unexplained reasons, he chose to make what was to prove a life-altering tour of the west of Ireland, accompanied by Dombrain. Why did he go? When asked that question some years later, Hill merely said: 'I was looking over the country generally'.[82] This was the trip, in 1834, in which he first visited Gweedore in west Donegal and, supposedly, formulated a plan to return, acquire land and raise up the natives to a wonderful new life. According to Dombrain, Hill observed 'the lack of any management on many estates' and 'spoke of his idea of purchasing a property and working out his own means as to raising the people to a moral and social scale of civilisation'.[83] Another of Hill's friends, Reuben John Bryce, believed that 'social improvement' of the peasantry was upmost in Hill's mind, writing that 'his single-minded anxiety [was] for the elevation of the humbler classes'.[84] Regardless of these alleged ambitions for social reform in Donegal, it does appear that, after just one visit, Hill fell in love with the county's scenery.

78 *Dublin Evening Packet*, 6 March, 21 June 1834; *Dublin Evening Post*, 1 April 1834.
79 *Dublin Evening Packet*, 7 Dec 1833; *Newry Telegraph*, 20 Dec 1833.
80 *Northern Whig*, 9 Jan 1834.
81 *The Warder*, 30 Aug 1834.
82 *Destitution*: 6632.
83 Ibid.
84 Bryce letter to *Belfast News-Letter*, 12 April 1879.

Love was definitely on his mind at the time. Seven years after his thwarted marriage proposal to Cassandra Knight, a brief news item appeared in several English newspapers in October 1834:'Lord George Hill, the brother of the Marquess of Downshire, is about to lead to the hymeneal altar a rich and accomplished young Lady; namely, Miss Knight, of Godmersham Park, near Canterbury'.[85]

---

85 *Morning Post* and *London Evening Standard*, 6 Oct 1834.

3

THE LORD MARRIES HIS LADY

Love is an emblem of eternity. It confounds all notion of time, effacing all memory of a beginning and all fear of an end – Madame de Staël[1]

Hill's willingness to wait seven years in order to marry the woman of his choice says much about him. Once his mind was made up, it was not for changing. Call it an example of a strong will and it can be viewed as commendable. Call it obstinacy and it can be regarded as irrational. It would be churlish to see his lengthy commitment to Cassandra Knight as anything other than laudable. But how did he know the right moment to reopen their relationship?

There are no records of the couple having maintained contact between August 1827 and August 1834, and it is doubtful if they did. By reading newspapers, it would have been possible for Cass, or members of her family, to have monitored some of Hill's activities. She would have known that he had remained single. For him, however, news about Cass must have been sparing.

So, how did he hear that Cass, living quietly with her sisters and brother Charles at Godmersham Park, Kent, had become engaged? It stretches credulity to believe that his sudden arrival on the scene within weeks of her engagement was merely a coincidence. There is evidence which suggests he was tipped off. Seventy or so years after the event, Cass's niece, Fanny Margaretta Rice (by then the Dowager Countess of Winchilsea), confirmed that 'someone' had 'told Uncle

---

1 *Corinne, or Italy* (1807), Chapter II.

George of the proposed marriage'.[2] The countess, who was only 13 at the time may have recalled it accurately or, just as possibly, may have been recalling a family rumour.

There was opposition within the Knight family when Cass accepted a proposal from a vicar, the Rev. Musgrave Alured Henry Harris, youngest son of a late military commander, Baron Harris of Seringapatum and Mysore.[3] It was a strange match for Cass, which upset her eldest sister, Fanny, Lady Knatchbull, who thought the 'infatuation' to be 'odious' and decried the 'absurd engagement'.[4]

She sought help from other family members to persuade Cass to change her mind, and it was their aunt – Cassandra Austen, sister of Jane – who finally convinced her to reject Harris.[5] Within weeks of the break-up, Fanny recorded her 'extreme joy and astonishment' at Lord George's arrival at the Knight-Austen family home in Chawton, Hampshire, where he proposed marriage to Cass for the second time.[6]

How had Hill managed to convince his mother to change her mind? Evidently, the Duke of Wellington played a part. She consulted him about the status of the Knight family, rightly anticipating that he would know of them because he had a house in Hampshire near the Knights' family seat. Wellington gave them a clean bill of health, calling them 'a very respectable family'.[7] So, Hill did not defy his mother: she simply gave in. One of her acquaintances told a friend: 'Old Lady Downshire has been opposing it all along, but has at last consented'.[8] She accepted that George, after seven years as dance partner to an assortment of attractive and eligible noble ladies, was not going to marry any of them. Now aged 70, Mary's failing constitution also softened her opposition.

The upshot was the marriage on 21 October 1834 of 32-year-old Lord George Augusta Hill to 27-year-old Cassandra Jane Knight at St George's Hanover Square. The splendid church, Handel's favourite, was within sight of the grand mansion where Hill had spent several of his childhood years. Cass wore a white satin gown, set off with a grey satin pelisse (a

---

2 Davis (2021a): 6. The revelation emerged in correspondence between Lord George's eldest son, Arthur, and the dowager countess.

3 Hillan (2011): 94.

4 Ibid. 95.

5 Ibid.

6 Hillan (2011): 96.

7 Ombersley Archive, Wellington letter to MDS, 9 Sept 1834. Supplied by Martin Davis.

8 Captain John Hart to Viscountess Forbes, 17 Sept 1834. PRONI Granard Papers, Register of Irish Archives, K/3/1.

fur-trimmed cloak) and a pink satin bonnet. A diary record by her brother, Charles, indicated the gulf in social class between his and Hill's families.[9]

For the Knights, the match 'had social cachet', and Cass's newly elevated station had been evident on the journey to London from Kent. While she travelled, in company with her sister, Louisa, in a new carriage, attended by two servants, the rest of the Knight family were relegated to less stylish, and less comfortable, coaches. On the wedding eve, Cass's family were entertained to dinner at Lady Salisbury's imposing house on Arlington Street. George's mother and his two brothers, Atty and Marcus, were also at the table. Doubtless, MDS chose that evening to pass on the goodwill message to the couple she had received from the Palace. Queen Adelaide wrote to the dowager marchioness to praise the couple's 'constancy & fidelity', adding that 'the King and I join in very good wishes for yourself and the young couple'.[10]

Charles thought his sister a very nervous bride and even perceived her as 'a sacrificial victim'. He wrote: 'Cass'ra looked uncommonly well, but with her chaplet of orange flowers & white veil over it was rather like a victim'. He continued: 'Poor dear Cass could hardly speak at first, but got better as she went on'.[11] Outside the church, Cass was overwhelmed by the attention. When confronted by 'an immense crowd' as she stepped into the carriage, 'she pulled the blinds down'. Her husband would have none of it. He 'immediately pulled them up that his bonny bride might be seen, which pleased the mob very much & they cheered them off heartily'.[12]

The post-wedding celebrations for 'nearly one hundred fashionables' consisted of 'a splendid *dejeune a la fourchette*, served on massive silver' at Hitchcock's hotel in Albemarle Street.[13] There were speeches by Hill's eldest brother, Downshire, and Cass's father, Edward. Afterwards, the Knights were treated to a taste of the aristocratic world at a party, hosted by Lady Salisbury. Among 'the chief fashionables' were Hill's Anglo-Irish friends, such as the Marquess of Westmeath, his daughter, Lady Rosa Nugent, and the Hon. Charles Gore, son of the second Earl of Arran.

Charles expressed his family's joy at his sister's choice of husband: 'The more we know of [Lord George], the more we feel sure that he will make her happy, and the more we know of all his family the more we

9 Hillan (2011): 97-8.
10 Davis (2020b): 70.
11 CBK, 21 Oct 1834. Diaries 8 JAHM.
12 Ibid.
13 *Belfast News-Letter*, 31 Oct 1834; *Dublin Morning Register*, 28 Oct 1834.

have reason to be satisfied with the match'.[14] For Hill's mother, there was little satisfaction once she grasped the financial details. Cass's fortune stood at £5,800, which was just over half of Lord George's. His income was less than £900 a year, of which about £400 was earned as comptroller of Lord Wellesley's household. The marchioness was told by her solicitor: 'This annual sum would not, without the utmost prudence and economy, be nearly sufficient to sustain him and the Lady of his affection in their married state, at all consistently with their Station'. Therefore, he added: 'The extra Means to enable them to do so must rest with the never failing maternal Solicitude of his Noble Mother, to provide for the Welfare, Comfort and Happiness of all who are so near and dear to Her Ladyship.'[15]

Despite his duties on Wellesley's behalf, Hill did not return to Dublin after the wedding. He and his bride spent a short honeymoon at the marchioness's house in Roehampton, she having decamped to Brighton. The newly-weds then spent two weeks at MDS's estate in Worcestershire, Ombersley Court.[16] Towards the end of their visit they were joined by Lord Marcus and all then travelled to Brighton, where the marchioness had rented a large house in the fashionable Kemp Town district.[17] It was an early introduction to Cassandra of the Hills' peripatetic life. Similarly, she learned of the obligations expected of her new family's closeness to royalty by accompanying her husband to pay respects to the King at the Pavilion.[18]

After a fortnight, the couple travelled, via London, to the Knights' home in Kent for Christmas, where they spent seven weeks.[19] During their stay at Godmersham Park, Downshire arrived with his family for a week. A picture emerges of an endless house party with long countryside walks, shooting and riding in the daytimes followed by evenings of music, singing and games of charades. Hill forged a friendship with her brother, Charles, cutting down trees together, riding and shooting.[20] As widely forecast, the Marquess of Wellesley, was deposed as lord lieutenant, so George did not return to Dublin. Instead, he took a rented a house in

---

14 CBK, 21 Oct 1834. Diaries 8 JAHM.
15 Davis (2020b): 102. Letter to MDS from Thomas Handley.
16 *Morning Post*, 3 Nov 1834; *Worcester Journal*, 15 Nov 1834.
17 *The Sun*, 5 Nov 1834; *Morning Post*, 11 Dec 1834.
18 *The Sun*, 14 Feb 1835.
19 Hillan (2011): 101.
20 Ibid. 102.

London's Mayfair and, by August, with Cassandra pregnant, they were back with the Knight family.[21]

Hill's fascination with Irish culture and history was evident in his attempt to encourage Charles to take an interest in the subject. It proved to be an uphill battle, with Charles remarking disdainfully in his diary: 'I read some more of G. Hill's old book on the ancient history of the Irish, which is full of absurdities, but he thinks it is all founded on fact, & I daresay it is'.[22] In late November, Hill was in mourning for his aunt, the Dowager Marchioness of Salisbury, who perished, aged 85, in a fire at the Cecils' magnificent family seat, Hatfield House.[23] He had always been close to his father's eccentric sister, as had his mother. Within a couple of weeks, however, he was celebrating the birth of his first child, a daughter named Norah Mary Elizabeth.[24]

Throughout 1836, the Hills divided their time between Brighton, Worthing and Godmersham Park. They attended the king's levee at St James's Palace, and Cass was inculcated into her new aristocratic role, being presented to William IV by her sister-in-law, the Marchioness of Downshire.[25] The Downshires retook possession of the family's Hanover Square house, which had previously been let by MDS.[26] Her health declined rapidly over the early summer months and she died in August, aged 72.

Her impressive funeral reflected her status. Leading the procession from Roehampton were four mutes on horseback, a state plume of feathers, a man bearing the marchioness's coronet on a crimson velvet cushion, and a horse covered with black velvet emblazoned with escutcheons of the family arms. The hearse, with armorial bearings and the Downshire family crest on each side, was drawn by six horses caparisoned with velvets and feathers. Six mourning coaches, each drawn by six horses, were followed by the private carriages of her immediate family. Then came a line of some 40 carriages belonging to a swathe of the nobility. They included George III's son, the Duke of Sussex; three Dukes, including Wellington; the Dowager Duchess of Richmond; four Marquesses, including Wellesley, Londonderry and Salisbury; and Lords and Ladies too numerous for the journalists to list. But they did not miss the fact that one of the untitled

21 Hillan, op. cit. 102.
22 CBK, 19 Nov 1835, Diaries 9 JAHM.
23 *The Times*, 30 Nov 1835.
24 *Kentish Weekly Post*, 22 Dec 1835.
25 *Morning Post*, 6 May 1836.
26 *Morning Post*, 9 May 1836.

mourners was George IV's morganatic wife, and MDS's long-time friend, Maria Fitzherbert, now in the 80th, and final, year of her life. The dowager marchioness's remains were interred in a vault in the church on the Downshires' 5,000-acre Berkshire estate, Easthampstead Park.[27]

Her death was a major turning point for George and two of his brothers. In Atty's case, it elevated him to the title of the second Baron Sandys and the ownership of Ombersley Court with its large estate. He stood down as Lieutenant-Colonel of the Scots Greys and was also required to give up his County Down parliamentary seat.[28] (He was succeeded by Downshire's 22-year-old son, Arthur, Earl of Hillsborough, a loss for the Whigs because he stood, unopposed, as a Tory.) For George and Marcus, it meant a substantial financial settlement: each of them received £24,500.[29]

While Hill was awaiting his inheritance, and planning on how he would spend it, Cassandra went into labour.[30] Her second child – George's son and heir – was named Arthur Blundell George Sandys. Did the new mother have any inkling that she would raise her son in Ireland? Did she even have a clue about her husband's ambition to become an Irish landowner? Gweedore, the heart of George's story, beckons.

27 *Evening Chronicle*, 10 Aug 1836; *Morning Post*, 12 Aug 1836; Worcester Herald, 27 Aug 1836.

28 *Dublin Morning Register*, 5 Jan 1838.

29 Maguire, op. cit. 88; Davis, *Letters*:123. £24,500 would be approximately £2.7 million today.

30 Davis (2021a). Address recorded by George in his bible.

4

THE HILLS OF DONEGAL

Good was to be done to them whether they wished it or not
– Sophia Hillan[1]

Hill's decision to make a radical change to his life coincided with the end of the Georgian era when, in June 1837, the British throne passed to Victoria. The following month, he was presented to the young queen by his brother, the Marquess of Downshire.[2] It was to be one of his last visits to a palace. Once his mother's bequest reached his bank he took the first step towards his future by formally resigning from the army. He exchanged into the 47th (Lancashire) Regiment of Foot and immediately sold his commission as major.[3]

For the first time in his life Hill was rich. His £24,500 inheritance would, in today's terms, amount to about £2.75 million. What to do with the money, and with himself? There were investment opportunities opening up in England as the industrial revolution moved toward its zenith.[4] Capitalism was in the ascendant.

With manufacturing supplanting agriculture, nouveau factory owners were asserting their supremacy over the land-owning class. A campaign launched against the corn laws identified landowners as the unwarranted beneficiaries of a protectionist policy which had the effect of keeping bread prices high.

The growing opposition to landowners in England was confined to the emergent bourgeoisie. It did not involve their tenants, quite unlike Ireland

---

1 Hillan (2011): 125.
2 *The Times*, 20 July 1837.
3 *Morning Advertiser*, 24 March 1838. At the time, the value of an infantry major's commission was about £3,200 (today's equivalent: £297,000).
4 Ireland, which did not experience anything like an industrial revolution, remained a largely agricultural society (with the exception of Belfast).

where there was long-held hostility by the tenantry toward the people who owned the land they worked. There, landlords, who owned and controlled a vast swathe of the country, were perceived as foreigners. Most were English and many of them rarely, if ever, set foot in Ireland. The overwhelming majority were Protestant while their tenants were overwhelmingly Catholic. In Ulster (except for west Donegal), there was another split – most Protestant owners were members of the established Anglican church while their tenants were largely dissenting Presbyterians. They tended to have slightly less antagonistic relationships with owners than Catholics. And it was there, in counties Down and Antrim, that Hill gained his lessons in landlordism during visits to Hillsborough Castle, his brother's seat.[5]

These experiences may well have given Hill a false picture of landlordism. The Marquess of Downshire's estates were situated on good farmland and were well run by an agent respected for his tact and good sense.[6] Downshire had pioneered the introduction of new agricultural methods and machinery without upsetting his tenants.[7] He enjoyed a substantial income in spite of complaining that he had little surplus to invest in his farms.[8] His was far from a typical case. Across Ireland, many landowners found it increasingly difficult to profit from their holdings and were beginning to run into financial difficulties. Attempts by landlords to improve their income by raising rents, and evicting those unable or unwilling to pay, provoked controversies, including violent, and sometimes fatal, clashes. These conflicts were often reported in English newspapers, so Hill could not have been other than aware of them as he contemplated what to do with his windfall. It did not deter him from joining the landlord class.

Hill's friend, James Dombrain, played a crucial role in persuading him to buy land in Donegal. Seven years older than Hill, he had a far broader experience of life. Born in Canterbury to an inn-keeper in 1794, he joined the Royal Navy, aged 14, during the Napoleonic war. He saw action in the Mediterranean and was promoted to the rank of lieutenant just before the war reached its climax in 1815. At the end of hostilities, he joined the Preventive Water Guard, a branch of the British revenue service founded to combat smuggling. By the end of 1816, he was the service's assistant

---

5 Downshire also owned estates in Edenderry, King's County (now Offaly) and Blessington, Wicklow, plus an estate in England: Easthampstead Park, Berkshire.

6 Downshire was heavily dependent on his agent, William Reilly, Maguire (1974).

7 Ibid. 15.

8 Ibid. 25.

comptroller and, three years later, he was sent to Ireland to establish an equivalent force. Dombrain, who was given the title of Inspector General of the Irish Coast Guard, made a huge success of the service, creating a flotilla of ships, setting up a chain of coastal stations and recruiting a loyal force of officers. Most of its activities were concentrated along Ireland's west coast, where the guards disrupted the smuggling of tobacco and the illicit distillation of whiskey and poitín.[9] Occasionally, they found guns, allegedly imported to arm 'the Irish peasantry'.[10]

Dombrain revealed his humanitarian ethos during the 1831 outbreak of potato blight.[11] Aside from his concern for the people of Donegal, he also fell in love with the wildness of its scenery and was especially struck by Dunlewey, adjacent to Gweedore. The haunting valley and deep lake, known as the Poisoned Glen, stands amid the Derryveagh mountains and is overlooked by its highest peak, Mount Errigal. Having heard about its bleak beauty, he found it difficult to reach. His first attempt to get there, on horseback along 'a dangerous mountain track', failed. Months later, he managed it on foot.[12] He found a small cottage owned by a woman who used it during the summer while her cattle were grazing. She agreed to rent it to him and he soon decided to buy a substantial tract of land.

In order to build a large house on the lake shore, Dombrain had to negotiate for the necessary land with a man he regarded as a squatter who 'refused to quit until I paid 20 years' purchase of his rent'. Dombrain was piqued at the man's response. 'Even after receiving so large a sum of money he left his curse upon his house so that no one would afterwards inhabit it.' He added: 'I purchased other tenants out on similar terms but they quitted without leaving a similar blessing.'[13]

This anecdote exemplifies the tensions inherent in the relationship between English landlord and Irish tenant. In economic terms, it should also be viewed as the friction caused by the import of capitalism. An inbuilt inequality opened a chasm between the two sides in which the rights of the landlord, through the ruthless exercise of financial superiority, outweighed the rights of the tenants. But it wasn't money itself that divided them; it was what the money represented. It imbued the landlord, whether he was conscious of it or not, with a sense of entitlement. Dombrain, otherwise

9 Symes (2003): 60-61.
10 *Kentish Weekly Post*, 15 Feb 1831.
11 See chapter 2.
12 VB, 1: 123.
13 Ibid.

noted for his altruism, saw nothing intrinsically wrong with using the power of his purse to get his way. In his view, he was acting justly by paying for what he wanted. There was no question in his mind of his trampling on the tenants' rights because he was compensating them. Nor, apparently, did he worry about the emotional injury caused by uprooting natives from their long-held patches of land.

For displaced tenants, it was a different matter. They were relinquishing their homes and seeing their community broken up. Their powerlessness, manifested through their lack of money, obliged them to do as the landlord required. That reality coloured their perception of incomers (hence the tenant's parting curse) because it reinforced a feeling of deprivation, of helplessness, of hopelessness. In so many ways, the attitudes and actions of both the compassionate Dombrain and his resentful tenants prefigure the situation that would arise between Hill and his tenants.

When Dombrain introduced Hill to Gweedore in 1834 he clearly enthused him with his love for the area, encouraging him to buy land adjacent to his own estate. For Hill, who had spent most of his life in the capital cities of England and Ireland, Gweedore – some 280 kms from Dublin – must have had its aesthetic appeal: rugged coastline, boulder-strewn mountains, purple-heathered bog, fast-flowing icy streams, dramatic skies. Its tautologous Irish name, *Gaoth Dobhair* (aqueous estuary) referred to its location at the mouth of the Crolly river where it flowed into the Atlantic. Everywhere was water, running down the mountainsides, falling from the sky, oozing up through sodden bogs. In a panorama devoid of people, it could have been mistaken for a peaceful rustic utopia. This was romantic Gweedore.

In realistic Gweedore, scenery was immaterial for its inhabitants. Amid what visitors regarded as a picturesque wilderness were thousands of people eking out a living. On poor soil, they were growing oats and potatoes, and grazing cows, sheep and pigs. Their tiny houses, mostly single-roomed, were clustered in groups known as clachans. Some shared their living space with their animals. They farmed under a communal system known as rundale in which a number of tenants, usually from one clachan and often linked by kinship, held joint leases on the holding.[14] The land closest to the houses, the infield, was divided into individual plots for cultivating crops. Pasture, the outfield, was generally shared

14 Derived from the Irish words 'roinn' for a division or share and 'dáil' for 'portioning out'.

by all.[15] Small plots, which were not fenced, were usually scattered over a wide area while animals were allowed to roam free. Plots were also periodically sub-divided to accommodate newer family members, making them ever smaller. Some families moved seasonally with their animals between mountain pasture and the coastal lowland (booleying, aka transhumance).[16] To outsiders, all this seemed like anarchy.

It appears that in some estates landlords had retreated from any responsibility for their tenants, allowing them to regulate themselves. Rent and taxes went uncollected.[17] Debts built up. It could not have been a more unpromising prospect for a would-be landlord, a world away from the situation Hill had witnessed on his brother's rolling acres in east Ulster. And Downshire was anything but warm about the people in counties outside his domain. In 1834, he wrote to Hill to say he had lost his 'enthusiasm' for 'the peasantry in the South' and complained that 'the state of the Country people is so vicious now, that it will take years, if ever, to bring them back to good Order'. He concluded: 'It is duty now alone that actuates me'.[18]

Hill also knew about the state of distress in west Donegal in advance of becoming a landlord because, in 1836, it was Dombrain who alerted the Dublin authorities to the dire conditions in which thousands of people were living. He acted as an intermediary for two men, a priest and a schoolmaster, who sought to draw the attention of the Lord Lieutenant, the Earl of Mulgrave, to the shocking level of poverty in the region. H.O. Freil (probably Hugh Friel), parish priest of West Tullaghobegley, which included Gweedore, wrote a letter to two Donegal newspapers about his 'distressed congregation' of 700 families. He said 'nine-tenths' of them were 'starving' and praised benefactors for their £50 contributions 'to alleviate the distress'. They included Mulgrave and Dombrain.[19] Some of the money was used to buy 60 tons of potatoes and to import 140 tons of meal. When Mulgrave visited Donegal, Freil led 'the entire parish of Tullaghobegly' to confront the lord lieutenant on his way to Doe Castle and presented him with an address about his parishioners' plight.[20] Mulgrave was accompanied by Dombrain, who then took him to his Dunlewey house for an 'elegant repast'.[21]

15 McCourt (1955).
16 Evans (1957).
17 Ó Gallchobhair (1962): 22ff.
18 Davis (2021a): 10.
19 *Derry Journal*; *Ballyshannon Herald*, 21 June 1836/24 June 1835.
20 *Derry Journal*, 2 Sept 1836.
21 Ibid.

Although Freil's letter was republished in other papers elsewhere in Ireland, his efforts attracted little publicity compared to a report compiled by schoolmaster Patrick McKye. Cast in the form of a petition, it was presented to Mulgrave via Dombrain. It pointed to the paucity of implements available to the area's population (supposedly 4,000), claiming that they shared one plough and had few shovels, harrows and rakes, making it difficult, if not impossible, to work their small farms.[22] According to McKye, 'no other garden vegetables, but potatoes and cabbage' were grown. He described the people as being 'in the most, needy, hungry, and naked condition of any people that ever came within the precincts of my knowledge'. They lacked proper clothing, with many unable to afford shoes. Families slept together, mostly on beds of 'straw, green and dried rushes … their bedclothes are either coarse sheets or no sheets, and ragged, filthy blankets'.[23]

McKye wrote:

> There is a general prospect of starvation at the present prevailing among them … the principal cause is a rot or failure of seed in the last year's crop, together with a scarcity of winter forage, in consequence of a long continuation of storms since October last in this part of the country. So that they, the people, were under the necessity of cutting down their potatoes, and give them to the cattle to keep them alive. All these circumstances connected together have brought hunger to reign among them.[24]

'The peasantry', he continued, 'are on the small allowance of one meal a day, and many families cannot afford more than one meal in two days, and sometimes, one meal in three days. Their children crying and fainting with hunger, and their parents weeping, being full of grief, hunger, debility, and dejection, with glooming aspect looking at their children likely to expire in the pains of starvation. Also, in addition to all, their cattle and sheep are dying with hunger, and their owner forced by hunger to eat the flesh of such. 'Tis reasonable to suppose that the use of such flesh will raise some infectious disease among the people.' School rolls had fallen because of the 'hunger and extreme poverty of children'.[25]

McKye, with a touch of sarcasm, contended that the landlords would be sure to contradict his account, telling Mulgrave 'it would blast their

---

22 Hill, *Facts from Gweedore*: 16. All quotes from 5th edition (1887) unless otherwise stated. Hereafter, *Facts*.
23 Ibid. 14.
24 Ibid. 15.
25 Ibid.

honours if it were known abroad that such a degree of want existed in their estates among their tenantry'. He called instead for an investigation by an 'unprejudiced gentleman' who would find 150 naked children 'and some hundreds only covered with filthy rags' in houses shared with animals. He listed three people who would authenticate his findings: the parish priest, the chief constable stationed at Gweedore, and Dombrain. The petition was shown to Hill by Dombrain 'as a matter of curiosity'.[26] It was to become a central plank of Hill's promotional literature ever after.

As Hill prepared to become a Donegal landlord there were other bad omens for him to consider, such as outbreaks of civil disobedience and occasional outbursts of violence in which landlords, and more often their agents, were targets. One trigger for lawlessness was the obligation on Catholics and Presbyterians to pay tithes to fund the established Protestant church. With the Irish Tithe Bill limping through the House of Commons, there was continuing opposition to payment. In late summer 1838, two Catholic clergymen in Donegal were pressured into paying tithes, one of whom was imprisoned.[27] It meant that Church of Ireland clergymen were often unpopular. At least two of them were victims of arson attacks.[28] The most serious incidents were due to poverty and its result, hunger. There was a continual suspicion that landlords were seeking to profit from people's misery. When rumours spread in Dunfanaghy that potatoes were being loaded on to a ship, thereby denying local people of their main foodstuff, a crowd of 200 gathered near the dock to try to prevent the shipment. A riot broke out, several arrests were made and eleven men were convicted for taking part in an affray. After the jury recommended mercy, two were jailed for two weeks with hard labour while the others got a week.[29]

In Ballyshannon, throughout 1837, there was a series of violent confrontations over fishing. People objected to the decision by a wealthy Church of Ireland rector, George Tredennick, to allow a Scotsman, James Hector, to use bag nets to catch salmon. Local protesters, joined by people from along the Donegal and Sligo coast, regularly attacked Hector's nets and boats. One incident generated a surprising amount of publicity. A newspaper report, headlined 'Rising of the peasantry', told of 1,000 people armed with guns, swords and scythes gathering to

26 *Destitution*: 6936.
27 *Newry Examiner*, 8 Aug 1838; *Belfast Commercial Chronicle*, 11 Aug 1838; *Morning Advertiser*, 13 Aug 1838; *Derry Journal*, 28 Aug 1838.
28 *Londonderry Sentinel*, 6 Jan 1838; *Morning Chronicle*, 2 Jan 1838.
29 *Londonderry Sentinel*, 4 Aug 1838.

destroy Tredennick's boats and burn Hector's nets and fishing tackle.[30] This wildly exaggerated story was retold to the House of Lords, by the Earl of Glengall, when he complained about the poor being unable to afford fishing boats. 'It is notorious', he told fellow peers, 'that the coasts of Ireland abound with fish in greater quantities than the coasts of any other portion of the globe; yet so great is the poverty of the people, that they are unable to avail themselves of the blessings which Providence has so liberally placed within their reach'.[31] More than a year later, Tredennick received a letter threatening his life and two of his cows were killed in barbaric fashion.[32]

None of this can have escaped Hill's attention. It was, after all, Dombrain who regarded the people as having 'habits of self-will and lawlessness'.[33] And against this background of rumbling discontent, Hill also had to take on board the broader political realities of the period. The insistent calls for repeal of the Union by Daniel O'Connell had the effect of building a nation-wide sense of unity among Irish people of all classes. His campaign, although not directly threatening to the power exercised by Anglo-Irish landlords, had the effect of undermining their confidence in the future and united them in opposition to repeal. One of the most vociferous was Hill's brother, Lord Downshire, and Hill underlined his own anti-repeal stance by supporting a meeting in Belfast called to oppose O'Connell.[34]

Apparently undaunted by the negative signs, and quite possibly inspired by the challenge, Hill was determined to become a landlord. He had demonstrated his unshakeable single-mindedness by waiting seven years to marry Cassandra. Now, his stubborn streak would come to fore again. It says something about his strength of character – or, arguably, his naivety – that he decided to purchase a large slice of Gweedore in the belief that he could triumph where others had failed. He entered into a series of negotiations to buy estates from landlords who were only too eager to offload them – at a price. His initial purchases involved separate deals with four landlords over four years.[35] His first acquisition was an estate of 11,164 acres, bought from Captain William Stewart of Horn Head, a former high sheriff of Donegal. It cost Hill £4,380, which

---

30 *Saunders's News-Letter*, 29 May 1837.
31 *Hansard*, Lords, 19 June 1837, para 1534.
32 *Waterford Mail*, 3 Aug 1838.
33 VB 1: 123.
34 *Northern Whig*, 21 Jan 1841.
35 *Destitution*: 6641.

included £310 rent arrears.[36] Months later, he spent £1,300, including £50 fishing arrears, to buy 1,092 acres from another member of the same family, Major William Stewart.[37] Four islands were included in these deals, including Gola with its 150 inhabitants.

While Hill was preparing his initial reconstruction plans in September 1838, he and Cass stayed nearby to what a newspaper called his newly-purchased 'extensive estate'.[38] They rented St Ernan's, south of Donegal Town, a large house standing on a little island reached by a short causeway. It was owned by Captain John Hamilton, a land-owner who had been praised for raising substantial funds during the 1831 potato blight. He would later win plaudits for organising relief works in the 1840s hunger, which sank him into debt.[39]

In 1839, Hill extended his holdings by paying £5,300, including £100 in rent arrears, to acquire 7,850 acres from James Watt, who owned a whiskey distillery in Derry and lived at Claragh, Ramelton, very close to another property Hill would eventually acquire. It was not until 1842 that he obtained his fourth portion, some 2,677 acres, paying £1,200 to a 'Mr Barton'.[40] Around the same time, he paid a further £2,614 to Watt in order to share a weir.[41] It was the land bought in 1838-39 which was the most important because it was on these estates that he first introduced his social and agricultural reforms and carried out his substantial building projects. The stand-out fact to note from those transactions is that his acquisition of almost 23,000 acres cost him £12,180, a sizeable chunk of his £24,500 inheritance.

The relatively high levels of outstanding arrears that Hill accepted as part of the purchase prices can be attributed, on the landlords' side, either to their apathy or to their poor management. None of them were resident on these estates, although all had houses relatively nearby. None employed land-agents at the time. On the tenants' side, poverty was the main reason for non-payment. None of this could have come as a surprise. Did Hill not wonder why the Stewarts and Watt had sold to him so readily? The bigger question, of course, is to ask what possessed

---

36 Memorandum Book, PRONI D3054/3/1/2 (Hereafter Memo Book).
37 Ibid.
38 *Freeman's Journal*, 15 September 1838.
39 He detailed his travails in a memoir, *Sixty Years' Experience as an Irish Landlord*. His story was not too dissimilar from that of Hill.
40 Probably William Hugh Barton of Waterfoot, Co Fermanagh
41 Memo Book.

him to become a landlord at all? What induced a man of his privileged background and class to buy more than 20,000 largely unfertile acres and assume responsibility for the livelihoods of some 3,000 tenants? Although he went on to write in some detail about his achievements, he left behind no coherent explanation of his motivation.

Was he hoping to make money? Or was it, as Dombrain suggested, purely an act of philanthropy? The first makes little sense. If profit was his main incentive there were countless, risk-free investment possibilities open to him in England. Given the inflation rate at the time, even depositing his windfall in a bank would have guaranteed him a decent, if modest, return. He could not possibly hope to have made much money, let alone a fortune, from the rents paid by the subsistence farmers of Gweedore. We are therefore compelled to consider the second answer as much more likely. For his critics, both contemporaneous and more recent, his claim to have acted out of altruism has proved too difficult to accept. In their view, he was little different from the exploitative rack-renting absentee landlords who squeezed profits from the Irish peasantry in order to live high on the hog in England. Even those willing to concede his heart was in the right place, believing he set out with good intentions, argued that his actions had unintended negative consequences.

But this Lord George we are meeting in 1838 is in a different frame of mind and nursing a different bank account from the Lord George we will encounter in 1857. There is ample evidence to show Hill had no head for business and, for now, he is in the foothills of what looks to have been a spending spree. Acquiring the estates was only the beginning. One of his first acts was to buy out the tenants who rented the rough-and-ready quay and the fishing rights at Bunbeg, where the River Clady flows through a ravine into the sea. For ten years, brothers Edward and James Gallagher had run a successful salmon export trade and also worked a large farm on the surrounding 60 acres.[42] Hill, envisioning the quay's potential as a proper harbour and commercial centre, paid the Gallaghers £300 each as compensation for giving up their tenancy.[43] As tenants-at-will they could have been evicted without a penny.[44] Once Hill acquired the quay he immediately instituted the construction of a harbour,

---

42 Rummel (2013). Cf. Ó Gallchobhair (1975).

43 *Destitution*: 6843, 6848.

44 Edward acquired property on the Marquess of Conyngham's neighbouring estate while James emigrated to America following a failed attempt to set up a bakery.
Destitution: 6710, 6714.

which was designed to accommodate ships of 150 tons at high tide.[45] It was necessary to blast rocks in order to build a huge corn store on the pier, work that cost £750.[46] On the exterior wall he erected a plaque inscribed with a biblical quote, from Proverbs, in Irish: '*Is cúis áthais don Tiarna meáchan cóir, ach is gráin ina chothromaíocht é cothromaíocht neamhchothrom*' (A just weight is a pleasure to the Lord, but an unequal balance is an abomination in His sight). It remains in place to this day. He also built a general store, bakery and a harbour-master's office. In the following years would come five coastguard cottages, a school-house (later transformed into an Anglican church, St Patrick's) and a glebe house for a clergyman.[47] In addition, he had a two-storey house, later known as Heath Cottage, built for his personal use.[48]

For a district without adequate road links, the advantage of a little port was obvious, and it was to prove a valuable lifeline. Indeed, more than 180 years on, it continues to be an asset to the local community. For his tenants at the time, the building of the harbour was of far less import than his intention to institute far-reaching reforms to their way of life. He appears to have been influenced by a book claiming that the poor could be raised up by cultivating 'waste lands'.[49] His early meetings with tenants seemed to go off rather well. He visited every one of them to establish 'a mutual acquaintance' and to acquire 'an insight into their condition and character'.[50] They were both astonished and delighted that he could address them in Irish. Evidently, it made it difficult for them to believe he could be a lord.[51] It is unclear where he learned Irish. Some evidence (though not entirely convincing) suggests he may have picked up the basics as a child in Hillsborough from his nurse, 'a native Irish speaker from mid-Down'.[52] What is more certain is that in 1827, during his army posting to Ulster, he was introduced to a Presbyterian Irish language scholar, Reuben John Bryce, and showed an immediate interest in Bryce's society

45 *Facts* 5: 36.
46 *Destitution*: 6647. Elsewhere, it was recorded as £550. Davis (2021a): 11. The store was 84 ft long (25.6 metres) with three lofts and capable of holding 400 tons of grain. Its first export cargo, 30 tons of oats bound for Glasgow, was recorded on 20 September 1840.
47 *Destitution*: 6649,6650,6789.
48 Aalen and Brody (1969): 34. See https://www.buildingsofireland.ie/buildings-search/building/40817001/heath-cottage-meenderrygamp-gweedore-donegal
49 A copy of Alexander Whalley Light's *Plan for the Amelioration of the Condition of the Poor of the United Kingdom (more particularly Ireland)* was found in the Ombersley Court archive. Davis (2021a): 10.
50 *Facts*: 36.
51 Ibid. 36.
52 Davis (2021a): 10. Brendan Bonar letter, Sept 1969.

for preserving Gaelic.[53] Before then, according to Bryce, 'Lord George had been studying the language, and had already made great progress in it'.[54] Hill, who joined the society with his brother, Lord Downshire, kept in touch with Bryce for the following forty years.[55] Hill's friendship with the Irish scholar Owen Connellan also helped in his learning of Irish.[56] But Hill's message, whether delivered in Irish or English, was anything but welcome to the people of Gweedore. He wanted to do away with both their system of farming (rundale) and the arrangement of their housing (clachans). He also wished to re-set their rents.[57]

He began by hiring a surveyor, Robert Montgomery of Lifford, to conduct a lengthy, formal inquiry into his estate holdings. His entirely predictable recommendation, given the wishes of his employer, was for the termination of the rundale system. He proposed instead a wholesale reallocation of land to form strip, or squared-off, farms – known colloquially as 'cuts' – so that each tenant would have roughly equal portions of shore land, arable fields and mountain grazing. At the same time, the housing clusters should be broken up, with tenants having new houses located on their new cuts. No evictions would be necessary to introduce this reform.

When the tenants learned of the proposals, which Hill was eager to adopt, they 'felt all their prejudices outraged'.[58] They were unwilling to accept new houses if it meant separation from their neighbours.[59] They also suggested that the strips be sub-divided. Hill countered by pointing to the problems it would cause, such as lengthy cartage and a multiplicity of fences. Although he was willing to modify his plan a little, he would not be diverted from the overall extinction of rundale. One of his most enthusiastic supporters was John Pitt Kennedy, a locally-born agricultural reformer, who was also dedicated to the abolition of rundale in the belief it was chaotic and unproductive.[60] He thought farmers, whom he regarded

---

53 Bryce (1797-1888), president of the Royal Academical Institute in Belfast, was a co-founder and then joint secretary of the Ulster Gaelic Society. See Blaney (1996): 145.
54 Bryce letter to *Belfast News-Letter*, 12 April 1879.
55 According to the Gweedore Hotel Visitors' Book, Bryce stayed 16 Sept 1842, and his Gaelic Society colleague, Robert Shipboy MacAdam (Roibeard MacAdhaimh), stayed 30 May 1843.
56 See chapter 2.
57 *Destitution*: 6660,6671-4.
58 *Facts* 2: 16-17.
59 Woodham-Smith (1962): 24.
60 Captain in the Corps of Royal Engineers. Secretary to both the Devon Commission (1843) and the Famine Relief Committee (1845).

as 'poor ignorant people', would eventually come to see the benefits of a rational system.[61] He had some experience, having pioneered changes while acting as farm manager for a Donegal landowner with large estates around Ballybofey, Sir Charles Styles (possibly Style), whose daughter he married. His philosophy was clear from the title of his book on how to improve conditions for agricultural tenants: *Instruct; Employ; Don't Hang Them*: or *Ireland Tranquilized without Soldiers and Enriched without English Capital*.[62]

The change Hill instituted was carried out over a three-year period up to 1843. It was not popular, although Hill was ambivalent when commenting on his tenants' reaction. At one point, he claimed the tenants raised 'innumerable objections' before 'peaceably' consenting to the changes.[63] At another, he hinted at more trenchant resistance, saying that 'the opposition on the part of the people to the new system was vexatious and harassing, though ... not violent'.[64] And, at yet another, he said the tenants, having been 'called upon to assist in dividing the land ... expressed themselves frequently as being perfectly satisfied'.[65] However, the ending of rundale and the break-up of clachans certainly involved substantial upheaval, and there was no doubt that Hill, invested with the power of a landlord, would get his way.[66] He would not countenance any refusal to carry out his wishes. In that sense, it is fair to describe him as guilty of authoritarianism. Convinced of the rightness of his ideas, he imagined the long-term results of his reorganisation of his tenants' lives and livelihoods would be so beneficial that they would come to value the transformation.

Hill was, in effect, engaged in a social engineering experiment, which he made abundantly clear in his book, *Facts from Gweedore*. It is obvious too from the inscription on a plaque erected in the Bunbeg church he built, describing him as 'a self-denying Christian' who 'devoted his life and fortune to civilise Gweedore, and to raise its people to a higher social and moral level'. Several contributors to his hotel book used exactly the same phrase, suggesting that he, or someone close to him, was given to

---

61 *Facts* 2: 16-17.
62 Published in London, 1835.
63 *Facts* 5: 40.
64 Ibid. 41.
65 *Destitution*: 6660.
66 MacSuibhne (1995).

repeating the philosophy to guests.[67] His friend, Reuben Bryce, said Hill, prior to becoming a landlord, 'yearned for the power' to promote the peasantry's 'social improvement'.[68]

Hill sought to enlighten the people through changing both their agricultural arrangements and their domestic circumstances, all the while monitoring their responses to his initiatives. It could be said that his initiative treated the residents of Gweedore as if they were guinea pigs in a science lab. Not that he viewed it in those terms. All the signs indicate that he genuinely believed he was improving people's lives, a reminder that paternalism justifies itself through the belief of the protagonists that they are acting for the good of others, even if those people fail to appreciate it (as Hillan's quote at the head of this chapter indicates). Nor can we accuse Hill of boastfulness. Everything we know of him suggests he was a well-mannered, modest, even shy, man. But the insistent message of *Facts* is one in which he places himself at the centre of events, underlining that his leadership is the key factor.

He did not try to conceal that it was his position as a landlord which enabled him to introduce his reforms and there is no other way to describe that exercise of unaccountable power as anything other than autocratic. Although this does not make him a despot on a par with many of the more hard-hearted Anglo-Irish landlords of the period, his tenants were not in a position to make such comparisons. Their lived experience was of being forced to do Hill's bidding. As far as they were concerned, it would not be overstating matters to accuse him of employing an iron fist in a velvet glove. Even if we assume the purity of his motives, that he acquired the Gweedore estates as a philanthropic act, it was hardly surprising that the inhabitants remained suspicious. From their perspective, regardless of his good manners, his ability to speak some Irish and his expressed wish to improve their prospects, he was a rich member of the British aristocracy who, by accident of birth, had their fate in his hands.

While Hill wrestled with the problems of his new role as a landlord, his public life receded. He attended family occasions, but the nights of balls and parties were over. Early in 1839, he spent a brief time in London[69] before joining the pregnant Cassandra at the Knights' house,

---

67 VB,1: Warren Miller Jones, 7 Oct 1842; Anon, 30 May 1845; E. Chambers, 12 Sept 1846; Anon, 14 Oct 1846; John Storey, 30 Oct 1849. Cf. Dombrain's entry, 16 Sept 1846.
68 Bryce letter to *Belfast News-Letter*, 12 April 1879.
69 *The Sun*, 19 Jan 1839.

Godmersham, in Kent. In March, she gave birth to their third child, and second son, Augustus Charles Edward, named after Hill's late brother.[70] The couple stayed on for at least three months. A letter to Marcus at the end of June revealed Hill's absence from Gweedore. He wrote: 'I hear from Donegal that provisions are getting up very much'.[71]

Anxious not be an absentee landlord, Hill decided he must move to Donegal. As befitted a man of his class, that meant acquiring the obligatory Big House. While scouting for one, he set up home in Letterkenny, which boasted businesses and stores unavailable in the south and west of the county. The disadvantage was a 25-mile journey to Gweedore over very bad roads.

If Hill had read a November edition of the *Londonderry Sentinel* he might just have noticed an advert for a 'most eligible residence' at Ballyare in nearby Ramelton. The 'comfortable and commodious' house, with an accompanying farm, was being rented by a Royal Navy captain, William Boxer, but the owners were eager to sell.[72] We must presume Hill didn't see it. Instead, he rented a house at Barnhill, on Letterkenny's outskirts, where he and Cassandra settled in with four-year-old Norah, two-year-old Arthur and baby Augustus.[73] Cassandra also gave birth there in June 1840, but the child, a daughter, was still born.[74]

Hill's status granted him immediate entrée to Donegal's legal and political elite. He was soon sworn in to the Grand Jury, the body that operated, in effect, as a county council.[75] He found himself alongside five Donegal landlords: Edward Michael Conolly, MP for the county, with a large estate in Ballyshannon; Wybrants Olphert, with 18,000 acres around Falcarragh; Conolly Gage, owner of 2,500 acres in Castlefinn; Sir James Annesley Stewart, with 1,000 acres in Ramelton; and Lord Clements, son of the second Earl of Leitrim, who had substantial land holdings in five counties, including two large estates in Donegal totalling 43,000 acres.[76] Hill may not have agreed with their specific political agendas – Gage had voted against electoral reform in 1832, for example

---

70 *The Sun*, 13 March 1839.

71 Letter to Lord Marcus, 30 June 1839. PRONI Downshire Papers D671/C/348/19.

72 *Londonderry Sentinel*, 30 Nov 1839. The owners were three unmarried sisters: Catherine, Elizabeth and Emily Patterson.

73 *Dublin Monitor*, 23 Jan 1841; *Londonderry Sentinel*, 15 Jan 1842.

74 *Londonderry Standard*, 17 June 1840.

75 *Londonderry Sentinel*, 25 July 1840.

76 Malcomson, *Clements*: x.

– nor with the way they treated their tenants, but the landlords, as a class, had shared interests in maintaining and improving the county's infrastructure, and especially in the maintenance of law and order.

Hill soon discovered the potential dangers when John Marshall, owner of the Garton estate in Donegal, was shot from ambush while riding in his carriage on the way to church. Several shotgun slugs lodged in his shoulder. According to Marshall's servant, who gave chase, the gunman was dressed in women's clothes, a familiar disguise for ribbonmen or Mollies (Molly Maguires).[77] Hill contributed £25 towards the £100 reward offered to anyone prepared to confide 'private information' to the police to facilitate the capture of the perpetrator of the 'atrocious outrage'.[78] No-one came forward and there was no arrest. Marshall's wound was said to be a contributory factor to his death two months later.[79]

All of Hill's Grand Jury colleagues had long experience, either as landlords or as the sons of landlords. Would this newcomer amaze them, or merely amuse them, with his fresh approach? They approved of his choice of agent, 'the able and intelligent' Francis Forster, owner of a small estate and a large house, in Burtonport.[80] He, like his father, had been an agent for the Marquess of Conyngham, an absentee landlord with an extremely poor reputation among his tenants. According to one account, the Forsters had attempted to extract rents from impoverished tenants but, having failed to do so, resisted Conyngham's order to evict them because they feared revenge from the tenantry.[81] Forster's diplomatic abilities, both as an agent and a magistrate, earned him some favourable opinions, but even an admirer noted his 'unremitting zeal' and 'perseverance' in carrying through Hill's land reforms.[82]

Within two years of buying his estates Hill managed to attract positive newspaper coverage for his innovations. Doubtless, 21st century public relations executives would have viewed this as something of a media coup. He had discovered, possibly by accident, the power of publicity. It was in September 1840 that the *Derry Journal* carried a lengthy anonymous letter (republished days later by the *Dublin Morning Register*) which

77 *Derry Journal*, 18 Aug 1840.
78 *Londonderry Standard*, 26 Aug 1840.
79 *Derry Journal*, 13 Oct 1840.
80 Bennett (1847): 67.
81 Campbell (2015): viii.
82 Bennett, op. cit. 80. In February 1845, Forster named a son after George's family: Arthur Sandys.

hymned Hill's efforts to redress 'the distress and destitution of the Guidore (sic) district' by 'giving the energies of the peasantry proper direction'. It praised his attempts to 'suppress the ruinous and demoralising practice of illicit distillation' and for inaugurating 'works of public utility, such as making new roads, enclosing and draining new mountain farms'. It mentioned his introduction of 'prizes and premiums' to 'encourage and stimulate [tenants] to habits of industry, comfort, and cleanliness' and Forster's part in distributing the awards. The writer, identified only as 'W', quoted a priest, Hugh McFadden, as hailing 'the dawn of a new era' and predicting 'the agricultural reformation of Guidore'.[83]

Without being able to identify W it is impossible to know if it was written by a genuinely independent witness or if Hill, through Forster or Dombrain, engaged in subterfuge to promote the Gweedore reforms. It is noticeable that the style and substance of the letter foreshadowed material that later appeared under Hill's own name. The claims in the letter certainly set him apart from his peer group. Nor was it an isolated example. Although landlords with titles were often treated in press reports with undue flattery,[84] a search across a dozen leading Irish newspapers throughout the late 1830s and early 40s failed to turn up praise for any landlord equal to that enjoyed by Lord George Hill.

Meanwhile, he maintained a close relationship with his brother, Downshire, attending a 'great agricultural meeting at Hillsborough'.[85] In company with others of his class, he gave his support to various charities, such as the Irish Society of London, which promoted schooling in the Irish language,[86] and the Benevolent Society of St. Patrick, which helped children born to Irish parents in London.[87] He was drawn towards societies that encouraged advances in farming; he was a regular donor to the Agricultural Improvement Society of Ireland,[88] and took on the vice-presidency of the association that promoted the cultivation of flax.[89] He also donated money towards the purchase of instruments for Letterkenny's Temperance Society band.[90]

In the autumn of 1841, he finally found his Big House. His first hope, to buy the bishop's palace in Raphoe, was dashed by a refusal from the

83 *Derry Journal*, 22 Sept 1840; *Dublin Morning Register*, 24 Sept 1840.
84 Cf *Londonderry Sentinel*, 1 July 1843.
85 *Newry Telegraph*, 2 April 1840.
86 *Belfast Commercial Chronicle*, 18 May 1840.
87 *The Globe*, 2 March 1841.
88 *Dublin Evening Mail*, 28 April 1841.
89 *Londonderry Sentinel*, 3 July 1841.
90 *Londonderry Sentinel*, 15 Jan 1842.

Ecclesiastical Commissioners.[91] So Ballyare House in Ramelton was a second choice and also a problem because it wasn't quite big enough, requiring extensive, and expensive, renovation. While the works were being carried out, he and Cassandra, who was pregnant once more, moved temporarily from Barnhill to Gortlee House, on a hill overlooking the Ballyraine quayside. Soon after, another anonymous letter appeared in the *Londonderry Sentinel* in praise of Hill, whose 'tenantry speak of the lordship as the kindest, the most humane and benevolent of mankind'. It continued: 'His lordship and Lady Hill's charities are unbounded: they truly feed the hungry and clothe the naked; and it is not the poor seeking for relief, but his lordship and Lady Hill searching out for objects and poor housekeepers to dispense their bounty to; and their manners are so mild, so affable, that the poor feel not that embarrassment that they would do in the presence of most others'. It was signed 'An Observer' followed by an editor's note: 'We publish the above at the urgent request of the writer, a respectable individual; although we fear that we shall, by so doing, incur the censure of the estimable personages alluded to by our correspondent'.[92]

The correspondent referred to Lady Hill as 'gentle and amiable in her manners and disposition as she is beautiful in person and majestic in appearance'. This complimentary, and rare, mention of Cassandra in print came just two months before tragedy. On 12 March 1842, at Gortlee, she gave birth to a daughter (named Cassandra Jane Louisa), and three days later, she died, aged just thirty-five.[93] The cause, most likely, was puerperal fever.[94] Her death must have been devastating for Hill, although he chose to console himself by ascribing her fate to Divine Providence in a letter to his brother, Downshire:

> I had only time this melancholy morning to inform you [of] my sad loss – my dearest wife was wonderfully well until Sunday eve – when she got a chill – after that, inflammation set in, which the most vigorous measures could not subdue, & the poor dear creature breathed her last this morning at 11 – The Lord knows what is best for us – & nothing happens but with his permission. It remains for me to submit humbly to his holy will – he has helped me for some years with a most affectionate and faithful wife, & my regret at her being taken from me, is much diminished by the knowledge of the hope that was in her, & I

91 *Londonderry Sentinel*, 8 April 1879.
92 *Londonderry Sentinel*, 15 Jan 1842.
93 *Morning Post*, 19 March 1842.
94 Hillan (2001): 111.

trust she is now happy for ever. I know all your kindness to us & my dearest Cassandra was ever sensible of the affection showed to her by my dear sister and nieces who I know will share my grief.[95]

On the back of the letter he wrote: 'Poor Cassandra: Death'. Three stark words to convey the traumatising sadness of a widower with four children under the age of seven, including a new-born baby. Cassandra's heart-broken family reacted swiftly to the news. Two of her brothers, George and Charles, and her sister, Louisa, travelled to Donegal from Kent, which Charles described as a 'journey of wretchedness'.[96] After Cassandra's burial in the Church of Ireland graveyard in Letterkenny, the brothers returned to England and Louisa – Cass's unmarried elder sister – stayed on to care for the children while Hill settled affairs in Gweedore, where his hotel was nearing completion, and at Ballyare, where extensive building work was under way.

At the end of April, he and Louisa shepherded the children on the long trip to the Knights' family home in Godmersham, Kent. Soon after, he rented nearby Updown House.[97] Louisa, two years older than Cassandra, appears to have taken on the task of running Hill's household without demur, and with the blessing of her family. It was viewed as 'a practical solution',[98] and Hill felt confident enough in August to leave them for Ireland. He travelled first to Hillsborough to spend time with Downshire, and then they rode together across Ulster to visit George's new house.

Under the headline 'A Landlord Worthy of Example', the *Londonderry Sentinel* reported that the brothers had arrived at 'Lord George's place, near Ramelton, where Mr Hagerty, the architect of Derry, has nearly completed an extremely commodious residence on the banks of the Lennon'.[99] Next day, they went to Gweedore to stay at Hill's new hotel, situated a couple of miles inland from Bunbeg harbour on the Clady river. It was Downshire who made one of the first entries in the Visitors' Book:

I dined and slept last night in this here inn built by my brother Lord George and have found everything in it, the bed, entertainment very comfortable ... This inn has been extremely well built and is well suited to its situation and I hope that Lord George's excellent object, that of

95 LGH to Lord Downshire, 15 March 1842. PRONI, Downshire Papers, D671/C/348/20.
96 CBK, 11 April 1842. Diaries 13 JAHM.
97 *Kentish Gazette*, 14 June 1842. The owner was a prominent judge, Sir John Bayley.
98 Hillan (2001): 116.
99 *Londonderry Sentinel*, 3 Sept 1842. William Hagerty was listed in the *Belfast and Province of Ulster Directory* for 1852. Cf. Hagerty's adverts in *Londonderry Sentinel*, 2 Oct 1841, 29 July 1848.

improving the mountainous district, possessed as it is of many natural advantages, will ere to be crowned with well merited success.[100]

Several newspapers republished the *Sentinel* report praising Hill's 'excellent inn' and his wider work in Gweedore, such as the 'extensive corn, timber, and iron store' and 'a general shop and store for dry and soft goods, which has conferred the greatest advantage upon the country people'. There were mentions of the premiums given to industrious tenants; the abolition of the 'pernicious' rundale system; the wisdom of his building of the Bunbeg harbour; and the success of a salmon fishery launched jointly by Hill and Dombrain, 'the spirited proprietor of the neighbouring estate'.[101] None of this press adulation could compensate Hill for the loss of his wife. He now had a Big House, but no-one to fill its spacious rooms and play in its ornate gardens. For the next couple of years he would live between Ballyare House in Donegal and Updown House in Kent.

---

100 VB, 31 August 1842.

101 *Londonderry Sentinel*, 3 Sept 1842. Cf. *Dublin Evening Mail*, 7 Sept; *Newry Telegraph*, 8 Sept; *Warder & Weekly Mail*, 10 Sept; *Belfast Commercial Chronicle*, 12 Sept.

5

'A PUBLIC BENEFACTOR TO HIS COUNTRY'

The whole code relating to landlord and tenant in this country was framed with a view to the interests of the landlord alone
– Lord Chief Justice of Ireland, Edward Pennefather, 1843[1]

Wealth and poverty are relative terms, but they are rarely viewed dispassionately. This was particularly true in early Victorian Britain, where the gap between rich and poor was both wide and conspicuous. And it was even more the case in Ireland where, with the continuing dominance of a rural economy and little sign of industrialisation, the division between land-owners and the rest was so pronounced. Yet within that upper class, there were, of course, inequalities. By the standards of his peer group, Hill was not a wealthy man. As far as his tenants were concerned, his social class and his title, along with the fact that he had been able to acquire the land on which they lived and worked, demonstrated otherwise. In addition, there was his religious persuasion and his Englishness. The colonised are rarely well disposed towards the coloniser. The few reports that exist of his character suggest that he was neither flamboyant nor high-handed. Earnest, kindly and unpretentious, he may have been. But the chasm between his lifestyle and that of his tenantry was unbridgeable.

Nowhere was this division more obvious than in Hill's decision to build a hotel in an area of deprivation. His intention was to attract well-heeled visitors to enjoy the scenery and field sports of Donegal.

---

1 John O'Connell MP, *Hansard*, April 1846, col 1041. Pennefather was a substantial landowner himself, with an estate in Tipperary.

Described as no more than an inn by his brother,[2] it was anything but an ostentatious building – two storeys, rectangular, and without any exterior ornamentation. Nor was it overly large, with six bedrooms and three sitting rooms.[3] Hill gave it an estate agent's gloss by describing it as being 'fitted up and furnished with every attention to comfort and convenience'.[4] A female visitor agreed about the comfort but reported that the rooms lacked 'aesthetic taste', adding: 'Perfect was the cleanliness of the tiny bedrooms, each with its iron bedstead and its strips of carpet across the spotless floor, its plain deal wash-stand and chest of drawers, its tidy curtain, and – oh, rare luxury in Ireland! – blinds that act, windows that open, and doors that shut'.[5] According to Hill, the sitting-rooms 'had the benefit of all the sunshine' and looked out on to the river where a boat was moored for guests who wished to 'amuse themselves fishing'. Ponies were available 'to assist ramblers in their excursions'. And every Sunday, 'a resident minister of the Church of England' was on hand to perform divine service.[6]

The hotel's visitors' books[7] are replete with praise for the excellence of the accommodation and the service, including 'the marked attention in civility of the domestics'.[8] Most of the 850 entries view the hotel as an 'oasis in the surrounding wilderness'.[9] Guests were wholly complimentary about the accommodation, with some being moved to compose lines of doggerel:

I've stopped in Hotels – I will say of each degree
From fam'd London City to my own town Tralee –
A thousand I've stopped in and may add much more
But all far eclipsed by Lord G's at Guidore[10]

It attracted members of the Ascendancy, senior government officials, doctors, clergy, magistrates, journalists, and a sprinkling of wealthy travellers from Europe and the USA. As his tenants could not help but recognise, the Gweedore Hotel was quite unlike any other building for miles around, a haven of plenty in a land of poverty. Food was supplied

2 See previous chapter.
3 *Bradshaw's Illustrated Handbook for Tourists in Great Britain and Ireland*: 46
4 *Facts* 5: 48.
5 Craik (1887): 120
6 Ibid.
7 Two are preserved at Donegal County Council offices. VB hereafter
8 VB 2: 194, Alexander Stewart (Ramelton), 29 July1864.
9 VB 1: 161, illegible signature, 12 Oct 1847.
10 VB 1: 54, J Crainer, 18 Nov 1844.

from what Hill liked to call 'my model farm', the surrounding twenty acres trenched, drained and fenced by his tenants.[11] For Hill, the hotel may have provided a modicum of income to offset his expenditure on building new cottages. For the tenants, it appeared to be a money-making enterprise which served to exaggerate the gulf between their situation and that of their 'master'. Living in style among poor people – even if the style was deliberately understated, as it was in this case – was bound to create resentment. Hill could not surmount the fundamental differences between himself and the people of Gweedore, failing to grasp that there was no middle way between landlord and tenant. By inhabiting different spheres, they had wholly incompatible perspectives.

To make matters worse, Hill was eager that his guests should witness his good works by visiting the farms on his estate. As a public relations exercise, it was a success, which is evident from the tributes in the visitors' books. If the tenants had read them, they may well have gasped at some of the contributions:

> May industry daily an impetus gain
> Lord G Hill reigning – Lord of our domain
> Happy each peasant – increasing our store
> Success then to commerce at Lord G's Guidore[12]

It has been convincingly argued that an 'effusive master narrative' emerges from even the most superficial study of hotel visitors' books.[13] This was a case in point. Hill was hymned for his 'self-sacrifice',[14] 'laudable zeal'[15] and 'judicious management'.[16] In order to point to the differences between what they were seeing and the wretched conditions that existed in Gweedore before his arrival he had a framed copy of Patrick McKye's 1836 petition on the hotel lobby wall.[17] Improvement was his insistent message, and he was duly rewarded with a chorus of praise: 'The great improvement going on in the neighbourhood ... is a convincing proof of the momentous good that could be done in Ireland if its landlords or even a few of them were like minded with

---

11 *Destitution*: 6750.
12 VB 1:54, J. Crainer, 18 Nov 1844.
13 James (2012).
14 VB 1: 166, Treshail, 2 Sept 1847.
15 VB 1: 203, John Storey, 30 Oct 1849.
16 VB 1: 66, S Keighley, 30 May 1845.
17 Davis (2021a): 11.

his Lordship'.[18] 'I have been delighted by seeing the neatness and comfort of the cottages which I have visited on the estate.'[19] 'Honour to the noble Lord who has set, and still continues to set, so fine an example of benevolence, patience and true love of country.'[20] Hill's 'patriotism' is a running theme in the inscriptions.

Throughout the years 1841 to 1844, there were many newspaper articles and letters to editors praising Hill's 'laudable and most liberal improvements' in Gweedore.[21] His fame for 'doing incalculable good' spread across Ireland, from County Down to County Cork, where readers learned of his lordship's 'progress ... in hitherto backward and much-neglected districts', which was said to prove 'what care, perseverance, and a desire to act justly towards every one, will do'.[22] One of those who extolled Hill's improvements was a priest, Hugh McFadden, who acted as a judge for the annual awards given to the Gweedore tenantry. He signed a report expressing 'gratification' for 'the great benefits which his lordship has conferred upon this extensive district' and 'the rapid and progressive improvements' which included 'the neat and comfortable cottages' with 'clean, orderly, and well-ventilated rooms, comfortable and suitable beds and bedsteads, with a supply of bed clothing and furniture'.[23] This encomium was to have a significance some fifteen years later. Fellow landlords applauded too. At the inaugural exhibition of the Donegal Farming Society, Hill's health was toasted by Colonel Joseph Pratt, owner of Cabra Castle in Cavan, who told of having been 'astonished to see the rapid improvement on Lord George's estate'.[24] Pratt's own record as a landlord was somewhat less laudable. Just the year before, several of his tenants were arrested for assaulting his bailiffs in a rents dispute. As a result, Pratt was obliged to reduce the rents.[25]

During these years, the fraught relationships between landlords and tenants over land tenure in Ireland were being explored in an official

18 VB 1: R. Linney, 16 Aug 1843.
19 VB 1: 46, M. Grimshaw, 18 Sept 1844.
20 VB 1: 172, Henry Carre, 2 June 1848.
21 *Londonderry Sentinel*, 16 Sept 1843. The report was republished verbatim in *Saunders's News-Letter*, 19 Sept; *Dublin Evening Mail*, 20 Sept; *Ballyshannon Herald*, 21 Sept; *Dublin Evening Packet*, 22 Sept; *London Evening Standard*, 25 Sept; *Londonderry Standard*, 30 Oct 1844; *Cork Examiner*, 23 Dec 1844.
22 *Newry Telegraph*, 5 Oct 1844; *Cork Examiner*, 22 Dec 1843.
23 *Londonderry Sentinel*, 16 Sept 1843. Cf. *Derry Journal*, 5 Feb 1858.
24 *Dublin Mercantile Advertiser*, 18 Oct 1844.
25 *Drogheda Conservative Journal*, 14 Jan 1843.

inquiry set up by the prime minister, Sir Robert Peel. Known as the Devon Commission, and sometimes the Land Commission, its work began in November 1843.[26] In Hill's evidence, about the iniquities of land subdivision by tenants, he related two anecdotes that were to be quoted for decades afterwards. He told of a man whose 'farm' was split into forty-two distinct patches, and, unable to locate them, he abandoned the idea of cultivating them. He also told of twenty-six individuals with claims to just a half-acre.[27] All the commissioners were landlords, which provoked Daniel O'Connell's scathing remark: 'You might as well consult butchers about keeping Lent as consult these men about the rights of farmers'.[28] Yet the commission's lengthy and detailed report, issued in February 1845, was, in two respects, surprising: it agreed that land had been acquired by confiscation and, secondly, conceded that leases were overly favourable to landlords. However, it was not prepared to recommend any form of intervention to redress the balance.

Its commitment to property rights underlay its rejection of the so-called Ulster Custom, which would have granted tenants the so-called 3Fs: fair rents set by an independent arbitrator rather than a landlord; free sale of holdings to others without landlord interference; and fixity of tenure, which meant that, as long as tenants paid the rent, they could not be evicted. In other words, the proprietorial rights of the landlord remained sacrosanct. Similarly, the commission reiterated 'the just rights of property' when supporting the remedies employed by landlords – the seizing of goods and evictions – to recover rents from defaulting tenants.

Hill, in company with fellow landlords, was relieved that his rights had been upheld. At the beginning of 1845, there was official recognition of his seven years as a prominent member of the land-owning class of Donegal when he was appointed as the county's High Sheriff.[29] A couple of months later, he had to cope with another family tragedy. His eldest brother, the energetic and supposedly fit Marquess of Downshire, died unexpectedly, aged 56. While touring his Wicklow estate, Blessington, he 'was attacked with apoplexy' (probably a stroke or cerebral

---

26 Its chairman was William Courtenay, the 10th Earl of Devon.
27 These claims were repeated in *Facts* (2): 18, 21. Over the years, the figures were often wrongly remembered by politicians and journalists. For later examples, see *Belfast News-Letter*, 9 March 1870; *Cork Constitution*, 22 April 1870.
28 Shaw Lefevre (1887): 234.
29 *The Times*, 31 Jan 1845.

haemorrhage) and tumbled from his horse.[30] His death was marked with paeans in the press about the 'deeply lamented nobleman',[31] 'the most amiable, benevolent and useful man',[32] and the 'venerated landlord'.[33]

According to an obituary in *The Gentleman's Magazine* 'his mind was constantly occupied in plans for the improvement of his numerous tenantry, by whom he was greatly beloved … a better, more liberal, indulgent and kind landlord did not exist'.[34] *The Times* was much more interested in recording Downshire's religious credentials. 'There were few occasions on which he neglected to testify his devotion to the British Revolution of 1688, and the Protestant Reformation of the sixteenth century. He, therefore, earned for himself with one party all the honour of a great patriot, and with the other whatever discredit attaches to the name of an 'Orange-Tory'.[35] It regarded him as a Conservative and an orthodox member of the Church of England, who was trenchantly opposed to Tractarian doctrines and practices in Ulster. Hill adopted a similar stance.[36]

The 90-mile journey of Downshire's body from Dublin to Down attracted a cortege said to have numbered 3,000, which included many hundreds of his tenants from his Kildare and Wicklow estates.[37] They were joined at the funeral in Hillsborough by several hundreds more of his Ulster tenantry plus 'upwards of 200 clergymen of the Established Church, and not less than 150 ministers of the Presbyterian Church'.[38] Among the chief mourners were George and Atty (Lord Sandys) and, of course, the new and fourth Marquess of Downshire, Hill's 32-year-old nephew, who gloried in the name Arthur Wills Blundell Sandys Trumbull Windsor Hill.

The new marquess had a distinct advantage over his industrious father because the historic debts had been eradicated. So, he inherited estates with an annual rental of more than £95,000. His riches enabled him to commemorate his father's life with a memorial that echoed Nelson's columns in London and Dublin. In 1848, a 130ft high

30 *Freeman's Journal*, 14 April 1845.
31 *Illustrated London News*, 3 May 1845.
32 *Belfast Commercial Chronicle*, 16 April 184.
33 *Statesman* and *Dublin Christian Record*, 15 April 1845.
34 Cf. *Hampshire Telegraph & Naval Chronicle*, 19 April 1845.
35 *The Times*, 16 April 1845.
36 *Newry Telegraph*, 22 March 1845.
37 *Statesman and Dublin Christian Record*, 22 April 184.
38 Ibid. 25 April 1845.

Corinthian sandstone column, with the third marquess's figure on top, was erected on a hill. It was visible for miles around, as it is today.

Downshire's death occurred while Hill was preparing the publication, in Dublin and London, of a book about his Gweedore experiment. This slimmest of slim volumes was to win him fame in his lifetime and, although he could not possibly have foreseen it, it would also ensure that his name would live on into future generations. In truth, *Facts from Gweedore: With Hints for Donegal Tourists*, (hereafter, *Facts*) was more of a pamphlet than a book. It was an unconcealed attempt to preach the virtues of his creating a new agricultural system while denigrating the vices of the one he replaced.

Its publication happened to coincide with the arrival in Gweedore of Thomas Campbell Foster, dispatched to Ireland by the editor of *The Times*, John Delane, to report on 'the true condition of the Irish people'. Delane gave Foster, a trainee London barrister, a highfalutin title, '*The Times* Commissioner', and devoted plenty of column inches to his series of 'letters', which appeared in the newspaper from August 1845 until January 1846, and were later published together as a book.[39] In one letter, Foster – who enjoyed his stay at Hill's hotel[40] – wrote warmly about Hill's efforts and in another, three days later, quoted approvingly from *Facts*.[41] These letters were reproduced verbatim in many other newspapers in Ireland and England.[42] The mentions helped to boost sales and served to raise Hill's profile.

Foster, aware that he would face accusations of prejudice, tried to pre-empt his critics by asserting: 'I came here as no partisan, either political or religious'.[43] However, his urging of the Catholic Irish to ignore calls for repeal of the Union and to halt their hostility towards Protestants did suggest an obvious bias.[44] That alone would have earned him a hostile response from Daniel O'Connell and his followers. But Foster also attacked the ageing Liberator directly by reporting that O'Connell's tenants on his

---

39 Foster (1846).
40 'An inn as comfortable as any in England', VB 1: 82, 5 Sept 1845.
41 *The Times*, 9 Sept, 12 Sept 1845.
42 Cf. *Bell's Weekly Messenger* (London), 17 Sept; *Leeds Intelligencer*, 20 Sept; *The Vindicator* (Belfast), 20 Sept; *Belfast Commercial Chronicle*, 17 Sept; *Dublin Weekly Register*, 20 Sept; *The Pilot* (Dublin), 15 Sept; *Wexford Independent*, 17 Sept; *Northern Whig*, 16 Sept.
43 Foster, op. cit. 81.
44 Ibid. 96.

estate in Kerry lived in 'wretched hovels'.[45] This resulted in widespread condemnation of Foster in those Irish newspapers loyal to O'Connell.

O'Connell's son, John, criticised Foster's reports at great length during a meeting of Loyal National Repeal Association in Dublin's Conciliation Hall.[46] He argued that Foster's championing of Hill was a case apart, out of the ordinary, and that the welfare of the Irish people could not depend on the goodness of one man. Tenants needed rights rather than the reliance on the character of an individual landlord. He didn't wish to criticise Hill, but sought to explain why his tenants were reluctant to accept his reforms. The depth of distrust of landlords made the people wary of change. In reality, there was no check on the landlord class to do as they wished, a power which allowed them to discourage Irish enterprise. That point was hammered home by another speaker, a Captain Broderick, who contended that the worst aspect of rule by landlords was their failure to encourage the development of manufacturing industry.

Foster also earned rebukes for his choice of language, writing of 'the aboriginal Irish' as a 'people utterly ignorant, and both mentally and physically degraded'.[47] He insulted tenant farmers by insinuating that they could not understand how they would reap greater rewards by cultivating more land, arguing that they preferred short-term misery to long-term prosperity because they were incapable of strategic thought.[48] This condescension was only partially offset by his eyewitness accounts of the appalling conditions suffered by some poor tenants.

During his visit to Donegal, he contrasted 'the misery and wretchedness which the neglect of an absentee landlord produces' with 'the Comfort and Happiness diffused by a landlord attentive to his duties'.[49] It was something of a false dichotomy, in which he chose to cast Hill as the good guy and his absentee neighbour, the Marquess of Conyngham, as the bad guy. He compared the supposed benefits enjoyed by Hill's tenants with the 'misery' of Conyngham's 'wretchedly poor' rack-rented tenantry. But it was the tenants who were the main targets for his scorn because, in his opinion, they could not thrive without adequate leadership. He wrote: 'With a non-resident landlord, a non-resident agent, no capital spent amongst them, no

---

45 Ibid. 394-7.
46 *Freeman's Journal*, 16 Sept 1845; *Dublin Evening Mail*, 17 Sept 1845.
47 Foster, op. cit. 120-1.
48 Ibid. 95.
49 Ibid. 98.

encouragement given to them, and no one to teach them anything, either by precept or example, how are they likely to improve?'[50]

Hill must have been gratified by this burst of publicity and the resulting high sales of *Facts*, which were good enough to justify the issue of a second edition some six months later. In fact, over the course of 45 years, five separate editions were published (1845, 1846, 1854, 1868, 1887), the final one appearing posthumously. Every edition stated that it was 'compiled from notes by Lord George Hill' and he was referred to throughout in the third person, strongly suggesting that it was written by someone else. The most likely candidate as author of the first three editions, and possibly the fourth, is James Dombrain.[51]

Although the basic story did not change from edition to edition, there were amendments, additions and deletions. Illustrations came and went. Some editions carried lithographs of Bunbeg harbour and the grain store executed by Harriet Windsor-Clive, Lord Downshire's sister-in-law, during her visit in October 1844.[52] In the fourth, there was a lithograph of Hill's hotel, overlooked by Mount Errigal, by an unidentified artist. By far the biggest departure was the fifth edition, which amounted to a significant redraft. It was far longer and much more informative than the others, with substantial textual differences. Given that it was published eight years after Hill's death and sixteen years after Dombrain's death, its authorship is a matter of speculation. A 'prefatory note' refers only to 'the present Editor', and there is no clue to the person's identity.

Whoever was responsible, the tone and style of writing is a departure from that of the previous editions. It is more descriptive, and makes a conscious attempt to create an atmosphere of a romantic *Gaoth Dobhair*. At times, it adopts a sense of distance, reading like a newspaper report. At others, it introduces barely credible anecdotes. It is much sharper in its criticisms of the Gweedore people. There are odd factual differences.[53] But the overall message remains the same. Life in Gweedore before Hill was wretched; life after Hill was far, far better. The fifth edition is the one drawn on by most critics, especially its 1971 reprint with a lengthy introduction by the cultural geographer Estyn Evans.[54]

---

50 Ibid. 109.
51 MacArthur (2001).
52 *Newry Telegraph*, 5 Oct 1844.
53 In the fourth, George is said to have acquired 'upwards of 24,000 acres and 2,500 inhabitants'. In the fifth, it was 'upwards' of 23,000 acres with 'about' 3,000 tenants.
54 Facsimile reprint, Queen's University, 1971.

Facts has long been the subject of dispute, splitting readers into two camps: devotees and detractors. Initially, and for many years afterwards, the former far outnumbered the latter. In the modern era, however, historians and several other academics have been much more critical of Hill's account of his achievements and the portrayal of himself as a model Irish landlord. As a result, far fewer people than in the 19th century now accept the book as entirely factual. Complaints about its accuracy are understandable because it is a blatantly self-referential tract. It amounts to a piece of propaganda. Moreover, seen from the cultural perspective of the 21st century, its condescending tone borders on racism.

In outline, the basis of his story was simple. Hill sought to contrast the bad old Gweedore and its badly-behaved people of the era before he arrived with the good new Gweedore, and its better-behaved people, a transformation for which he claimed responsibility. That was the reason for his pamphlet beginning with the verbatim republication of McKye's 1836 petition. It set the scene of pre-Hill deprivation before he added his own portrait of misery, which ran something like this:

Gweedore was previously inhabited by people known for their violence who were by ruled by insubordinate bullies and lawless distillers.[55] The revenue police could do little or nothing about the illicit distilling of whiskey and poteen, which required so much of the people's corn there was none left to make meal. Rent arrears went back many years. When tithe collectors arrived in 1834, accompanied by 50 policemen, they were repulsed and unable to collect any money. The system of unfenced farming was chaotic and inefficient, with families continually dividing and sub-dividing land into increasingly small parcels. These plots were known as 'a cow's grass' (roughly three acres), supposedly regarded as sufficient grazing to support a cow.[56]

There were further divisions, known as a foot, a half foot and a cleet, making the cultivation of crops hopelessly inefficient. The consequences of this 'ruinous' system, known as 'rundale', were 'fights, trespasses, confusion, disputes and assaults', which Hill called 'evils'.[57]

The people lived an 'Arab mode of life', moving with the seasons.[58] Their main 'cabins' were scantily furnished, with 'one or two wooden stools, an

---

55 *Facts*, 5: 27.
56 Evans, *Facts* 5: ix.
57 *Facts* 5: 22.
58 Ibid. 25.

iron potato-pot, sometimes an old crazy bedstead, filled up with heather or potatoes, and little or no bedclothes'.[59] Many shared their homes with their animals. 'Famine and disease were periodical.'[60] People were unable to travel because there were no roads worthy of that description and, anyway, the nearest market towns were many miles away. Many people spoke only Irish, or, at least, pretended they could not speak English.

Then came the positive contrast – 'the vast difference between things as they are, and things as they were'[61] – in the transformed Gweedore that emerged following Hill's innovations. Each tenant has a fresh house, with a thatched roof and white-washed walls, with comfortable beds and suitable bed-clothing.[62] They have pots and crockery. Men work a defined area of farm-land, and have extended the amount of land under cultivation. Accordingly, this has improved the quantity and quality of the output, which includes turnips and flax, along with oats and potatoes. Tenants are able to consult 'an experienced agriculturist', appointed by Hill, to advise on the best way to manage their farms.[63] There are fewer disputes between people because they do not live so closely in clustered groups of houses. Rents, which have been held down, are paid punctually and in full, as is the county cess (the local tax). Only 'a few widows' are in arrears.[64] People no longer resort to 'tricks, subterfuge, and craft' to avoid their responsibilities. No-one has been evicted. People eat better by consuming bread and biscuit. They have access to medicine. There is a school, with a clock and a bell, which is rung at stated hours each day in order to encourage 'regular and punctual habits'.[65] Weavers' looms have been supplied to women and the socks and stockings they produce are properly marketed.[66] Travel is easier because of new roads and bridges.

He admitted that not quite all had gone to plan. Hill could not realise his wish (and that of Dombrain) to stamp out the distillation of poteen because corn, converted into alcohol, proved much more lucrative than selling it simply as grain.[67] Too few parents allowed their children to go to

---

59 Ibid.
60 Ibid. 15.
61 Ibid. 47.
62 Ibid. 45.
63 Ibid. 43.
64 Ibid. 6.
65 Ibid. 49.
66 Davis (2021a): 13.
67 *Facts*, 5:6.

school.[68] He preferred to accentuate the positive, pointing in particular to the success of one of his main innovations: the use of incentives, known as premiums, to stimulate production and best practice. These premiums were offered to tenants twice a year, spring and autumn, and were granted after consideration by Hill's selected panel of judges.

Some of the judges' reports were published in newspapers, replete with praise for the benevolence of 'his Lordship'. He hosted a celebratory dinner after the first set of premiums had been awarded and the judges told how 'the poor people could not believe that they would be permitted to dine' with their landlord. 'They anxiously inquired ... if it was really true that they were to go in'.[69] Hill was not, as many of his readers seemed to believe, a pioneer of the awards incentives. His brother, Downshire, had previously introduced a similar arrangement, as had Lord Leitrim, landlord of an estate centred in Carrigart. At least two years before Hill started to pay premiums, it was widely reported in Irish newspapers that Leitrim had offered 'liberal' payments to his tenants 'for the growing of green crops and house-feeding cattle'.[70] Nor did Hill fund the premiums. He acknowledged that they were grants from the London-based Irish Peasantry Improvement Society.[71]

Most editions of *Facts* carried a three-part illustration of a Donegal townland of 205 acres drawn by the agricultural reformer Captain John Pitt Kennedy, described as Secretary for the Land Commission.[72] The first map showed the land as divided under the rundale system into 29 holdings split into 422 lots; the second, the 29 strip farms as desired by 'the proprietor'; and third, the tenants' preference for multiple narrower strips.[73]

Facts gave Hill a wholly favourable press profile in Ireland and England. In the *Derry Journal*, which had yet to complete its journey from militant Orangeism to militant nationalism, several articles commended Hill's 'true method' in raising 'the peasantry to comfort and contentment'. One went so far as to claim that were his reforms adopted by the landlords on 'neglected' estates they would 'keep away from the poor man's door the approach of the insidious demagogue, who ... finds too apt materials for unqualified and seditious invective'.

68 Ibid. 9.
69 Ibid. 45.
70 *Ballyshannon Herald*, 14 Dec 1837.
71 *Facts*: 8, 44, 55-6. *Destitution*: 6677.
72 *Facts* 2: 16-17.
73 *Destitution*: 6772.

In other words, a more benevolent landlordism would nullify support for Daniel O'Connell.[74]

Recognition in Westminster arrived soon after publication with passing references by three MPs. Henry Ward, the member for Sheffield, argued that it was time to curb the powers of badly-behaved (usually absentee) landlords and cited Hill as an example of what could be achieved by sympathetic land-owners. He said: 'Lord G. Hill's recent publication afforded the most signal proof that even in the short space of seven years, the efforts of a resident landlord of moderate means, but guided by good sense, good temper, and sound judgment, might be crowned with complete success'.[75] Vernon Smith, MP for Northampton and formerly the member for Tralee, commended Hill for having 'wonderfully and creditably improved' his land, which had previously 'been divided in the most curious manner'.[76] There was approval too from Montague Gore, later the author of a slim book *Thoughts on the Present State of Ireland*, which advocated the need for investment and industrial education.[77]

But the icing on Hill's cake arrived with lavish praise from the prime minister, Sir Robert Peel, who defended his refusal to legislate against Irish landlords by urging them instead to consider their 'duty' by exercising their power with 'liberality and forbearance'. Look, for example, at 'the improvements effected ... by Lord George Hill'.[78] Peel, in a flight of whimsy, even dared to put words in Hill's mouth by imagining him making an internal pledge: 'I will perform my duty as a Landlord. I will persevere against all difficulties. I will not be deterred by any opposition I may encounter from my tenants or neighbours, but I will persevere in my attempt to improve the condition of the people.'[79] Hill's efforts were, in Peel's view, all the more creditable because he had chosen to purchase his estates rather than inheriting them. To continual shouts of hear, hear, Peel recited a list of rhetorical questions: Had the noble lord not succeeded despite the ignorance and prejudices of the people? Had he not effected his revolution 'by kindly feeling'? Had the value of his property not improved? Have his rentals not increased?

---

74 *Derry Journal*, 3 Dec 1845.

75 *Hansard*, 17 April 1846, col. 758.

76 Ibid., col.763.

77 Ibid., col. 769.

78 *Hansard*, 27 April 1846, col. 1128.

79 Ibid. Sometimes wrongly attributed to George himself. Cf. Somerville-Large (1995): 250 and Hillan (2011): 119.

More cheers punctuated the rest of Peel's accolade: 'That gentleman [Hill], by the example he has set, has entitled himself to be regarded as a public benefactor to his country. I honour and respect the motives which have led him to adopt this course, and I envy him the gratifying reflections of his own conscience.' Peel reiterated his message: forget legislation, think rather that 'the immediate practical improvement of Ireland will be most efficaciously promoted by a combination of the Landlords, resident and absentee, to follow the example of Lord G. Hill to improve their property, and to increase its productiveness while at the same time they conciliate the affections and goodwill of those who stand towards them in the relation of tenants'.[80]

As flattering as this was for Hill, Peel's intention was obvious. He was using him as a way of avoiding political engagement in the unfolding tragedy of Ireland. He was, in effect, using Hill in order to play Pontius Pilate, washing his hands of responsibility for what was happening in a country where landlords held sway.

---

80 Ibid. col. 1129.

6

AN GORTA MÓR

The Almighty, indeed, sent the potato blight, but the English created the famine
— John Mitchel[1]

And once in port I exorcised my ship
Reporting all to the Inspector General.
Sir James, I understand, urged free relief
For famine victims in the Westport Sector
And earned tart reprimand from good Whitehall.
Let natives prosper by their own exertions;
Who could not swim might go ahead and sink.
'The Coast Guard with their zeal and activity
Are too lavish' were the words, I think.
— Seamus Heaney[2]

Robert Peel's hymn of praise for Lord George Hill was a breath-taking example of cynicism because, at the time he made the speech, Ireland was suffering from the blight that robbed its people of their staple food. The Great Hunger, *An Gorta Mór*, the so-called Irish famine, had begun while Peel was prime minister. He did, in fairness, institute traditional, if inadequate, relief measures. But his departure from Downing Street in June 1846 heralded the arrival of a much less sympathetic, and less adroit, prime minister in Lord John Russell.

His adherence to the economic policy of *laissez faire*, allied to his belief that Irish landlords should bear the financial responsibility for

1 *The Last Conquest of Ireland (Perhaps)*: 219.
2 For the Commander of 'The Eliza', 1966.

Ireland's problems, was catastrophic. Between the years 1845 and 1852, one million people died of starvation and more than two million fled the country.[3] In Russell's view, and far from his alone, the potato blight and its consequent tragic effect, was not a sufficient reason for official intervention. He wrote: 'The common delusion that the government can convert a period of scarcity into a period of abundance is one of the most mischievous than can be entertained. But, alas! The Irish have been taught many bad lessons, and few good ones'.[4]

Hill did not agree, and his actions during what he called a 'period of unparalleled distress and suffering' reflect well on him.[5] There is an abundance of contemporaneous material from a diverse range of sources documenting his performance. As chair of the Donegal relief committee he persistently lobbied the Dublin-based Relief Commission chairman, Randolph Routh, and also the senior civil servant responsible for administering relief policy, Charles Trevelyan, for greater understanding of the plight of people in the west.[6] Hill sent several letters to William Stanley, the commission's secretary, to bewail the high price of meal. Each time, he was informed that the government could not intrude in the market. He urged Routh to allow the sale of food below cost price, requested the provision of seed, and arranged the setting up of soup kitchens at Dunlewey and at a townland on his own estate. His own monetary contribution to relief was recorded in the commission's files.[7]

Hill was also patron, trustee and honorary secretary of the Irish Relief Association for the Destitute Peasantry, which sought private donations and, 'regardless of its ultra-Protestant leanings ... proved highly effective in providing relief to all denominations'.[8] Hill supported other money-raising charities, such as a fishing company,[9] and was involved in initiatives aimed either at promoting novel forms of agriculture or the stimulation of new enterprises. To that end, he became vice-president of the Horticultural Improvement Society of Ireland;[10] joined the Society for the Promotion and Improvement of the Growth of Flax in Ireland;[11]

---

3 Kinealy (1994).
4 Letter to Lord Lansdowne, Oct 1846. Cited by Foster (1988): 320.
5 *Facts*, 3: 5.
6 *Morning Post*, 27 April 1847.
7 Famine Relief Commission Papers 1845-47, RLFC3/2/7/12.
8 Kinealy (2013): 262.
9 *Morning Post*, 25 March 1847.
10 *Dublin Evening Mail*, 1 Jan 1846.
11 *Northern Whig*, 5 May 1846.

and was named as a provisional director of a company exploring the possibility of compressing peat as a form of fuel.[12] One of his most important contributions came as a result of his having set up a mill in Bunbeg: 'most useful in famine time', observed Thomas Carlyle.[13] During 1847, it ground 688 tons of Indian corn, for which the government paid him £1 per ton; he regarded it as 'a fair rate'.[14] Hill pleaded for rye and barley seeds, but succeeding in getting only the former.[15]

Hill's key ally was Sir James Dombrain – he had been knighted in 1843 – who served on the Relief Commission along with another of Hill's friends, John Pitt Kennedy. Dombrain and Hill kept in close touch throughout 1846-47 and often worked in tandem to ensure food reached Donegal. When Dombrain tipped off Hill that a coastguard cutter was on its way to Sligo with a cargo of meal, Hill urged Routh to send a similar load to Bunbeg 'with as little delay as possible ... as the wants of the people are daily increasing'.[16] Most often, it appears that the supplies were sent instead to Killibegs.[17] Dombrain became a thorn in the side of the commission, which relied on his coast guard boats to distribute grain to depots. At one point, he disobeyed direct orders by Routh and Trevelyan not to give away corn meal for free to supply centres in Donegal and Westport, County Mayo. Routh observed that Dombrain had 'very inconveniently ... interfered'.[18]

It was the Westport incident that inspired Seamus Heaney's Swiftian poem, quoted at the head of this chapter. But it was only one instance of Dombrain's defiance. In September 1846, he informed Routh that his coastguard officers, having witnessed distressing scenes in which people were dying of hunger, had issued meal without charging for it.[19] As a result, Dombrain was rebuked in a Treasury minute for his 'gratuitous issue' of food: 'He had no authority, he was informed, to give meal away free. His proper course would have been to call upon the leading persons in each distressed locality to form themselves into a relief committee, and raise a fund by private contribution, which

---

12 *Ulster General Advertiser*, 18 April 1846.
13 Carlyle (1882): 243.
14 *Destitution*: 6785-6787.
15 LGH to Routh, 1 Jan 1847.
16 LGH to Routh, 13 Sept 1846. RLFC3/2/7/12.
17 *Derry Journal*, 20 Jan 1847.
18 24 June 1846. Cited by Woodham-Smith ((1962): 85.
19 Dombrain to Routh, 5 Sept 1846.

might possibly be increased later by government donation.'[20] Dombrain replied tartly: 'No committee could have been formed. There was no one within many miles who could have contributed one shilling ... The people were actually dying'.[21] Regardless of those deaths, Dombrain and his coastguards 'were not popular in Whitehall'.[22]

Dombrain left Donegal in early 1846, selling his Dunlewey house and estate to James Russell, a hop merchant.[23] From this point on, when visiting Donegal, Dombrain would stay at Hill's hotel, as his contributions to the visitors' book indicate.[24] They remained friends and collaborators, and were together in Bunbeg in August 1846 to greet the arrival of a schooner named the *Lady Dombrain* following its maiden voyage from America to deliver a cargo of timber.[25] Both men were less concerned about the arrival of wood than the lack of food.

There were many witnesses to Hill's good works during the hunger years, but their opinions carry one significant caveat: they were guests at his hotel and their views were inscribed in its visitors' book. That said, there was nowhere else for people visiting west Donegal to stay, and they were not required to praise him. One of the most important was James Saumarez Dobree who, as the Deputy Commissary-General, was working under direct instructions from Routh. Dobree explained that his mission was to 'recommend the best means of relief' within Donegal, and thought Hill's store at Bunbeg would make an ideal depot for imported corn. He added: 'What an example does the progressive improvement about Gweedore offer to all Irish landlords'.[26]

Routh was slow to take up Dobree's idea. In frustration at the delay, the Catholic priest in Bunbeg, Hugh McFadden, complained to the Lord Lieutenant, the Earl of Bessborough, that his parishioners were beginning to think Dobree's promise to be 'illusory' and 'would fervently beg and implore of His Excellency to order a cargo of 80 tons of Indian corn meal ... to be landed at Bunbeg'.[27] Unknown to the priest, a 15-ton consignment of meal (maize) had been sent, not to Bunbeg, but to Dombrain's coast guard

20 Symes (2003): 67.
21 Dombrain to Routh, 18 Sept 1846.
22 Woodham-Smith, op. cit.: 116.
23 Russell pulled off something of a farming marvel by producing 'a crop of turnips from the bog which would stagger the credulity of any agriculturist', *Derry Journal*, 2 Jan 1847.
24 Symes, op. cit.: 64.
25 *Derry Journal*, 19 Aug 1846.
26 VB, 5 Sept 1846.
27 Hugh McFadden to Earl of Bessborough, 14 Oct 1846.

service. He passed it on to Hill who acknowledged its arrival in a letter to Routh in which he urged him to send more because of 'the greatest demand'. His main concern was about the price being 'much higher than expected', arguing that since there was no competition among merchants there was 'no necessity for adhering to a market price'.[28] His plea was ignored.

One unexpected visitor to Hill's hotel in 1847 was Asenath Nicholson, an American philanthropist who travelled around Ireland throughout the famine and wrote a book about her experiences.[29] Captivated by the 'noble-hearted' and 'indefatigable' Hill, whose 'simplicity was his dignity and strength',[30] she accepted his before-and-after account of life in Gweedore and simply copied passages word for word from *Facts*. Her view of Hill's tenants smacked of condescension. When they were first introduced to bread, she wrote, 'can you believe it? Savage as they were, they loved it.'[31] She continued in similar vein: 'If Lord George Hill could transform those wild mountain goats, even to common civilised bullocks, what could not be done with any and all of the wild game of Ireland?'[32]

Yet, in a letter to a newspaper, Nicholson was candid enough to concede that not all of Hill's tenants were 'free from want'.[33] A couple of years after her visit, Hill contacted her in order to emphasise that none of his tenants perished during the hunger: 'Say that no person died of famine at Gweedore, though many of the aged and infants, from being scantily fed, died earlier than otherwise they would, as well as from change of diet; also that the people are reviving in a great degree'.[34] His claim was noted in some newspaper reviews of Nicholson's book, *Lights & Shades of Ireland*, which included her *Annals of the Famine*.[35] Many years later, Hill repeated it to a House of Commons committee.[36] The lack of fatalities on Hill's estates during the hunger years has been one of the reasons he has enjoyed a largely positive reputation among a swathe of the population in 20th and 21st century Donegal.

Another hotel visitor, Thomas Emerson Headlam, MP for Newcastle-upon-Tyne, thought Hill had 'done his part well in struggling with

28 LGH to Routh, 14 Oct 1846.
29 Nicholson (2017).
30 Ibid. 62, 64, 66.
31 Ibid. 63.
32 Ibid. 66.
33 *Dublin Evening Mail*, 13 Aug 1847. Cf *North British Daily Mail*, 4 Sept 1847.
34 Nicholson, op. cit.: 66.
35 *Northern Star & Leeds General Advertiser*, 19 Oct 1850.
36 HC, 1857-8, Vol XIII: 383.

the greatest calamity of modern times and is deserving of honour and respect from all who wish for the future regeneration of Ireland'.[37] Barry Hewetson, whose wife, Hannah, was a member of the Belfast Ladies' Association for the Relief of Irish Destitution, told of Hill 'doing all that man can do' for the starving people of Donegal, adding: 'He is occupied, from morning till night, sparing himself neither trouble nor personal fatigue'.[38] A guest who signed himself E.G.H. of Newry wrote to his local newspaper to commend Hill as 'the best practical example of what can be successfully accomplished' through agricultural reforms aimed at preventing the sub-division of land. 'I consider Lord George Hill's system a perfect model of colonisation for the Irish cottier.'[39]

By the time the French historian Amédée Pichot reached the Gweedore Hotel in August 1847 his travels across Ireland had convinced him of the inefficiency of official relief efforts. By contrast, he was enraptured with Hill's work. 'Lord Hill has turned the peat bog fertile', he wrote in the final sentence of a poem (in French) in the visitors' book.[40] Back in Paris, he wrote a magazine article in which he told 'how a single man, by the perseverance of his reason and his courage, can tame all the bad wills, defeat hereditary prejudices, discipline the most prejudiced and the most obstinate minds, and finally substitute his sole rule for an anarchic routine'.[41] In a memoir of his travels, he devoted a chapter to Hill, praising 'his reason and his courage'.[42]

Pichot was not alone in his admiration of his host. Here are three typical contributions to the hotel visitors' book during the famine period, selected at random. Andrew Durham thought Hill's tenantry should 'congratulate themselves on having a landlord residing amongst them, anxious to instruct and improve them, disposed to anticipate and alleviate their wants and to elevate their moral and social condition'.[43] Henry Carre wrote: 'Honour to the noble Lord who has set, and still continues to set, so fine an example of benevolence, patience and true love of country'.[44]

---

37 VB, 24 Sept 1849.
38 *Northern Whig*, 9 March 1847.
39 *Newry Telegraph*, 6 April 1847.
40 VB, 15 Aug 1847, 152.
41 *Revue Britannique*, March 1847.
42 Pichot (1850). According to Macarthur (2001), Pichot was accompanied by the painter Paul Balze who is thought to have compiled an album of sketches during their visit to Gweedore. The pictures disappeared.
43 VB, 14 October 1846.
44 VB, 2 June 1848.

And J.G. commented: 'Would to God there was a Lord G Hill in every parish in Ireland'.[45] His view was mirrored in a newspaper comment: 'Would to Heaven that Ireland had many landlords like Lord George Hill. His exertions at Gweedore reflect immortal honour on him ... Let others learn what he has done and do likewise'.[46]

Two other contributions deserve special mention. *The Nation*, a newspaper founded by three rebellious members of Daniel O'Connell's Repeal Association, surprisingly greeted Hill's *Facts* with a warm notice: 'Heaven smiles upon this western Oasis of Gweedore; and we are right glad that Lord G. Hill has permitted this little book to be published. It is truly a voice crying from the Wilderness'.[47] Doubtless, that opinion was influenced by the fact that two of the paper's moving spirits, John Mitchel and John O'Hagan, had stayed at the hotel in the summer of 1845, and had been 'much pleased with the accommodation'.[48] In a magazine article, under his pseudonym, Slieve Gullion, O'Hagan later wrote: 'Lord George Hill – blessings on him – has established an admirable hotel'.[49] He was also impressed by the 'immense business' carried out at the Bunbeg store, calling Hill 'a common benefactor to the whole country round'.[50]

From the polar opposite political persuasion, the staunch Orange title, the *Londonderry Sentinel*, ran a 3,000-word adulatory review of Hill's sequel to *Facts*, entitled *Hints to Donegal Tourists, with a Brief Notice of Rathlin Island*.[51] The timing of the book's publication was very odd. As the writer remarked, it was bound to 'draw shoals of visitors to Donegal' to enjoy 'its coast and lake scenery' and 'scenes of extraordinary beauty and sublimity'. Did Hill really think it tactful to attract well-heeled tourists to a country suffering so much misery?[52] A counter argument is that by bringing such people to the west of Ireland, he was hoping to stimulate charitable contributions. Private donations of money, which eventually totalled more than £1 million, along with gifts of food, clothing, bedding and supplies of seeds, 'played a significant role in saving lives' in the course of the hunger.[53]

45 VB, 5 Sept 1846.
46 *Southern Reporter & Cork Commercial Courier*, 5 Dec 1848.
47 *The Nation*, 25 April 1846.
48 VB, 19 Aug 1845.
49 O'Hagan (1913): 398.
50 Wall (1970): 167.
51 Dublin: Philip Dixon Hardy & Sons.
52 *Londonderry Sentinel*, 4 Sept 1847.
53 Kinealy (1998): 109.

Hill was not alone in acting to alleviate the suffering of his tenants. Several of his neighbouring landlords, aside from reducing rents or overlooking arrears, do appear to have provided food, on occasions at least. Wybrants Olphert wrote three letters to Routh about the desperate state of the starving people.[54] McFadden, the priest, backed him up by telling Routh that the people were 'in a perishing condition ... wretchedly poor' and lacked the transport to reach a food depot, 'should one exist'.[55] These genuine attempts to urge official action cannot conceal that the majority of the county's 'landholders controlled the market for agricultural goods' and, in so doing, 'imposed their own Hiberno-Victorian world-view, with its puritanical ethos and parsimonious attitudes, on the more profligate and pauperised sectors of Donegal society'.[56]

Hill acknowledged that his estates 'would have been absolutely desolated' without the charitable aid supplied by the Society of Friends, the Baptist Society and the Irish Peasantry Improvement Society of London. Otherwise, he would have 'shared the fate of many a worthy proprietor in the south and west of Ireland'.[57]

Landlord interventions apart, one of the major reasons for the people of west Donegal surviving the famine was the tradition of knitting socks and stockings, and selling them to Scottish and English dealers. This industry, which pre-dated Hill's arrival, provided substantial income. One other positive pointer to Hill's efforts should not be overlooked. As distinct from every neighbouring locality, Gweedore's population was greater after the famine than before it.[58] That was a remarkable outcome when set against the fact that more than 13,000 people died in Donegal by 1850,[59] and that 30,000 emigrated from the county between the years 1846 and 1851. When the Quaker philanthropists James Hack Tuke and William Forster reached Donegal in December 1846, the sights in Dunfanaghy appalled them. 'I visited a number of the poorest hovels', wrote Tuke. 'Their appearance, and the condition of the inmates, presented scenes of poverty and wretchedness almost beyond belief.

54 Olphert to Routh, 9, 19 Feb 1846; 21 Dec 1846.
55 McFadden to Routh, 27 Oct 1846.
56 MacLaughlin, Atlas: 457.
57 *Facts*, 3: 5.
58 Seosamh Ó Ceallaigh, 'The Sheep War in Ghaoth Dobhair & Cloughaneeley', Dunlewey symposium, 12 August 2023.
59 Cited in speech by President Michael D Higgins, National Famine Commemoration, Milford, Co. Donegal, 21 May 2023.

One dirty cabin – not more than twelve feet square – contained several persons. Two or three of them were full-grown men – gaunt and hunger-stricken – willing and wishful to obtain work, but unable. The mothers, crouching over a few embers of turf ... looked misery itself.'[60]

Tuke told of conditions in the Glenties workhouse, where 'the living and the dying stretched side by side' on 'dirty straw ... the pale, haggard countenance of the poor boys and girls told of sufferings, which it was impossible to contemplate without pity'. Travelling on through snowstorms, Tuke wrote of being 'really glad' to reach the Gweedore Hotel, where he extolled Hill's 'admirable zeal and enlightened benevolence'. His tenants 'are no doubt suffering severely, but he has given them work, has provided them with cheap food, and is constantly employing himself for their benefit'.[61]

So, even allowing for the fact that many eyewitnesses to Hill's work were guests at his hotel and consequently subject to his propaganda, the evidence of his good works throughout the Great Hunger is overwhelmingly positive. But we cannot overlook the fact that the tragedy also engendered this pernicious statement by Hill:

> The Irish people have profited much by the famine; the lesson was severe; but so rooted were they in old prejudices and old ways, that no teacher could have induced them to make the changes, which this visitation of Divine Providence has brought about, both in their habits of life, and in their modes of agriculture.[62]

His pronouncement is an echo of the opinions of both Lord John Russell and Charles Trevelyan, who wrote: 'Supreme Wisdom has educed permanent good out of transient evil'.[63] It can be read either as unduly callous or as an example of hard-nosed realism. It is likely that 'the Irish people' who suffered from the ravages caused by the shortage of food – including Hill's own tenants – would have viewed it as condescending, supercilious and insensitive. Lordly, in the very worst sense of that adjective. As for his description of potato blight as 'this visitation of Divine Providence', that could have been plucked from the religious lexicon attributed to medieval plagues. It ignores the scientific and climactic reasons for the spread of the *phytophthora infestans* organism, the blight known in Donegal as

60 Tuke (1846). Cf O'Brien (1896): 173.
61 Tuke (1846): 252.
62 *Facts*, 3: 9.
63 Trevelyan (1848): 1.

fiabhras dubh (black fever).[64] Nor does it take account of the poverty which underlay the people's dependency on a single variety of potato, the Irish lumper. Worse perhaps, it conveniently overlooks the British government's refusal to abandon its economic fundamentalism.

In one of the worst periods of the famine, spring 1847, Hill got married for the second time, to his late wife's sister, Louisa. She had been caring for his four children in Kent, bringing them occasionally to George's Ramelton house.[65] On one visit, she spent more than two months there.[66] In the course of the five years following Cassandra's death, love – laced with a large dose of pragmatism – blossomed between them. 'It was not surprising that an attachment had grown up between Lord George and herself', wrote Louisa's sister, Fanny.[67] She explained that marriages between a man and his dead wife's sister were prohibited by law. It was the bizarre outcome of an attempt by the well-meaning Lord Lyndhurst to achieve the opposite. Aware that such marriages threatened the legitimacy of their heirs, he introduced a bill in the Lords in order to validate them. His fellow peers responded by enacting a law which did indeed validate them, but only those that had occurred before August 1835. Any which took place after that were deemed, by virtue of the *affinity* between the couple, to be invalid.

In a further example of Hill's tenacity when faced by an apparently insurmountable barrier, he decided to sidestep the ban by marrying Louisa in one of the many countries where it was allowed. So, in May 1847, he and Louisa took their wedding vows in Wandsbek, Denmark (now Germany). It was not carried out in secret, being widely reported.[68] This kind of marriage was not a new departure within Louisa's family because her uncle, Rear-Admiral Charles Austen (younger brother of Jane Austen, Louisa's godmother), had married his deceased wife's sister. George and Louisa returned to Ireland the following month,[69] and there was no public controversy about their marriage, one of many among all classes.[70] Nor was there any question of a prosecution. Although their marriage would not be recognised

---

64 Gallagher (1982): 61.
65 FCK to Miss Chapman, 17 Sept 1845 CKS/951/C109.
66 Marcus, *Marriage*, 300.
67 FCK to Dorothy Chapman, Aug 1847, CKS, Knatchbull Archive U951/C109/34.
68 Cf *The Times*, 20 May 1847; *The Observer*, 23 May 1847.
69 *Dublin Evening Packet*, 24 June 1847.
70 Frost (2008): 55.

under English law, they were able to produce a marriage certificate, which had the effect of giving their union 'public sanction'.[71]

Hill's tenants were reportedly sympathetic – 'the common people approving highly', as his brother, Lord Marcus, put it – and thinking him 'wise' to have married Louisa because it was far better than to have brought a stranger into the family. Marcus was addressing a commission set up to inquire into the state of the marriage laws in the face of opposition to the ban.[72] Hill's family were hugely supportive, as was his wider circle of friends, several of whom gave evidence to the commission. Asked if the couple had been received in society, Marcus replied: 'I have no reason to doubt it'.[73] He listed several people in Ireland, including 'neighbours of distinction', who had called on Louisa.

On the day of her marriage, Louisa was forty-two years old. During her spells in Ramelton, she had often been obliged to run the house alone because of George's frequent absences in Gweedore and occasional visits to Dublin. She also embraced his project with some enthusiasm by drawing on her friends and her sister, Fanny, to publicise *Facts*.[74] Her other major contribution was to market the socks and stockings made by George's tenants. Some of the money was used to build an Anglican church in Bunbeg, a house for the clergyman, and to provide him with a stipend. This was done to serve the small Protestant population, all of whom had been recruited by George. Famine, it was noted, 'did not take precedence over missionary zeal'.[75]

However, as the people's misery increased over the months of 1847, the Hills did dedicate their fund-raising activities to the purchase of food rather than the church.[76] A letter from Louisa to her sister, Fanny, provides an insight into her character, illustrating her compassion for George's hungry tenants but a surprising degree of ignorance about their plight. She appeared not to know of the awful dilemma people faced in choosing to enter a workhouse. In writing of 'the utter wretchedness of the poor children about here', which 'is miserable to see', she continued:

> All need clothing ... and it is impossible to clothe three thousand and we are obliged to do nothing in that way – added to this it would do very little

71 Ibid. 60.
72 Marriage 1848. Cf Frost: 61.
73 Para 305.
74 Hillan (2011): 125.
75 Ibid. 125-6.
76 Louisa to FCK 1847, CKS Knatchbull Archive U951/C109/35.

good – for they will neither [dress] the children in the clothes or mend them & had rather go about in dirt and filth than go to the Poor House & be fed and clothed & have the children educated ... this last year of bad suffering and privation has destroyed their energies & produced a kind of torpor which comprehends nothing.[77]

Her belief in the workhouse as a safe haven to escape hardship was utterly misguided. Hill, who served on the Dunfanaghy workhouse board of guardians,[78] understood that entry was denied to anyone occupying more than a quarter of an acre on the grounds that they were not deemed to be destitute. So, in order to qualify for a workhouse place, people were required to relinquish their land, thus rendering them destitute. Men and women confronted by this woeful paradox suffered three times over: first, as they eked out a pitiful existence while trying to avoid giving up their land; second, coping with the heartache of being forced to change their minds; third, existing as landless paupers inside a forbidding institution. Workhouses were grim places and grew even worse in the final months of 1846 as they filled to capacity.[79] Families were split up. Bedding was rudimentary. And they were breeding places for diseases, such as typhus and dysentery. Why was Louisa unaware of this reality?

In fairness to her, and to Lord George, and to all those charitable landlords who did offer relief measures to their tenants, they were confronted by a disaster on a scale which required greater help than they, as individuals, could ever hope to provide. Louisa's acknowledgement in her letter – 'it is impossible to clothe three thousand' – said as much. But the destitute were in no position to view matters dispassionately. Even if landlords were encountering financial losses, it is highly doubtful if people could perceive any change in their circumstances. Outwardly, life within the Big House appeared to continue as serenely as before.

A glimpse of the declining fortunes of Irish landlords emerged during a court case involving the Marquess of Conyngham and his estranged wife, who argued that the £2,400 a year he paid to her was insufficient for her needs. 'The feature of most interest to the public', said the newspaper reports, 'was the fact that though his lordship's income from his Irish estates should be about £30,000, it does not in reality amount to more than

---

77 Ibid.
78 He is listed as an attendee at the inaugural meeting, 31 Aug 1841. http://www. workhouses.org.uk/Dunfanaghy/.
79 Kinealy (2013): 27.

£12,000'.[80] The reports referred to Conyngham's 'ruinous mismanagement' of his Donegal estates, 'as depicted in *The Times* Commissioner's letters with such remarkable vividness, especially contrasted with the same writer's account of the adjoining estates of Lord George Hill'.[81]

Hill received a further plaudit in the widely-read and respected *Illustrated London News* in an article critical of Irish landowners for their failure to invest in their holdings. The result, it contended, was that 'the Irish cotter is as much a serf as the Russian peasant, with the difference that he is worse fed' and it concluded: 'The state of property there has as much to do with the absence of capital, as the disposition of the people; their mistrust, suspicion, and a disbelief in the real intention of any person to benefit them, can be removed by time and a little management; that has been proved by others besides Lord George Hill at Gweedore'.[82]

The lack of capital investment in Ireland was a common theme by critical journalists, politicians and also by George Nicholls, the Poor Law Commissioner. Almost a decade before the Great Hunger, he observed that Ireland was 'suffering under a circle of evils' due to 'want of capital'.[83] Running alongside this analysis was a broad streak of anti-Irish sentiment exacerbated by the 'influx of Irish' into England, which 'is becoming a national evil'.[84] Once again, Hill was singled out for praise. His efforts were said to 'prove, that, *properly directed*, the resources of Ireland are amply sufficient for the comfortable support of its people'.[85]

While Hill was learning about the effects of *laissez faire* economics in Donegal, down south in County Cork, a young man was learning his trade as a journalist by reporting on the effects of the Great Hunger in his county. Denis Holland, aged just twenty, was witnessing the ravages wrought by lack of food in Skibbereen, a town of such suffering it was to become a byword for famine.[86] His newspaper, the *Southern Reporter & Cork Commercial Courier*, summarised its correspondent's reports by remarking: 'The west of Cork, around and beyond Skibbereen, is turned into a human abattoir by famine, and the

80 The modern equivalents for those sums are respectively: £255,400, £3.2 million, and £1.28 million.

81 *Liverpool Standard*, 16 Feb 1847; *Cork Examiner*, 19 Feb 1847.

82 *Illustrated London News*, 20 Feb 1847.

83 Nicholls (1836).

84 *Norfolk Chronicle*, 2 Dec 1848.

85 Ibid.

86 *Destitution*, 2438-9.

people fall in scores. The slaughter is suppressed: the English Press has no sympathy to spare. The victims are Irish – mere Irish.'[87]

The impact of what Holland saw during his visit was to influence his political views and his journalism. It hardened his already pronounced anti-English stance and moved him towards the militant branch of Irish nationalism. Three years before he reported on the 'famine', he had been in Skibbereen to attend one of Daniel O'Connell's monster repeal meetings, which was said to have attracted a crowd of 500,000.[88] 'So extraordinary a spectacle I have never seen before or since', he later wrote.[89] Then, he was wildly enthusiastic about O'Connell, recalling that while sitting at the front of one meeting 'the great orator' twisted his long hair.[90] By the time of the famine, Holland had become increasingly critical of the Liberator's stance, finding it unacceptable that O'Connell 'had begun already to emasculate the warlike manhood of Ireland by his astounding doctrine that 'no political amelioration was worth the shedding of a single drop of blood!'[91] This said much about Holland's direction of political travel.

Unlike Hill's background, about which so much is known and recorded, there are few clues to Holland's start in life. Born in Cork city in February 1826 to William Holland and Cath Callanan, he spent his boyhood in the central Marsh district.[92] It is likely he came from a Catholic middle class family, and hinted as much towards the end of his life by writing: 'There are few men in Ireland so profoundly intimate with the thoughts and feelings of the Irish middle class as I am; for I have been a student and observer'.[93] A brother, John Callanan Holland, was also a journalist.[94] They were related through their mother to a distinguished poet, Jeremiah Joseph Callanan, and to a lesser poet, Katharine Murphy.[95]

---

87 *Cork Examiner*, 5 Dec 1846.

88 *Cork Examiner*, 23 June 1843.

89 'Honest Tom Steele', *The Emerald*, 18 Dec 1869. Holland dated the meeting wrongly as 1845.

90 *The Emerald*, 28 Aug 1869.

91 *The Emerald*, 18 Dec 1869.

92 Baptised 23 Feb 1826, St Mary's parish, Cork city. Register of births: 249. *The Emerald*, 1 Jan 1870.

93 *The Irishman*, 12 May 1866.

94 *The Globe*, 21 June 1880; *Cork Daily Herald*, 2 March 1891. John died, aged 89, in 1921, *Gloucestershire Echo*, 24 Dec 1921.

95 Holland took one of his pen names, Allua, from a line in Callanan's most famous poem, 'Gougane Barra'. For the Murphy link, see 'Our Poets. No XIV: Katharine Murphy (Brigid)', *The Irish Monthly*, Vol. 13, No. 146 (Aug 1885).

He appears to have been something of a child prodigy because he was able to read and write fluently from an early age. It is not known whether he could speak Irish but he occasionally liked to Gaelicise his surname as *an Ollainn*. He was educated at the Capuchin friary overseen by Father Theobald Mathew, the noted temperance crusader. He founded a society to stimulate debate about the benefits of teetotalism, and Holland became an enthusiastic member, giving its second lecture, on 'the physiology of the Saxon and Celtic races'. He later admitted that it was 'a very ambitious' choice of topic 'for one so young'.[96] Over the years, he would often return to the subject.[97] He was a life-long admirer of Mathew, referring to him as 'Father Toby ... my beloved and revered friend'.[98] His closest pal among the friary boys was Joseph Brennan, who became a poet, journalist, admirer of John Mitchel and leading Young Irelander.[99]

Holland's family are thought to have moved to Bandon, because Holland popped up, aged sixteen, as secretary of the town's Total Abstinence Society. His letters to newspapers defending the society revealed an early penchant for belligerent prose alongside a contempt for what he called 'the Orange Press'.[100] Within a year, his interest moved far beyond temperance matters as he urged O'Connell to stage a repeal meeting in Bandon.[101] He also signed up subscribers willing to pay 'repeal rent' to fund O'Connell's campaign.[102] Feeling it necessary to explain to his former mentor, Father Mathew, that his growing attachment to repeal was separate from his being a representative of 'abstinence men', he choose to do so in an open letter.[103] Repeal of the Union rather than the denial of alcohol was soon dominating his life and he proved to be a diligent fund-raiser.[104] His writing skills were also recognised by the *Dublin Journal of Temperance, Science, and Literature*, which published articles by him in 1843 signed 'D.H. of Cork'.[105]

In March 1844, Holland became an official Repeal Association volunteer, on the recommendation of O'Connell's son, John, in recognition

---

96 *The Emerald*, 16 Oct 1869.
97 See chapter 13.
98 *The Emerald*, 28 Aug 1869.
99 *The Emerald*, 16 Oct 1869.
100 *Cork Examiner*, 1 April 1842, 20 June 1842, 13 July 1842; *Southern Reporter & Cork Commercial Courier*, 21 June 1842, 14 July 1842.
101 *Dublin Weekly Nation*, 8 April 1843.
102 *Cork Examiner*, 10 April 1843.
103 *Cork Examiner*, 3 May 1843; *Southern Reporter & Cork Commercial Courier*, 6 May 1843.
104 *Cork Examiner*, 29 July 1843, 12 Aug 1843, 21 Oct 1843, 8 Nov 1843.
105 DIB https://www.dib.ie/biography/holland-denis-a9290.

of his attachment to the cause and his recruitment of members.[106] His letter-writing skills and nationalist outlook carried him on to the staff of the *Cork Examiner*.[107] It was the natural choice. Apart from it being his local paper, it suited his politics, having been founded earlier in the decade by John Francis Maguire in order to campaign for Catholic emancipation, to support O'Connell and to raise the issue of tenant right.[108]

Debating proved to be Holland's forte. In company with Joseph Brennan, he took an active part in the debates of the Cork Historical and Literary Society, often speaking in opposition to Maguire.[109] He did not stay long with the *Examiner*, moving across to the city's other leading paper, the *Southern Reporter*, which was owned and edited by Michael Joseph Barry, a poet and author with pronounced repeal sympathies who became disillusioned with O'Connell. It led him, as it did Holland, towards the Young Ireland movement. Both men were enthused by the ideas of John Blake Dillon, Thomas Davis, Charles Gavan Duffy and, particularly, John Mitchel.

Like Mitchel, Holland would eventually end up staying at Hill's hotel. However, it would be more than a dozen years until that headline-making visit. Before we reach there, it's time to meet Hill's most celebrated visitor: Thomas Carlyle.

---

106 *Cork Examiner*, 13 March 1844.
107 DIB. Bourke (1967): 30.
108 Maguire, later an MP, was to serve on the select committee that inquired into destitution in Donegal.
109 *Cork Examiner*, 31 Oct 1849, 21 Nov 1849, 23 Oct 1850.

7

'A MAN YOU LOVE AT FIRST SIGHT' or THE MAN WHO MAKES HIS TENANTS MISERABLE?

The interest of the landlord is always opposed to the interests of every other class in the community—David Ricardo[1]

By 1848, it would not be an exaggeration to describe Lord George Hill as famous, and his celebrity continued over the succeeding years. Hardly a week passed without a newspaper in Ireland, England and Scotland reporting that someone – be it politician, philanthropist or poet – had heaped praise on his name. In the first five months of 1848 alone, I counted more than 100 articles which commended him and all his works.[2] He was eulogised as a model Irish landlord, usually as a counterweight to the criticism levelled at the majority of fellow landowners. His supporters fell into two distinct categories: the compassionate and the cunning. In the first group were humanitarians whose central concern was the alleviation of the misery suffered by Irish people and who sincerely viewed Hill as a paragon worthy of emulation. In the second were politicians who saw the advantage of using Hill's supposedly unique virtues to highlight the negligence of his fellow landlords and thereby suggest Ireland's problems were the fault of its landowners rather than its government.

---

1 *An Essay on the Influence of a Low Price of Corn on the Profits of Stock* London: John Murray (1815): 20.
2 Examples, all in 1848: *Dublin Evening Post*, 18 Jan; *The Examiner* (London), 22 Jan; *Derry Journal*, 26 Jan; *Dublin Evening Packet*, 27 Jan; *Hampshire Telegraph*, 29 Jan; *Sligo Journal*, 4 Feb; *Coleraine Chronicle*, 5 Feb; *Downpatrick Recorder*, 18 March; *The Sun* (London), 22 March; *Morning Post*, 23 March; *Bell's Weekly Register*, 25 March; *Cork Examiner*, 27 March; *Banner of Ulster*, 28 March; *Tyrone Constitution*, 31 March; *John O'Groat Journal*, 7 April; *Hereford Times*, 8 April; *Morning Post*, 19 May.

Hill's widespread acclaim as a landlord showed how far he had travelled from his days as a sought-after dance partner at aristocratic balls. Then, the smart young officer in his dress uniform was noticed only in passing in society columns which recorded the comings and goings of England's 'fashionables'. Now, in middle age, he was the central figure in articles that charted Ireland's unfolding tragedy. Many hundreds of thousands had lost their lives and hundreds of thousands more had fled the country, so it would be crass to equate Hill's problems with theirs. But there cannot be any doubt that the potato blight had derailed his project and devastated his bank account. According to Thomas Carlyle, no rent was paid 'in famine year' (presumably 1847) and in the two following years income had proved 'uncertain' and 'trifling when it does come'.[3] At the height of Hill's fame, with journalists and MPs extolling his efforts, only he was aware that while they were celebrating his past his future looked decidedly bleak.

His personal life, however, was more settled and secure. The issue of the ban on men marrying a deceased wife's sister (or, of course, women marrying a deceased sister's husband) rumbled on in the background. When an MP raised the 'delicate' matter in the Commons,[4] at least one Irish newspaper remarked on its relevance to Hill's 'prominent' family.[5] That reference may have raised a wry smile at the Hills' Ramelton residence, because 44-year-old Louisa was heavily pregnant with George's fifth child at the time. She duly gave birth to a boy, named George Marcus Wandsbeck, after the Danish town where the couple had married two years before. At the time, Cassandra's eldest child, Norah, had reached her fourteenth year and was said by a cousin to be 'the prettiest and nicest girl'.[6]

Hill's profile in Dublin and London, where newspapers continually referred to his deeds, remained high. A typical flattering article in the *Morning Advertiser*, repeated in several papers, was headlined, 'What an Irish landlord may do'.[7] Hill also won local favour by stepping in to save a thief from seven years' transportation by presenting a character reference to the assizes. The man was given a six-month jail sentence instead.[8] So

3 Carlyle (1882): 248.
4 *The Sun*, 28 Feb 1849. *Hansard*, 22.02.1849, Col.1102.
5 *Southern Reporter & Cork Commercial Courier*, 24 Feb 1849.
6 Louisa Rice, cited by Hillan (2011): 147.
7 *Morning Advertiser*, 2 Dec 1848.
8 *Ballyshannon Herald*, 26 July 1849.

extraordinary was Hill's status that when a neighbouring landlord, John Obins Woodhouse, decided to sell the lease to the townland of Meenaclady he saw an advantage in advertising it as 'immediately adjoining the Donegal estate of the enterprising and philanthropic Lord George Hill'.[9]

Just occasionally, he was drawn back to his old Dublin Castle days. In the spring, he dined with the Lord Lieutenant, the Earl of Clarendon, and Prince George, grandson of George III and cousin of Queen Victoria.[10] In August 1849, he was among the guests invited to the Viceregal Lodge to celebrate the Irish visit of Victoria and Albert.[11] The week before, he had played host to the cantankerous Carlyle, who was on the final leg of a tour of Ireland.

The celebrated historian had been expected to arrive at Gweedore with Charles Gavan Duffy, the Young Irelander who had been charged with sedition along with his fellow nationalists – William Smith O'Brien, John Mitchel and Thomas Francis Meagher – following their failed 1848 rebellion. Unlike the other three, who were convicted and transported to Van Diemen's Land (Tasmania), Duffy was freed after his fifth trial. He was aware that Carlyle had supported him by writing a letter to the Lord Lieutenant. Despite their political differences, which included Carlyle's extremely low opinion of the Irish, they remained friends and his decision to travel with the grouchy Carlyle was aimed at showing him the true state of Ireland's poverty-stricken people. But Duffy was called away to Derry just as they arrived in Donegal, and it was left to Carlyle alone to record his impressions of Hill.

Almost without exception, everyone who has written about Lord George quotes Carlyle's opinion of him as a 'handsome, grave-smiling man of 50 or more; thick grizzled hair, *elegant* club nose, low cooing voice, military composure and absence of loquacity; a man you love at first sight'.[12] Given that there are so few intimate descriptions of Hill, this one has stuck. Similarly, Carlyle's staccato word picture of George's Big House in Ramelton is one of only two accounts of it from that period: 'high rough hedges, gates, farm-looking place; and round the corner of some offices we come to an open smooth kind of back

9 *Armagh Guardian*, 16 Dec 1850. When the Dunlewey estate was put up for sale, George was again mentioned in the advert: *Saunders's News-Letter*, 1 Oct 1855; *London Daily News*, 20 Oct 1855.
10 *Freeman's Journal*, 8 May 1849.
11 *Cork Examiner*, 10 Aug 1849.
12 Carlyle (1882): 230. George was aged 47 at the time.

court, with low piazza at the further side: from piazza then at the back entrance (the only one handy to this mansion)'.[13]

He failed to take much notice of Louisa, calling her 'a nun-like elderly lady', and guessing her name to be either Georgina or Augusta, later settling for 'Lady A' and describing her as 'a delicate, pious, high and simple lady'.[14] He paid a little more attention to George's children as 'nice little modest boys and girls' who were addressed by their father in English, German and French. By coincidence, the children's German tutor was Richard Plattnauer, who happened to be a former protégé of Carlyle's wife, Jane. 'Poor Plattnauer', as Carlyle referred to him, had a record of mental instability, having spent periods in institutions in London and Switzerland, but he worked conscientiously for Hill for more than two years and later became tutor to the children of George's nephew, the Marquess of Downshire.[15] (Hill's children were also tutored in Irish.)[16]

The morning after a late supper of Irish stirabout, which Carlyle refused to eat, calling it 'a frightful parody of "Scotch porridge"', Hill took Carlyle and Plattnauer to Gweedore.[17] They travelled over 'a black dismal 22 miles of road', stopping at a half-way house, where Carlyle noted how his host, speaking in Irish, was known to everyone. 'Excellent, polite, pious-hearted, healthy man', he wrote of him. On arriving at 'Lord George's domain' he thought his 'improvements' were 'manifold' but 'swallowed in the chaos'.[18] He was unimpressed with the 'huts' and 'ragged potato patches' of Hill's tenants, and pessimistic about their prospects: 'nothing else one can see of human that has the smallest real promise here; *deluidit craiturs* – lazy, superstitious, poor and hungry'.[19]

His conversation with George about his tenants' initial response to his reforms was revealing. Unlike the relatively smooth transition hinted at in *Facts*, his candour with Carlyle indicated he had been required to face down some militant opposition:

---

13 The back door remains the most handy entrance. Some ten years after Carlyle, Ballyarr was visited by the Earl of Carlisle, the Lord Lieutenant, who noted the 'peculiarity of there being no door to the house, we got in by bending much under a very low window'. Carlisle to Lady Campbell, 21 June 1858 N.L.I. MS 40, 028/6.

14 Ibid. 230, 231, 251.

15 Carlyle Society (2010).

16 Ó Gallchobhair (1962): 24.

17 Carlyle (1882): 231.

18 Ibid. 240.

19 Ibid. 242.

How these people conspired to throw down Lord George's fences, how they threatened to pay no rent, at first, but to *shoot* agent if compelled, and got their priest to say so; how they had no notion of work by the day (*came* from 8 to 11am) and shrieked over hook-nosed Aberdeen [the agent's manager] when on Saturday night he produced his book and insisted on paying them by the *hour;* – how they are in brief, dark barbarians.[20]

He viewed Hill's approach as 'the largest attempt at benevolence and beneficence on the *modern* system (the emancipation, all-for-liberty, abolition of capital punishment, roast-goose-at-Christmas system) ever seen by me, or like to be seen'. His admiration for George was tempered by his belief that no good would come of it: 'Alas, how *can* it prosper; except to the soul of the noble man himself who earnestly tries it?'[21] Before leaving the hotel, Carlyle wrote in the visitors' book of his 'joyful astonishment' at what he had witnessed, adding: 'Could bid all Irish landlords, "See examine; go and do likewise!" Join, with all men, in wishing every prosperity to such an enterprise'.[22] Later, reflecting on his host, Carlyle reiterated his respect for him: 'In all Ireland, lately in any other land, I saw no such beautiful soul'.[23]

Yet it was Carlyle's friend, Gavan Duffy, who launched the campaign that led directly to the tarnishing of that beautiful soul. As editor of *The Nation*, Duffy threw his weight behind the Ulster Tenant Right Association, a movement founded by James MacKnight, editor of the *Londonderry Standard,* and William Sharman Crawford, the radical MP and progressive County Down landlord, along with several Presbyterian ministers. Duffy's initial act was to republish an 1848 address by MacKnight in which he argued that landlordism should be regulated by law. Duffy realised that the Encumbered Estates Act of 1849, which did not recognise the Ulster Custom of tenant-right, united Presbyterian and Catholic farmers in a common cause. In putting agrarian reform on the political agenda, the Tenant Right League, as it became, challenged the power of landlords at a time when many were facing financial ruin.

It was in Duffy's newspaper, at the end of 1850, that the first crack in Hill's halo emerged in public when it carried an anonymous letter from 'A Gweedore Tenant'. Although the writer's main target was Hill's agent,

---

20 Ibid. 243.
21 Ibid. 249.
22 VB, 4 Aug 1849, p184.
23 Carlyle (1882): 253.

Francis Forster, he did not spare his employer. His sarcastic reference to Hill's book inspired the editor's choice of headline: 'New "Facts from Gweedore" and its neighbourhood'.[24] Forster was accused of seeking 'the accumulation of riches' on his estate in Annagry by redistributing land – as Hill had done – and raising rents. After his poor tenants refused to pay, he was said to have called in bailiffs to remove their cattle, which the people prevented from happening, aided by a squad of police who did not intervene. Forster's next move was to persuade magistrates, all of them landlords, to issue arrest warrants. According to the writer, 'it is feared that Mr Forster has two objects in view – to rack-rent Lord George's tenants as well as his own'.

Three weeks later, *The Nation* returned to the issue with another letter, signed by a James McBride of Bunbeg, and a copy of a lengthy 'memorial' sent to the Lord Lieutenant. Once again, despite Forster being identified as the villain of the piece, the headline – 'More Facts from Gweedore' – was a conscious attempt to embarrass Hill.[25] These documents forged a link between one instance of alleged landlord malpractice and its wider political implications, identifying 'Englishmen' who own 'our property' as the culprits. Support for landlords by the Lord Lieutenant, Lord Clarendon, meant that tenant farmers were therefore 'victims of government misrule'. As a response to that state of affairs, said the letter, the Tenant League has 'undertaken... the task of redeeming a noble people from the most degrading feudalism'.

According to McBride, following the stand-off between Forster and his tenants, Clarendon authorised the deployment of armed police who held tenants at bayonet point as Forster's bailiffs collected rents, evicted those who did not pay and seized potatoes and property which was auctioned off at Hill's Gweedore Hotel. A further letter, signed by 'A Tenant Leaguer, Gweedore', argued that Clarendon's 'cool indifference' to the tenants' plight should 'make us shake off all apathy, and throw ourselves, heart and soul, into the Tenant Right agitation'.[26] Lord George was being treated to his first taste of bad publicity, albeit at one remove. Worse, much worse, was to follow.

Apparently unaware of the growing unrest, he sought ways to increase his income by taking an interest in two railway enterprises.[27] He also

24 *The Nation*, 28 Dec 1850.
25 *The Nation*, 25 Jan 1851:13.
26 Ibid.
27 *Dublin Evening Mail*, 3 Dec 1849; *Derry Journal*, 19 Dec 1849.

became a vice-president of the Chemico-Agricultural Society of Ulster.[28] For Hill, who donated a collection of Irish manuscripts to the Belfast Museum, the past seemed more relevant than the present.[29] But 'a spirit of insubordination' and the supposed rise of ribbonism in Donegal could not be ignored.[30] In January 1851, Hill was one of the Donegal landlords, acting in their guise as magistrates, who called on Clarendon to proclaim part of the county, including Gweedore, under the Crime and Outrage Act. As a result, an extra twenty police officers were drafted into the area. Ratepayers, who had to fund the force, vainly sought to have the decision reversed on the grounds that there were only 'isolated instances' of crime.[31] This difference of opinion was a manifestation of the growing split between the interests of landlords and those of an independent, emergent class of businessmen, many of them Catholics.

The magistrates' feared trouble because the court in Lifford was about to deal with an unusually large number of eviction notices. Some 154 'ejectments' were being sought by Donegal landlords, who were described by the *Londonderry Standard* as 'the chief actors in the clearance system'.[32] It named them as Lords Conyngham, Wicklow and Leitrim, Sir Edmund Hayes MP, and three clergymen. The newspaper was scathing about Leitrim, insinuating that the workhouses in Milford and Letterkenny would need 'extra wings' to cope with his evicted tenants. It concluded: 'Surely these cases of eviction are proof of the poverty of the country, that the land is not able to pay the rent and taxes that are imposed upon it'. Although Lord George was not among those 'chief actors', he was on friendly terms with all of them and, in Leitrim's case, was willing to do business with him over a potential mining project.[33] Hill was pronounced guilty by association.

One landlord, Colonel Joseph Pratt, owner of a large estate in Stranorlar, attracted persistent hostility. He had praised Hill's reforms six years before.[34] Now, his tenants were resisting his demand for rent increases. In December 1850, Pratt's bailiff, James Johnston, was waylaid by four armed men, who beat him, shot his horse to death, and robbed him of £165 in rent collections.[35]

28 *Journal of the Chemico-Agricultural Society of Ulster and Record of Agriculture and Industry*, 4 April 1853.
29 *Dublin Evening Mail*, 15 Sept 1852.
30 *John Bull* (London), 4 Jan 1851; *The Nation*, 4 Jan 1851.
31 *Dublin Evening Post*, 7 Jan 1851. Cf. *Londonderry Standard*, 5 Jan 1851.
32 *Londonderry Standard*, 9 Jan 1851.
33 See chapter 8.
34 See chapter 5.
35 *Ballyshannon Herald*, 6 Dec 1850.

Eight months' later, Johnston's sub-bailiff, David Moore, was 'mutilated unmercifully' when beaten to death by two men wielding spades.[36]

The London-based *Morning Post* claimed that the local population was sympathetic towards the perpetrators rather than the victim because they opposed the payment of *any* rent. What they want, it said, is 'the possession of the land in fee simple, or, at the very least, an absolute and unlimited right of squatting'.[37] It cited Hill's 'little treatise', *Facts*, as one of 'the best authorities' on the 'miserable and unproductive' rundale farming system preferred by 'the squatting population', and argued that, unless the people were willing to respect the rights of property 'the more politic course' would be 'to induce their emigration *en masse*'.

Hill, who opposed emigration as a solution to Ireland's problems,[38] continued to plough his own furrow in the belief that his tenants, unlike those of Pratt, Leitrim and Conyngham, appreciated his changes. In the autumn of 1851, a *Belfast News-Letter* article about Gweedore – a 'remote locality, now famed for the active benevolence displayed by its noble proprietor' – carried the latest report from the judges chosen (by Hill) to award 'premiums' to the best-performing tenants.[39] They expressed their 'delight' at the improvements to the estate, which were 'more apparent than in any year since the famine', and urged the people to 'fully appreciate' Hill's 'philanthropic exertions'.

Those exertions encouraged him to join a group of men who believed they could transform Ireland's agriculture by creating 'a permanent class of small landed proprietors' on land that had become available in the wake of the Great Hunger.[40] According to its mission statement, the Farmers' Estate Company of Ireland would provide loans to impoverished tenant farmers who would, in theory, 'joyfully grasp' the chance to take on loans repayable over a lengthy period at a reasonable rate of interest.[41] The board included the brewer Benjamin Lee Guinness, paper manufacturer Sir Edward McDonnel, politician William Maunsell, and Hill's long-time friend, Sir James Dombrain, who had left the coastguard to become a

---

36 'Dreadful murder in Donegal', *Dublin Evening Packet*, 14 Aug 1851; 'Barbarous murder in County Donegal', *Londonderry Sentinel*, 15 Aug 1851; *Ballyshannon Herald*, 22 Aug 1851.
37 *Morning Post*, 19 Aug 1851.
38 *Facts* 5: 56ff.
39 *Belfast News-Letter*, 31 Oct 1851. Cf. *Londonderry Sentinel*, 31 Oct 1851; *Downpatrick Recorder*, 8 Nov 1851.
40 *Northern Whig*, 13 March 1852.
41 *The Times*, 1 March 1852; *The Tablet*, 13 March 1852.

commissioner with the corporation overseeing Dublin's port. I could not locate any records of the company's performance.[42]

More positive publicity for Hill arrived with a lengthy article in the *Dublin University Magazine*, which was favourably cited in a host of papers.[43] The anonymous writer, relying on Hill's account of the rundale system in *Facts*, regarded it as having been based on 'a communistic principle' and claimed that it engendered civil wars between 'poor ignorant people'. Of Hill, it said: 'He has not shrunk from the exercise of authority nearly absolute, but he has exercised it manifestly with a design of training beings endowed with human faculties'. Here was praise for the benevolent landlord tinged with a disconcerting dose of realism.

Despite the widespread belief in Hill's good works and his tenants' supposed respect for his non-confrontational management style, he was subject to a surprising amount of 'outrages' in the 1851-56 period. According to police reports, two of his bailiffs were attacked when trying to distrain cattle for unpaid rent; a boat belonging to one of those bailiffs was destroyed; a bridge wall on his estate was knocked down; the tails of seven cattle belonging to his agriculturist were hacked off; the premises of his Scottish baker, John Mason, were burgled; Mason received threatening letters because of his being a Scot; Hill's own office was burgled; his gamekeeper was assaulted; and a notice was posted urging his tenants not to pay their rent. These incidents, most of which went unreported in newspapers, were recorded by the constabulary.[44]

It was a letter to a newspaper, *The Nation,* in January 1856 that signalled a turning of the tide against Lord George.[45] Signed by 'A Gweedore Man', it amounted to a full-frontal assault on Hill and may well have been written by the same person responsible for the 'Gweedore Tenant' letter which had attacked Hill's agent, Forster, five years before. There was a similar mixture of sarcasm and satire:

> Permit me to direct your attention to the miserable and deplorable condition of Lord George Hill's tenants on his property at the Gweedore. 'Lord George Hill', you and many will exclaim, '*his* tenants miserable!' Year

---

42 Lynch and Vaizey (1960): 12. This history of the Guinness family makes a passing reference to Lord George's innovations, but does not mention the company.
43 'Gweedore', *Dublin University Magazine*, No 241 (Jan 1853): 9-22.
44 A return of the outrages specially reported by the constabulary as committed within the barony of Kilmacrenan, county Donegal, during the last ten years, H.C. 1861 (404), lii, 585. Cited by Mac Shuibhne (1995): 558.
45 *Dublin Weekly Nation*, 26 Jan 1856.

after year, did not the public ear ring with the praises of his Lordship's improvements at Gweedore, and of his kind and liberal concessions to his tenants, and of the comforts and happiness among them? Was not Lord Hill held up as a 'bright example', no less, 'to the landlords of Ireland'... The fact is that no improvement affecting the tenantry has been or is being carried on at Gweedore. I challenge an instance of such improvement – to give employment – to introduce skill in agriculturing – to assist in preparing the ground for cropping – to contribute towards placing the seed within the reach of the poorer land holder – to give a stimulus to labour by opening some field for honourable enterprise – to direct the energy of the tenants along the shore to deep sea, or any fishery – to take advantage of the existing acts of parliament in developing the capabilities of the soil, the reclamation of the many thousand acres of waste land in Gweedore... Have these or any of these been done at Gweedore? No; it was not his Lordship's cue.

The writer claimed that Hill's 'entire expenditure at Gweedore was dictated by the most calculating and close-fisted policy, and solely incurred with a view to his own pecuniary advantages'. As a result, his tenantry were wretched. 'The greater part of them have neither cow, nor sheep, nor living thing, except a few poultry, whose produce goes to the huxter's shop, to help them in keeping their body and soul together. Numbers of them do not taste milk or butter of their own from generation to generation.' They had few clothes and little or no furniture in 'their poor hovels'. They had relied instead on Indian meal supplied by their priest, John Doherty.

And then came the sentence that was to have serious ramifications for Hill: 'On his accession to this property he appropriated to himself, without compensation, about five or six hundred acres of top-land, on which he grazes a large quantity of black and white cattle'.

By their nature, anonymous letters lack credibility. It was noticeable that the editor of *The Nation* initially rejected it and took more than two weeks to change his mind.[46] The editor of the *Derry Journal*, having received a similar letter from 'A Gweedore Tenant', agonised for almost a month and decided against publication.[47] As for *The Nation*, there was no follow-up, and no other paper remarked on it. If it upset Hill, he did not respond, at least in public, and the affair passed without apparent controversy. But the allegation about his appropriation of grazing land proved to be the opening shot in a battle that would severely dent Lord George Hill's public image.

---

46 *The Nation*, 12 Jan 1856: 8.
47 *Derry Journal*, 19 Dec 1855; *Derry Journal*, 16 Jan 1856.

8

WHERE SHEEP MAY NOT SAFELY GRAZE

The war between landlord and tenant has been carried on for eighty years. It is evident that this relation, which ought to be one of mutual confidence, is one of mutual hostility; nor do I see that they can be left to fight out that battle with any prospect of a better result. Murder on one side; ejectment on the other – are as common as ever
– Lord John Russell[1]

Despite his strained finances, Lord George Hill invested in several enterprises in the hope of improving his fortune. Early in 1857, he became a director of a company to explore and exploit Ireland's mineral wealth, the West of Ireland Mining Company.[2] Among the other investors were two Donegal landlords, Sir James Stewart and Alexander Stewart, along with the Irish railway pioneer William Dargan and the English shipbuilder Sir George Edmund Hodgkinson. According to a statement of intent, the directors' 'desire' was 'to promote the prosperity of the country, with much commercial benefit to themselves'. It also stressed that the project was 'not one of those delusive schemes ... but a sound, legitimate enterprise'.

Little more was heard of this sound enterprise, however, and it was a very different profit-seeking scheme that was to dominate Hill's life in the coming years while effectively fracturing his relationship with his tenants. The first intimation of the problem emerged towards the end of 1856 with hyperbolic newspaper accounts of barbarism, outrages and

---

1 Lord John Russell. Letter to the Marquess of Lansdowne, 18 Nov 1847. Cited in Walpole, Spencer, *The Life of Lord John Russell* Vol 1 (London: Longmans Green, 1889).
2 *Freeman's Journal*, 7 Jan 1857; *The Times*, 20 May 1857.

assaults after land had been rented by Hill and neighbouring landlords to 'strangers from England and Scotland' in order to graze sheep.[3] The reports, carried in scores of papers, also told of an attack on the home of a shepherd working for Hill's neighbour, John Obins Woodhouse, by forty men armed with pistols and sticks. In a 'classic Molly Maguire action', they killed one of his sheep dogs, stole his watch and issued an ultimatum: he must leave in eight days.[4] They said they would not allow any 'Scotch or English people' to take their mountains.

A month later a lengthy letter from 'A Donegal Man' – adopting a style somewhat similar to 'A Gweedore Tenant' – appeared in Denis Holland's Belfast-based newspaper, *The Ulsterman*.[5] It defended the action against the landlords by arguing that the tenants had long 'enjoyed the right, or privilege, of grazing their cattle on the mountains', which was 'their only means [of] clothing themselves and children'. The stock they raised also 'enabled them to make their rents and meet other contingencies'. The writer went on to accuse the landlords of raising rents to levels that caused the tenants 'misery and want and wretchedness'. Even so, the tenants were willing to pay more if they could use the land but the landlords were not interested in having anyone except 'Scotch and English graziers. "No Irish need apply."' Where was the justice, he asked, in ousting tenants from land where 'they and their forefathers grazed their cattle from time immemorial?'

This was the opening skirmish in a battle that would soon be dramatised as 'a war'.[6] The following month, 160 sheep were stolen from one of Hill's shepherds and 60 were taken from Olphert's estate.[7] The *Londonderry Standard* chose to view such incidents in the context of the people's defence of tenant right and compared the landlords' introduction of sheep-farming to the clearances in the Scottish Highlands.[8] 'The cultivation of brute beasts is preferred to the sustenance of human beings', it said, and quoted a letter in which the anonymous writer claimed that 'Scotch shepherds' had been guilty of destroying sheep belonging to people living

---

3 *Dublin Evening Post*, 18 Dec 1856; *Dublin Evening Packet*, 18 Dec 1856; *Manchester Guardian*, 20 Dec 1856.
4 Mac Suibhne (1995): 563.
5 *The Ulsterman*, 19 Jan 1857. See 'A Gweedore Tenant'.
6 Thomas Larcom, Under-Secretary for Ireland, believed 'there was much exaggeration on all sides'.
7 *Armagh Guardian*, 27 Feb 1857.
8 *Londonderry Standard*, 30 April 1857.

in the townland of Meenderrygamph, adjacent to George's Gweedore Hotel, because the animals had 'happened to trespass on the mountains'. When a witness to the killings was asked why there had been no attempt to launch a prosecution, the man replied: 'We are afraid of incurring the displeasure of Lord G. Hill and Mr. Forster, who are threatening to make the whole district a sheep-walk for Scotch and English'.

The *Standard* alleged that a consequence of Hill's improvements had been the removal of both top lands and mountain bog from the inhabitants of sixteen Gweedore townlands. At the same time, the tenants' rents had been raised by substantial amounts. 'Is it any wonder', asked the *Standard*'s editorial, 'that discontent, resentment, and even moodier passions, instigated by the loss of heart and hope, should be occasionally manifested?' It concluded with a plea for 'a searching investigation into the various rumours which have now gained currency', adding: 'If there is any error in these representations, we hold ourselves in readiness to correct that error ... We invite authenticated information respecting the system pursued about Gweedore and its neighbourhood'.

Over the following months, as clashes between immigrant shepherds and indigenous tenants multiplied, so did the rumours. Truth was consistently clouded by accusations and counter accusations. The landlords were able to exercise considerable power. They ruled the local courts and, through their access to the Lord Lieutenant, they were able to summon extra police officers whenever they wished. They also had the sympathy of the overwhelming majority of the press. Quite obviously, and crucially, they controlled the fate of their tenants. It does not mean they were guilty of the iniquities with which they were accused. But their superior position gave them a giant edge.

Hostility towards landlords was not confined to their tenantry. Cess-payers (ratepayers) were none too pleased by court decisions which compensated landlords from the local rates for losses incurred during what were known by the catch-all description 'agrarian disturbances'. These generally involved the theft or killing of sheep belonging to shepherds renting mountain land. As one newspaper report so delicately put it, 'the country people not entertaining friendly feelings towards them, they were visited nocturnally, and noticed to leave their holdings, and the destruction of some hundreds of valuable sheep was the penalty of disobedience'.[9] When magistrates sitting in Letterkenny agreed to pay the shepherds for their losses, the awards 'were opposed on the part of the cess-paying community'.[10] Three of Hill's Scottish shepherds – James Huggup, Joseph Wright and William Hunter – were granted payments of £561 5s, £333 15s and £135 9s respectively for the joint loss of 857 sheep. George himself was awarded £55 for the destruction of a house on his estate, although he had been seeking £123. Most of the magistrates were Hill's fellow landlords.

The killing of so many sheep – 'the wanton destruction of property' – was widely condemned, especially when the details of the 'malicious injuries' emerged in court. Lawyers representing the shepherds told how mutilated sheep carcases were discovered partially buried in bog holes. Some of the condemnation, however, was anything but welcome to Hill and his neighbouring landowners. The *Derry Journal* said:

> We cannot find language strong enough to condemn the barbarous method of revenge, for the wrongs inflicted upon them by landlord power, to which the people have resorted in the barony of Kilmacrenan, or to denounce the infamous Ribbon societies which we believe to be greatly on the increase in that quarter; but, at the same time that we hold up to public reprobation the perpetrators of these crimes, we cannot lose sight of the fact that it is in a great measure to the conduct of some grasping landlords that their existence is to attributed.[11]

The *Londonderry Standard* adopted a similar line: 'While every right-minded individual must both abhor outrage, and labour for its suppression, he cannot ignore the circumstances by which it is frequently provoked … we greatly fear that some of the proprietors of the disturbed districts … have not been pursuing the wisest or most equitable economy'.[12] There was some sympathy for the 'heavy penalties' imposed on ratepayers through compensation awards and by bearing 'the costs of the immense police force stationed in the localities'. The paper was concerned that 'the great body of cess-payers will not be able to pay these accumulated charges'.

The staunchly Protestant *Londonderry Sentinel* was wholly supportive of the landlords and, in so doing, represented the predominant Dublin

---

9 *Dublin Evening Mail*, 1 June 1857.
10 *Londonderry Standard*, 4 June 1857.
11 Cited by *Dublin Evening Post*, 4 June 1857.
12 *Londonderry Standard*, 4 June 1857.

and English media opinion of the period.[13] Most newspapers scorned 'journals of a certain stamp' that 'excuse the atrocities by libelling the landlords', as the *Dublin Evening Packet* put it. Hill's fame placed him firmly in the spotlight, being the landowner most frequently named in the articles. The *Packet* noted how critical papers pulled their punches when referring to him: 'None of the anti-landlord organs will dare to stigmatise him as an oppressor of the poor'.[14] Others agreed.

The message in *Facts from Gweedore* prevailed. 'His lordship is about one of the last men in Ireland who might be suspected of having an enemy amongst the people of this country', said the *London Evening Standard*, pointing out that he had 'converted the district of Gweedore from something little above the rank and value of a common to an attractive, fertile, and prosperous locality'.[15] During 'the potato famine', Hill had 'remained there, exerting himself, neither sparing his purse nor his person in the cause of the poor. This excellent nobleman, one might suppose, was not obnoxious to the ribbon conspirators of the district. Yet so it is.'

It was the *Packet*'s report, repeated in many other papers, which argued the landlords' case. 'It is complained that the peasantry in parts of Donegal were deprived of the liberty of grazing their cattle in certain districts by the newcomers. There is nothing extraordinary in this. When men purchase land they properly claim to be endowed with the rights of purchase, and if they do not resort to arbitrary measures using them, no man can find fault.'[16] Rather than settle the matter, this statement begged several questions about property rights; about tenant rights; about what constituted arbitrary measures; and, in a wider context, about the nature of landlordism itself.

The immediate upshot of the sheep-killing incident was, at local level, a grand jury inquiry to consider the compensation awards and, on the national stage, claims by the mainstream Protestant press that the tenants' villainy was being organised by Roman Catholic priests. At the inquiry hearings, people were re-examined about the disappearance of the sheep and the value of the animals. When one of the witnesses happened to mention Hill's name, the chairman of the jurors, John Vandeleur Stewart, landlord and owner of Letterkenny's largest mansion, Rockhill House,

---

13   *Londonderry Sentinel*, 10/17 July 1857.
14   *Dublin Evening Packet*, 6 June 1857.
15   *London Evening Standard*, 6 June 1857.
16   *Dublin Evening Packet*, 6 June 1857.

quickly intervened. They were not there, he said, 'to judge of the character of Lord George Hill ... such a line of examination was unusual and illegal'.[17] Freedom of speech was crushed. At what was regarded as a 'tedious inquiry',[18] it was finally agreed that the awards must be paid by the local ratepayers, which meant Hill's tenants, and others on neighbouring estates, would also be required to stump up their portions.

Meanwhile, several of Hill's tenants were accused of having stolen, driven away or killed sheep. Three were taken to Lifford jail to await trial,[19] and soon after a further five, plus one woman, were arrested in Gweedore.[20] When four of them – Daniel Gallagher, James McBride, Denis Coll and Paddy Coll – sought bail at a Dublin high court hearing, the judge was told they had been named by two of the men held in Lifford, James Boyle and William McGarvey, as sheep-killers. Bail was refused. More arrests followed swiftly. By early November, eighteen of Hill's tenants were in jail, having been remanded in custody on charges of destroying or maiming sheep.[21] Four more were arrested subsequently.

While they awaited trial at Donegal assizes, three priests, John Doherty, Hugh McFadden and James McFadden, took up the cause of their Gweedore parishioners. They saw themselves as community leaders and identified with the people from whom they were largely drawn. The Irish clergy were, after all, 'chiefly recruited from the class of small farmers and peasantry' and as a consequence shared 'all the passions of their class', including a suspicion of landlords.[22] The priests were the prime movers in forming the so-called 'Derrybeg Committee', which launched an appeal against the decision to levy the police rate. It was swiftly rejected, and their intervention earned them a large measure of notoriety and press condemnation for their trouble, being denounced as a 'knot of clerical agitators' and 'clerical triumvirs'.[23]

Accused by the *Dublin Daily Express* of being 'agitators' who held 'dominion' over Gweedore, they were said to have 'goaded the natives into wickedness'.[24] The paper also took the opportunity to criticise the

17   *Londonderry Sentinel*, 10 July 1857.
18   *Belfast Mercury*, 24 July 1857.
19   *Belfast Mercury*, 20 Oct 1857.
20   *Freeman's Journal*, 31 Oct 1857.
21   *Morning Chronicle*, 9 Nov 1857.
22   Grousset (1986): 229.
23   *Londonderry Sentinel*, 10 July 1857.
24   *Dublin Daily Express*, 11 July 1857.

nationalist press by claiming that the priests were authors of 'the most outrageous tissue of falsehoods' and 'libellous productions, published in *The Nation* newspaper and other papers of that class ... the *Derry Journal* [and] *Belfast Ulsterman*'. This conveniently overlooked the sympathy for the tenants' case advanced by the Presbyterian *Londonderry Standard.*

In an attempt to raise the stakes, the priests then sent a petition to the House of Commons. It was derided as a fabrication by the *Londonderry Sentinel*, which cited a report by the Public Petition Committee stating that only three signatures – those of Doherty and the two McFaddens – were genuine while 2,076 were 'palpable forgeries'.[25] This would be a recurring criticism despite the priests' explanation that they had filled in names 'on behalf of' parishioners who agreed with the sentiments in the petition (and many of whom were unable to write). Politicians and journalists remained sceptical. Newspapers were particularly critical of the priests' middle class supporters, such as the 'attorney for the Romish clergy of the shire', John McCrossan. The *Dublin Evening Packet* was astonished that the Omagh lawyer should attack 'the Benefactor of Gweedore' by arguing 'that the Donegal cottiers had been brought to the lowest state of physical distress by the harsh conduct of Lord George Hill and neighbouring proprietors'.[26] The *Dublin Evening Mail* was also exercised by the priests' petition being presented to parliament by Patrick McMahon, MP for Wexford and a member of the Independent Irish Party. It accused him of 'violating the privileges of the House of Commons by placing an irregular document upon its table'.[27]

The *Mail* was upset that anyone should think to complain about Hill. His 'exertions' in Gweedore 'for the subjugation of that desert ... are known to almost every man in the country ... the cost of them to that most worthy and patriotic man has been the incessant labour of fifteen of the best years of his life, and an outlay of not less than £20,000'. Drawing on details in *Facts*, and indulging in its own metropolitan, conservative and Protestant prejudices against people in the west of Donegal, the paper continued:

> When he undertook that work of the truest patriotism, about 2,400 savages occupied those bogs and mountains, living rather like the beasts of the field than human creatures. The famine intervened, and there are still in Gweedore a population undiminished in number, well-clad, comfortably-housed, supplied with the means of free communication, by excellent

25 *Londonderry Sentinel*, 17 July 1857.
26 *Dublin Evening Packet*, 21 July 1857.
27 *Dublin Evening Mail*, 20 July 1857.

roads, with other districts, and having all the necessaries of life within their reach, through the import and export trade of a port.

Newspaper editors were taking opposing positions based on their religious, class and political sympathies. They did not carry first-hand reports, however. The pro-Catholic press relied on word of the priests. The mainstream Protestant press relied on the word of the landlords. The *Londonderry Standard* relied on its belief in principle of tenant-right. But where did the truth lie? What was the reality of life in west Donegal? Was there any justification for the threats to Scottish sheep farmers and the killing of their flocks? One journalist decided to find out. Enter Denis Holland, editor and proprietor of *The Ulsterman*, militant nationalist, admirer of the Young Irelanders, and a long-time champion of tenant-right.

9

DENIS THE NEMESIS

The English parliament never did anything for Ireland on the simple
justice of her claim. The moral our history teaches is all the other way
— The Ulsterman[1]

Denis Holland was a young man in a hurry. We left him in his native
Cork, working for the *Southern Reporter & Cork Commercial
Courier*. In his spare time, he continued to be an avid debater and is also
thought to have attended Queen's College Cork.[2] If so, he did not graduate,
choosing instead to move to the *Limerick & Clare Examiner*. There, he
found himself in the middle of a political split between the two brothers
who ran the newspaper – Charles and James McCarthy – because they were
on opposing sides of the pro-repeal struggle. The former, the proprietor,
was a staunch O'Connellite, who advocated 'moral force', while the latter,
the editor, was a Young Irelander 'who favoured physical force'.[3]

Holland wasn't exactly in the middle. His initial admiration for Daniel
O'Connell had waned well before he reached Limerick. Although he
would eventually argue that O'Connell was 'one of the greatest Irishmen
that ever lived', he entirely rejected his pacific doctrine.[4] He was drawn
instead to the breakaway Young Irelanders whose ideas were aired in

---

1 Editorial, *The Ulsterman*, 12 Feb 1858.
2 Maume (2009). Bourke (1967): 30. According to the *Cork Examiner* (7 November 1849),
a Denis Holland was listed as a successful scholarship candidate for Queen's College's
literary department.
3 'Honest Tom Steele', *The Emerald*, 18 Dec 1869. Cf Bowen (2012 and 2013). Denis's
brother, John Callanan Holland, followed him at the *Examiner*.
4 *The Emerald*, 28 Aug 1869.

The Nation newspaper. At the end of 1847, that group, led by William Smith O'Brien and Charles Gavan Duffy, lost the support of one of their closest friends, John Mitchel, who was, as Duffy conceded, the paper's 'most valuable contributor'.[5] Mitchel resigned as the paper's leader writer because, unlike his comrades, he believed Britain was unlikely to relinquish its hold on Ireland without armed insurrection. Holland was somewhat sympathetic to that militant line, but he respected Mitchel more for his penetrating analysis of the causes of the Great Hunger and for his unstinting support of tenant right.

Holland was, first and foremost, a journalist rather than an activist, an agitator rather than a warrior. Despite his belief that it might be necessary to take up arms to secure Ireland's independence, he stood back from military activity and only very occasionally dared to advocate it. He admired from afar the Young Irelanders who launched the failed 1848 rebellion, such as O'Brien and Thomas Meagher. Claims that he joined James Fintan Lalor's conspiracy to launch an uprising in 1849 alongside Joseph Brenan and John O'Leary are highly doubtful. The evidence is thin to non-existent.[6] For Holland (just as it was for Mitchel), it was Lalor's radical analysis of rural Ireland that mattered, notably his conception that the only legitimate owners of land were the peasants. In accepting Lalor's viewpoint, both Mitchel and Holland concluded that there was no prospect of the illegitimate owners, the landlords, relinquishing their land without being forced to do so.

It did not mean that the force had to be force of arms, which was Mitchel's contention. Holland was ambivalent about the use of physical force, preferring to put his faith in the power of publicity by arguing the case against landlordism. As an intellectual supporter of tenant right, he made his case with the pen rather than the sword. A pen, it should be said, that was often dipped in vitriol. As a young jobbing reporter, however, he was required to keep his opinions to himself. It made his next move all the more remarkable because he decided to join a newspaper which promulgated views diametrically opposed to his own. The *Northern Whig*'s slogan, 'Pro rege sæpe, pro patria semper' (For king often, for country always), was hardly one Holland could be expected to support.

---

5 O'Sullivan (1944): 76.

6 Maume (2009). The specific source is unclear. See O'Bourke (1968): 20, 30; Legg (1999): 69; O'Sullivan (1944): 353-5. In L. Fogarty's biography of Lalor (*James Fintan Lalor: Patriot and Political Essayist*, Dublin 1918) there is no mention of Holland being among the conspirators.

Lord George Hill in his Blues uniform, painted by
Alfred Edward Chalon, 1831.

'Consider first the portrait of Lord George Augusta Hill in
his British cavalry uniform, a handsome head of dark
wavy hair, side-whiskered, otherwise smooth of face. He
stares blankly and obliquely out of the frame. Serious
without being solemn, the faintest hint of a smile
suggests he is holding his natural affability in check.
Despite the shining breastplate, there is no sign of a
military bearing. Instead, looking far younger in his
portrait than his thirty years, the enduring image it
presents is one of innocence.'

Lord George Hill's mother Mary, Marchioness of Downshire and 1st Baroness Sandys.

Lord George Hill's father Arthur, 2nd Marquess of Downshire. Portrait by Hugh Douglas Hamilton c. 1785–1790.

Cassandra Jane Knight, niece of Jane Austen. In 1834, seven years after his first thwarted proposal, she became Lord George Hill's first wife.

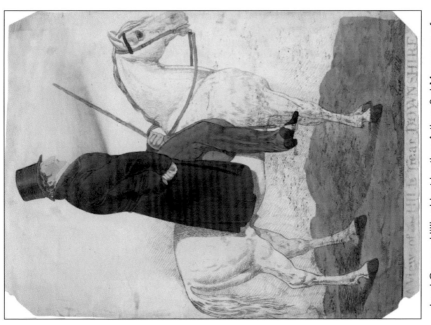

Lord George Hill's eldest brother Arthur, 3rd Marquess of Downshire (who died on his horse).

Hillsborough, the Downshire family's 'big house' inaccurately called a castle. Lord George Hill learned about landlordism during visits to his brother Arthur, 3rd Marquess of Downshire, at Hillsborough. He may also have picked up the basics of Irish as a child in Hillsborough from his nurse, 'a native Irish speaker from mid–Down'.

Dilapidated dwelling and its occupants, Gweedore 1889, a decade after Lord George Hill died. James Glass collection.

The Landlords of Gweedore

The 3rd Earl of Leitrim.
His evictions, 'angered almost the
entire press'; he was killed by three of
his tenants in 1878.

The 3rd Marquess Conyngham.
'An absentee landlord with an extremely
poor reputation among his tenants'.

© Donegal County Council

Lord George Hill's great friend and
mentor, Sir James Dombrain, owner
of the Dunlewey estate.

© Donegal County Council

Francis Forster, land agent for Lord
George Hill and a landlord in his own
right: 'it is feared that Mr Forster has
two objects in view – to rack-rent Lord
George's tenants as well as his own'.

Gweedore tenants engaged in collective work. James Glass collection.

A barefooted Gweedore tenant with her children. James Glass collection.

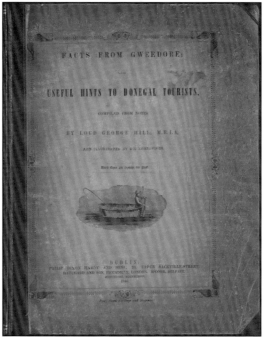

Front cover of the first edition of *Facts From Gweedore,* 1846 (above). The book includes idealised illustrations of Lord George Hill's key works in Gweedore, including his new harbour and storehouse at Bunbeg (below).

These were drawn by Harriet Windsor-Clive, Lord Downshire's sister-in-law.

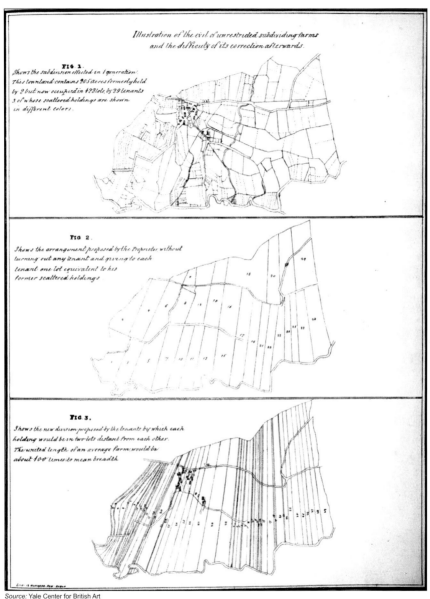

The above illustration from *Facts from Gweedore* shows the 'evil' of the pattern of landholding under the rundale system (Fig 1), Lord George Hill's proposed arrangement (Fig 2) and the 'new division' as proposed by the tenants (Fig 3).

Sketch of the Gweedore Hotel 1844, by Harriet Windsor-Clive.

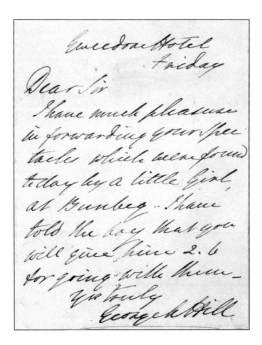

By his own hand, Lord George Hill writes to a hotel visitor – James Thomson Tennent of Letterkenny – who left his glasses behind: *Dear Sir, I have much pleasure in forwarding your spectacles which were found today by a little girl at Bunbeg. I have told the boy that you will give him 2.6 for going with them. Yours truly, George A Hill.*

Visitors to the Gweedore Hotel
during Lord George Hill's tenure

Asenath Nicholson
US philanthropist

John Mitchel
Republican revolutionary and politician

William Allingham
Donegal poet

Thomas Carlyle
Scottish author

A representation of the incident in which Inspector Martin was killed and for which Canon James McFadden (below) was charged with murder.

Canon James McFadden,
known as An Sagart Mór
(The Great Priest)

Lady Louisa, Lord George Hill's second wife, with her
son George Marcus Wandsbeck, born on 9th April 1849.
Portrait by Sir William Ross.

Lord George Hill in old age, circa 1875. Reports by people who met him at the time
'are suggestive of an elderly man living in a sort of genteel poverty'. He died in 1879.

(Left) Lord George Hill's eldest son Arthur who inherited the Gweedore estate, pictured here as Lieutenant (later Captain) and wearing his Indian Mutiny medal. He sold Ballyarr House and left Ireland in 1899, a few years after getting rid of the troublesome Gweedore estate and soon after the termination of a stint as Inspector of Irish Prisons. During the last years of Arthur's life, with his army pension proving inadequate to fund his lifestyle, he was obliged to borrow from his children. He lived to witness the partial disengagement of British rule from Ireland, dying, aged 86, in 1923. His obituaries noted he was Jane Austen's great nephew.

With permission of the executors of the late Lady Sandys

Sacred To The Memory
of
LORD GEORGE HILL,
A-SELF DENYING CHRISTIAN, HE DEVOTED HIS LIFE
AND FORTUNE TO CIVILIZE GWEEDORE, AND TO RAISE
ITS PEOPLE TO A HIGHER SOCIAL AND MORAL LEVEL;
AND AFTER HE HAD SERVED HIS GENERATION, BY THE
COUNSEL OF GOD, HE FELL ASLEEP IN JESUS AT
BALLYARE HOUSE, APRIL THE 6TH 1879,
His earthly remains are deposited in
Letterkenny Church-Yard,
THIS HUMBLE TRIBUTE OF AFFECTION IS ERECTED BY
A FEW OF THE CONGREGATION WORSHIPPING HERE.

With kind permission of Linda Ervine ©

© Roy Greenslade

One of Lord George Hill's projects was the building of a church at Bunbeg. Inside is this plaque commemorating his life and mission 'to civilize Gweedore, and to raise its people to a higher social and moral level'. The plaque is now discreetly concealed, with access to the church restricted.

The graves of Louisa (Lady George Hill) and her sister, Marianne, in Tully cemetery, on the hill overlooking Ballyarr House.

Ballyarr
(previously
Ballyare) House
Donegal, as
it is today.
Lord George Hill,
bought the house
in 1842. Carlyle
called it a 'farm-
looking place' with
a piazza at the
back entrance.

The paper, based in Belfast, a city of continual antagonism between its Protestant and Catholic residents, was owned by a liberal Presbyterian, Francis Dalzell Finlay, who was opposed to repeal and hostile towards Young Irelanders, especially Mitchel. In keeping with its slogan, the paper regularly applauded 'the people's attachment to the Throne and Constitution'.[7] Was Holland trying to test his ability to muzzle his own views while deepening knowledge of his trade? The only policy on which Finlay and Holland were broadly in accord was over tenant rights. Even so, the *Whig* was regarded as 'no friend to the Tenant League'.[8] Its great champion was the radical Protestant landlord and Liberal MP, Sharman Crawford. When Finlay introduced him to Holland, a friendship was forged and, together, they would go on to promote the League's campaign.[9]

Regardless of the political differences between the owner and his 23-year-old recruit, Holland impressed Finlay. So much so that when Finlay fired the *Whig*'s editor of twenty years, James Simms, he asked Holland to take over.[10] Holland, aware of the honour, conceded that he had 'only stepped over the threshold of manhood'.[11] In the following months, in what was expected to be a temporary appointment, the Catholic nationalist managed to prosper as editor of a Presbyterian Unionist paper. He did not attempt to change its overall stance, so the *Whig* went on being regarded as 'the able and indefatigable supporter of Lord Clarendon's administration'.[12] Perhaps he derived vicarious pleasure by publishing news reports favourable to his heroes. For example, the *Whig*'s readers learned of a New York celebration to toast Smith O'Brien and Mitchel as 'martyrs of liberty', having been convicted of sedition and transported to Van Diemen's Land (Tasmania).[13] They also read of 'sympathy in Philadelphia with the Irish exiles'.[14] More extraordinary still was a remark inserted into a report on Thomas Meagher's escape from Van Diemen's Land: 'it is to be hoped' that Smith O'Brien and Mitchel 'also escape'.[15]

---

7 *Northern Whig*, 2 Sept 1852.

8 *Londonderry Standard*, 10 April 1851.

9 He called Crawford 'a good and just man', *The Emerald*, 25 Sept 1869.

10 Simms revealed that his 'services' were 'dispensed with' in the first issue of his own newspaper, the *Belfast Mercury*, 29 March 1851.

11 *The Emerald*, 25 Sept 1869. James Simms resigned as editor in March 1851

12 *Belfast News-Letter*, 11 April 1851.

13 *Northern Whig*, 3 April 1851.

14 *Northern Whig*, 13 Dec 1851.

15 *Northern Whig*, 12 June 1852.

One editorial during Holland's *Whig* editorship, ahead of Belfast's 1851 July Twelfth celebrations, was remarkable on several counts.[16] It asserted that the 'curse' of the annual 'battles of the clans' – Protestants versus Catholics – had come to an end 'for ever' because of 'the inestimable exertions of Father Mathew'. Holland duly praised his temperance-crusading childhood mentor as an 'incomparable philanthrope' for having created the conditions in which such clashes had been relegated to 'remote corners' of Ulster. He concluded: 'We rejoice to think that our countrymen are, at last, awakening to a thorough appreciation of their olden folly... May we hope that our countrymen will learn to love one another, to forswear the enmity of creed and party … let us hope that … a new era has begun for Ireland – an era of peace and love … that may see the last death-pang of bigotry and faction.'

Did Holland really believe such idealistic, and wildly inaccurate, nonsense? If so, he had to eat his words a year later when the *Whig* reported on Orange rioting in Belfast during which a young man was killed, and two other men and a woman were shot and wounded. Several people suffered from serious injuries in fighting which sixty police, supplemented by a troop of dragoons, were unable to prevent. According to the reporter, 'the horrors of the … savage conflict … almost transcend description'.[17]

By that summer, Holland was becoming increasingly discontented by the need to do the bidding of a man with whom he fundamentally disagreed. His discomfort was compounded by the need, as part of his editing role, to rub shoulders with Belfast's Protestant governing authorities and the Dublin Castle administration, which included attendance at a banquet for the Lord Lieutenant.[18] In such circumstances, it was no surprise that he should want to leave and the split with Finlay was said to have been acrimonious.[19] What was a surprise was his decision to launch his own title because he lacked the necessary capital. He overcame that problem by forming a partnership with a Belfast printer, John P O'Hara.

It enabled him, on 17 November 1852, to present Belfast with the first issue of his tri-weekly newspaper, *The Ulsterman*. His page one prospectus made its distance from the *Northern Whig*, and every other

16 *Northern Whig*, 10 July 1851.
17 *Northern Whig*, 15 July 1852.
18 *Northern Whig*, 2 Sept 1852.
19 Maume (2009).

paper in that city at the time, abundantly clear. Holland wrote of the 'humiliating anomaly that the Catholics of Ulster, a great, a numerous, and important body' had no independent organ to represent them'. He continued: 'To supply this want, the projectors of *The Ulsterman* have resolved to publish a journal which in honesty, intelligence, national feeling and liberality may truly represent the Catholics of Ulster'.[20]

His new paper would, he pledged, avoid sectarianism by 'holding out the hand of national brotherhood to all, and zealously advocating the general interests of the country, to maintain the dignity and independent equality of the Ulster Catholics'. To that end, *The Ulsterman* would 'be thoroughly liberal' while campaigning for the extension of the franchise, 'and, above all, the obtainment for the Irish tenant of such security on his native soil as will raise our people from unparalleled privation to the prosperity which this fertile island offers to free and unrestrained industry'. He restated these principles at greater length on page two along with an address to 'Protestant brethren' who, he argued, were 'the willing victims of humbug and mountebankery ... tricked and cajoled' into ill-feeling towards Catholics.

In the third issue, in a column headlined 'Our Confession of Faith', he waxed lyrical about his paper's successful launch and was so effusive about Ulster and its people it was hard to believe he was a Cork man.[21] His central concern was for the marginalised Catholic population who were suffering 'abominable prejudice', people ...

who dwell in the heart of this great province, whose forefathers took root there when the mightiest nations of the antique world were yet in their infancy – whose race have grown and flourished there, in sorrow and in joy, in freedom and oppression, victorious or defeated, still strong and ineradicable, still clinging around, and with their very lifeblood nourishing the holy patrimony of our great Apostle – that this people, who are genial to its fertile soil, look on themselves as alien to the home which God gave them as their heritage, and unlike the rest of our old Irish race, shrink from the grand historic name of their native Ulster. No fashioning of words is competent to express how sad a thing to us is this. That the people, the ashes of whose forefathers, for countless ages have enriched and beautified the earth we tread on, should look thus coldly on the soil with which every association of race and kindred is connected, is a humiliation too great to hear in assenting silence. What would future ages say on reading so strange a story chronicled in the annals of Ireland?

20 There had previously been a Catholic, pro-repeal newspaper in Belfast, *The Vindicator* (1839-48), initially edited by Charles Gavan Duffy.
21 *The Ulsterman*, 24 November 1852.

This panegyric to the natives of Ulster, and its romantic view of Irish people in general, was typical of Holland's style. It also marks the beginning of his remarkable output. Over the course of his life, he wrote thousands of words a day and, although guilty of prolixity, his writings – a potent mixture of satire, scorn and sarcasm – were usually readable. And, just occasionally, he came up with a memorable phrase. 'The census returns', he wrote, 'speak of "improvement" from the worst to something better. They are eloquent on the increase of green crops and fat stock; but terribly brief on the extermination of immortal man.'[22] He called Irish MPs 'honourable members needy and unprincipled' who 'get snug berths' while 'the tenant farmers that risk everything in electing them, are still left at the mercy of their hostile and exasperated landlords'.[23] Under a one-word headline, 'Evictions', he wrote: 'The work of depopulation goes on'.[24]

In one of his essays he praised emigrating Irishmen as 'pioneers of civilization', calling them 'the bone and sinew' of America, while castigating *The Times* [of London] and all such enemies 'who have too often maligned and cursed our race'.[25] He continued:

> It is cheap to sneer at the Celt, and mock his poverty and misfortune; but, even from the lips of a sneering enemy the gigantic phenomenon of thousands of these Celts, brave, hardy, truthful, and enterprising, spreading over the world to lay the seeds of mighty states, must extort involuntary words of wonder and admiration... The great old Celtic race will never be exhausted ... There will always remain enough to work out the prosperity of our country; and we confidently anticipate the time when Ireland ... will yet rise up, great and free and happy among the kingdoms of the world.

Free at last to write what he liked, and at any length he desired, *The Ulsterman* was as much a magazine as a newspaper. Comment and analysis predominated. Naturally, Holland's overwhelming concern was with his words. O'Hara's overwhelming concern was with his money. It became obvious that Holland cared so little about finance – an early sign of a life-long problem – that he overspent wildly. The result was a sundering of his partnership with O'Hara after just 37 issues, obliging Holland to assume responsibility for the paper's debts.[26] Undaunted, he simply announced himself as 'proprietor and editor'.[27]

---

22 *The Ulsterman*, 1 Jan 1853: 2.
23 *The Ulsterman*, 12 Jan 1853: 2.
24 *The Ulsterman*, 2 Feb 1853: 4.
25 *The Ulsterman*, 26 March 1853.
26 *Belfast Mercury*, 23 March 1853.
27 *The Ulsterman*, 26 March 1853.

By chance, that very week he received a letter from a William Watson, who was furious about the way in which two papers, the *Belfast Mercury* and the *Belfast Commercial Chronicle*, had reported his hosting of a St Patrick's Day dinner. Watson had been criticised for causing offence to Protestants by having toasted the health of the Pope rather than the Queen.[28] In his letter, Watson argued that since Protestants were not invited to attend a dinner for Catholics it could not have caused them offence.[29] The exchange was fortuitous for Holland, who soon forged a friendship with Watson, a wealthy merchant, owner of several properties in Belfast, and a board member of the Belfast Bank.[30] They soon began campaigning together on issues affecting Belfast's Catholics.[31] They founded the Belfast Roman Catholic Institute – a club to provide 'cultural and recreational facilities for Catholic workmen'[32] – and the Belfast Literary and Debating Society, with Holland giving the initial lecture.[33] Most important to Holland was Watson's willingness to fund *The Ulsterman* without interfering in editorial matters.

From spring 1853 onwards, the newspaper built a respectable circulation and won a decent reputation as Holland honed his polemical style in countless essays that ranged from local to foreign affairs. In so doing, he differentiated his political line from that of the most popular pro-repeal title, *The Nation*. Under its editor from 1854, Alexander M. Sullivan, it sought common ground with the Catholic hierarchy. Holland, despite his devotion to Catholicism, made no such attempt, maintaining a radical stance.

He took every opportunity to highlight anti-Catholic prejudice. When Belfast corporation decided on the Sabbath closure of the waterworks, a park frequented by Catholic families on Sundays, Holland took direct action. While Liberal political leaders staged a protest outside, he discovered a back entrance and, to the delight of the crowd, appeared inside the locked gates and chided the politicians as 'the rankest impostures' for their tame demonstration.[34] This was something of a spontaneous stunt, but he could be measured too. When publicans believed their businesses were under threat

---

28 *Belfast Commercial Chronicle*, 19 March 1853.
29 *The Ulsterman*, 23 March 1853.
30 *Northern Whig*, 20 Oct 1855; *Belfast Mercury*, 27 Feb 1856; *Banner of Ulster*, 30 Aug 1856.
31 *Northern Whig*, *Belfast Mercury*, 9 May 1854.
32 De Burca (1968): 41. *Northern Whig*, 14 July 1859.
33 *The Ulsterman*, 24 Oct 1856. Denis's lecture, on 'the life and genius of Edmund Burke,' was well received: *Belfast Mercury*, 2 Dec 1856; *Banner of Ulster*, 4 Dec 1856.
34 *Belfast Commercial Chronicle*, 13 Aug 1855.

from so-called 'moral reformers' (Protestant preachers), Holland took up their case. He attended their protest meeting, advised them how to form a committee in order to press their complaints with the government, and agreed to serve on it.[35] For his trouble, the former advocate of temperance was made an honorary member of the city's spirit traders.[36]

His popularity was such that a rival Presbyterian paper, James Simms's *Belfast Mercury*,[37] praised Holland as 'our friend', the 'able editor of *The Ulsterman*' who 'has made for himself the high character of an honest and independent journalist', doing good service for press and the public.[38] It reported on a party where Holland was presented with a gold watch, suitably decorated with a harp and a wreath of shamrocks, a gift from the 'young men of Belfast' who admired 'the national spirit evinced by him' in *The Ulsterman*. He sometimes published work by budding young writers.[39] He also formed strong and enduring friendships. Through Sharman Crawford, he befriended Frederick Lucas, a co-founder of the Tenant Right League. A Quaker who converted to Catholicism, he went on to launch the Catholic weekly, *The Tablet*. Holland was also delighted to spend time with 'the dear old lady', Mary Ann McCracken, sister of the executed United Irishmen leader, Henry Joy McCracken.[40]

Holland's closest friend was a young solicitor from Newry, Charles Russell, who called into *The Ulsterman*'s offices soon after the paper's launch.[41] A Catholic nationalist, he contributed several articles to the paper, including reviews that were regarded as 'brilliant'.[42] Supportive, and sometimes critical, of Holland's writing, Holland felt confident enough in his friend's abilities to leave him in charge of the paper on the occasions when he was away.[43] It was said that the pair 'strove to unite all classes and creeds' in the hope of creating to create 'a national spirit'.[44] They proved to be a formidable and bold team, fighting any case where they perceived discrimination against Catholics. While Holland did so in

35 *Belfast Mercury*, 27 Sept 1856.
36 *Dublin Daily Express*, *The Ulsterman*, 29 Sept 1856.
37 Launched in 1851 by James Simms, former editor of the *Northern Whig*.
38 *Belfast Mercury*, 4 Oct 1856.
39 Cross (1931): 38-40.
40 *The Emerald*, 23 Oct 1869.
41 *Belfast News-Letter*, 11 Aug 1900; *Irish News & Belfast Morning News*, 18 Nov, 1901; *Belfast Telegraph*, 7 March 1903.
42 *Irish News & Belfast Morning News*, 8 May 1909.
43 O'Brien (1902): 51.
44 Ibid. 52.

The Ulsterman, Russell did so in the courts.[45] They campaigned together on behalf of a Liberal candidate in an election in Antrim and reportedly harangued the crowd. This was not Russell's normal style. He was already building a reputation for forensic court-room cross-examinations that would eventually see him triumph at the English bar and lead to his ennoblement as Lord Russell of Killowen, the first Roman Catholic since the Reformation to serve as Lord Chief Justice of England.[46]

Aside from his writing, Holland developed his early debating talents to become a regular lecturer and enthusiastic orator. He rarely attended a public meeting without getting to his feet to make a speech or to propose or second motions.[47] Whether in print or on the platform, it was noted that 'the Orange factions of Belfast quailed before the keen satire of his pen and the bold denunciations of his tongue'.[48] No setback, financial or otherwise, deterred him. When *The Ulsterman*'s offices were destroyed by fire, he found a way to print the paper elsewhere and gave the incident only the briefest of mentions.[49] Instead of dwelling on his own problems, his leading article in the first issue after the fire was devoted to a sardonic appraisal of England's claim to be 'the most glorious country in the world'.[50]

Holland became preoccupied by tenant right, devoting several editorials to the subject. With the Crimean war in mind, he asked: what do we in Ireland care whether England, France or Russia 'rules supreme ... the Irish tenant is still the same struggling serf he ever was'.[51] He contended that Presbyterian peasants, having been deluded into believing that tenant right existed, were being dispossessed by landlords who knew the 'right' was merely a custom, and therefore unenforceable in law. He hammered this home by reporting on examples where landlords purchased land over which the tenants wrongly supposed they had entitlement.[52] Although he boosted the

---

45 Examples of Russell's advocacy, see *The Ulsterman*, 26 Oct 1855; *Belfast Mercury*, 25 August 1856, 23 November 1855, 26 November 1855, 3 March 1856.

46 Russell married Holland's wife's cousin, Ellen Cecilia Mulholland, *Belfast News-Letter*, 12 Aug 1858.

47 Examples: *Belfast Mercury*, 1 Dec 1856, 21 March 1857; *Belfast Commercial Chronicle*, 30 June 1855; *Northern Whig*, 8 Jan 1857, 19 March 1857.

48 *Sunday Democrat and Weekly Catholic Advocate* (New York). Cited in *The Irishman*, 4 January 1873.

49 *Northern Whig*, 8 Jan 1856; *The Ulsterman*, 11 Jan 1856.

50 *The Ulsterman*, 11 Jan 1856.

51 *The Ulsterman*, 2 Jan 1856.

52 *The Ulsterman*, 16 April, 23 June, 31 Dec 1856.

Tenant League movement, he could also be critical of its well-meaning but 'spasmodic' plan of action.[53]

In time-honoured dog-eat-dog fashion, he enjoyed attacking rival newspapers, such as 'our Orange contemporary', the *Belfast News-Letter*, and the 'foolish' *Banner of Ulster*. He castigated the *Belfast Mercury* for publishing 'anti-Popish absurdities' and exhibiting 'virulent antagonism to "Popery"'.[54] He relished a libel case in which two Protestant titles, the *Downpatrick Recorder* and the *Downshire Protestant*, were ranged against each other.[55]

By far the most interesting *Ulsterman* editorial of the period claimed that Britain responded to political demands from its colonies only when threatened by force of arms. 'Of all the countries in the world England is the one most alive to the persuasiveness of force. She hates logic; but she bows to successful violence. The whole history of the empire, colonial and domestic, proves this truth.'[56] As for England's relations with Ireland, Holland contended that 'the same reverence for successful violence and incapacity to appreciate logic has been signally illustrated'. He concluded that 'the moral of British rule in Ireland' was its commitment to govern by force 'and by force alone'. Despite the broad hint that violence should be confronted with violence, there was no overt incitement to act, no call to arms.

The year of 1857 proved to be one of the most momentous in Holland's journalistic career, although it began badly. He was sued for criminal libel following an article, 'Irish serfs and slaveowners', in which he accused a County Down landlord, master of an Orange lodge, of mistreating his tenants.[57] The case dragged on until May, when the action was withdrawn after Holland issued a qualified apology.[58]

In the summer, he became embroiled in a controversy which erupted when riots broke out in the wake of the July 12th Orange Order celebrations. Although violence was an annual event, the clashes that year were unusual

---

53 *The Ulsterman*, 30 Jan, 16 May, 19 May 1856.
54 *The Ulsterman*, 'The Decencies of Journalism', 16 April 1856; 'No schism!', 23 April 1856; 13 June; 30 June 1856.
55 *The Ulsterman*, 28 July 1856.
56 *The Ulsterman*, 10 March 1856.
57 *The Ulsterman*, 5 Jan 1857.
58 'Criminal prosecution withdrawn', *Downpatrick Recorder*, 30 May 1857. Cf. *Freeman's Journal*, 23 Feb 1857; *Cork Examiner*, 25 Feb 1857; *Northern Whig*, 19 March; *The Ulsterman*, 20 March 1857; *Belfast News-Letter*, 30 May 1857

for their duration and scale.[59] Initially, the main assaults were directed at property, including several houses owned by Holland's friend and funder, William Watson. Tenants fled when the buildings came under fire before being wrecked by Orange gangs.[60] Matters took an even more serious turn when three Catholic teenagers, who were not involved in rioting, were shot and wounded. One of them, a 14-year-old boy, had to have a leg amputated. A 16-year-old girl was shot in her right eye.[61]

These incidents engendered demands among angry Catholics for armed resistance to combat 'Orange aggression'.[62] At a meeting of some 600 working men – 'the lower order of Roman Catholics', according to a Protestant paper[63] – there were calls to form a 'gun club'.[64] Holland may have attended as a journalist, but he did not stand to one side with his notebook. Instead, he stepped up to the platform to make a speech aimed at reducing the rising temperature. In his 'not very warlike' contribution,[65] he advised the crowd against responding illegally.[66] He argued that they should form a delegation to demand that the Dublin administration 'take proper measures' to prevent further 'Orange outrages'.[67] Next day, in the paper, he accused the authorities of 'the grossest neglect of duty', reminding them that he had previously warned of likely trouble.[68] He followed up by rushing out a 36-page pamphlet, entitled 'The Orange Plague', which repeated several of his editorials, his open letters to the Lord Lieutenant and a thoughtful letter from a reader.[69]

Rioting broke out again the following month when Catholics objected to open-air preaching by evangelical clergy. At last, Dublin Castle felt the situation was serious enough to order a commission of inquiry and called on scores of witnesses to give evidence, Holland among them.[70] He published several editorials and letters complaining about the intimidating

59 Holmes (2002).

60 *Belfast Mercury*, 20 July 1857; *Dublin Daily Express*, *Saunders's News-Letter*, 21 July 1857. Cf Farrell (2000): 144.

61 *Belfast Mercury*, 20 July 1856.

62 *Belfast Mercury*, 7 Aug 1857.

63 *Belfast News-Letter*, 7 Aug 1857.

64 Boyd (1969): 35-6.

65 *Freeman's Journal*, 21 Sept 1857.

66 Evidence to Royal Commission.

67 *Dublin Weekly Nation*, 15 Aug 1857.

68 *The Ulsterman*, 7 Aug 1857.

69 *The Ulsterman*, 10 Aug 1857. The letter by the reader, James McGouran, was headlined 'Suppression of Orangeism in Belfast'.

70 *Inquiry into the origin and character of the riots in Belfast in July and September 1857.*

nature of Protestant open-air preaching.[71] In response, the *Banner of Ulster*, in defending the practice, called *The Ulsterman* a Catholic organ under 'priestly surveillance', guilty of 'extreme scurrility', and an enemy of civil and religious liberty.[72] But Holland's argument gained a surprising supporter, *The Times* of London. According to its editorial, open-air preaching in Belfast was 'an assertion of lordship, supremacy and dominion' by Protestants over Catholics which was conducted 'more for religious affrays than for the serious object of the conversion of souls'.[73] When the commission's final report was issued, despite censuring *The Ulsterman* for its inflammatory language, Holland saw its criticism of 'the Orange faction' as a vindication for Ulster's Catholic population. He praised the commissioners for their 'right appreciation of the infamous workings of Orangeism'.[74]

By the time of the report's publication, however, Holland's interest was no longer confined to the riots, nor to Belfast. An editorial, 'The wail from Donegal', lamented 'the sufferings of the peasantry in those far wilds'. His readers knew something of those sufferings because he had devoted space throughout the previous two months to recording the 'oppression' of the 'unhappy land-serfs' living under 'the tyranny and heartlessness' of landlords in Ulster's western-most county. He derided the 'feeble mimicry' of the Tenant League and the efforts of two MPs calling for a commission of inquiry while peasants starved in Gweedore. His message was a thinly-veiled call for rebellion.

In late November 1857, Holland left his desk in Belfast to travel 190 kms (120 miles) to the west of Donegal. The editor was becoming a reporter once more. It is unclear exactly what decided him at that moment to make the journey. Was it the allegations in the anonymous letters published by *The Nation*, the *Derry Journal* and his own paper? Was it a thundering editorial in the *Londonderry Standard*? Was it the denunciation of the priests for their petition? One likely trigger was the denial of bail to four men charged with killing sheep, a report carried by *The Ulsterman*, in which Lord George Hill was named as the landlord responsible for letting 'thousands of acres of mountain districts to Scotch settlers'.[75]

Holland's reporting was never going to be impartial. Before setting off on his ten-day trip to west Donegal – a 'visit to the wilds' – he

71 'More of the street preaching humbug', *The Ulsterman*, 31 Aug 1857.
72 *Banner of Ulster*, 3 Sept 1857.
73 *The Times*, 9 Sept 1857.
74 *The Ulsterman*, 12 Feb 1858. Cf. Morris (2019).
75 *The Ulsterman*, 9 Nov 1857.

referred to the 'landlord rapacity' he expected to find in 'a tract of coast, unequalled anywhere else in Ireland for its cold, bleak, forbidding barrenness of rock and moor, and marsh'.[76] There, just as anticipated, he discovered 'a very howling sea of misery and suffering ... where human creatures, made to God's image, crouch and shiver by the little steaming turf heap... where the ragged cow and the little sheep are huddled together with father, mother, and children'.

It marked the beginning of his 'Landlord in Donegal' series, published in instalments over the course of 23 days. Written as pseudo-travelogues or letters, the pieces were oddly intimate, ponderously sarcastic, unashamedly partial, and overly repetitive, with few memorable turns of phrase. All the same, they were compulsive reading due to the sustained invective against an elite group which had grown used to controlling the narrative in its own backyard. It made the articles unique.[77] Both the *Derry Journal* and the *Londonderry Standard* had taken the tenants' side, but their tone had been measured by comparison with Holland's. Aside from the priests, no-one had used such colourful language to question the special character of 'landlord absolutism'. When they first raised the alarm about their 'poor flocks' the priests had been heavily criticised by most of the press. They had, Holland wrote, been 'bullied, and coerced, libelled and scandalised' by 'corrupt newspaper writers'.[78] This attack on his peers, even if deserved, was bound to attract a bitter response.

Every landlord got both barrels, including Charles Stewart, John Obins Woodhouse and Wybrants Olphert. Some came in for special censure. The third Lord Leitrim was likened to American colonisers (Yankees) who 'exterminate the red men' by facetiously calling it 'improving them off the soil'. Remarking on the splendour of Alexander Stewart's mansion, he observed: 'How odd that unbounded wealth should be found here, dwelling side by side with unspeakable poverty, misery, and toil'. His assessment of the 'very prudent and thrifty' Rev Alexander Nixon was stinging. His estate was 'a relic of feudalism', he wrote, and contended that 'this remarkable gentleman enjoys the singular pre-eminence of having on

---

76 *The Ulsterman*, 28 Dec 1857.
77 Unique enough to be reproduced widely in papers abroad, including America. Holland published them all in a short book, *The landlord in Donegal: pictures from the wilds* (Belfast,1858).
78 *The Ulsterman*, 28 Dec 1857.

his lands the most miserable and destitute peasantry even in Donegal'.[79] However, no landlord was mocked as relentlessly as Lord George. Holland devoted three lengthy articles to 'that benevolent individual', that 'model landlord', that 'special blessing on two legs, sent by Providence for the comfort of the neglected Celts of the wilds of Donegal'. He called him a 'pretentious philanthrope' and lampooned his book's title, remarking that it reminded him of Sheridan's celebrated jibe at a rival politician: he had drawn on his imagination for his facts. Aware of Hill's celebrity as one of Ireland's best-known 'improving' landlords, Holland set out to debunk his claims to have civilised previously barbarous peasants.

He dismissed *Facts* as a 'stupid book ... dull and prosy ... filled with old mother's tales and bald, pointless anecdotes about Celtic unthrift and laziness' while relating 'wonderful things of Lord George himself and his improvements'. His guide during his visit to Gweedore was its former parish priest, John Doherty, regarded by Hill as 'obnoxious'.[80] Hill had successfully prevailed on Doherty's bishop, Patrick McGettigan, to eject Doherty from the parish and he was transferred to the 'miserable village' of Carrigart.[81] But Doherty, having earned 'the mortal antipathy of landlordism', often returned to Gweedore, prompting Hill to complain to Dublin Castle.[82] There was an obvious similarity between the details in Holland's articles and the concerns raised by Doherty and his fellow priests. He described tenants' houses as 'mud and dry-stone cabins' standing on 'miserable ribands of land'. Adopting a conversational style, he wrote as if his readers were accompanying him:

> Jump down with me into the ditch, and enter one of these huts. Here is a space, of some ten feet-square, the sole residence of this poor man, with his wife and four children – shared with them by the little ragged mountain cow, which crouches beside the turf-heap in the corner. There is a small, broken deal table here. There is no chair, nothing to sit on but an old stool; and that heap of rags beside the fire-place, which will be the bed by and by. They are at dinner: what a horrid mess! Sticky potatoes and an abominable sea-weed which they call 'doulamaun'. Horrible! Your stomach sickens ... Yes, *these* are the tenants of my lord – these are the miserable beings whose sweat and labour are coined into rent for their master... Sweet Heaven! that human beings should be doomed to live as these creatures live – and

79 *The Ulsterman*, 8 Jan 1858.
80 N.L.I. MS 7632, Hill to Larcom, 9 Oct 1857. Cf. Mac Suibhne (1995): 565.
81 *The Ulsterman*, 30 Dec 1856. Cf Ó Gallchobhair (1962): 37.
82 N.L.I. MS 7632, Hill to Larcom, 9 Oct 1857.

then that the landlords who dwell in luxury on their unceasing labour should be heralded to the world with sounds of praise and fame![83]

Holland's eye-witness account, which echoed the statements of the priests, ran counter to the picture of a contented peasantry so skilfully painted by Hill over several years. His vivid reports were given greater validity by concentrating his fire on the landlord widely regarded among the political class as a paragon. Other Ulster newspapers chose an easier target in Lord Leitrim, whose evictions angered almost the entire press, Catholic and Protestant.[84]

Holland also touched on claims about Lord George's control of local business by contending that he had prevented freedom of trade. A Derrybeg store, run by a Protestant Scot, 'and a pet of the landlord', was allowed to operate a monopoly. He told how 'a thrifty, industrious peasant', Patrick Mulligan, was served with an eviction notice on Hill's orders because he tried to open a competing store. Once he had disposed of his wares he was allowed to stay on condition that never attempted to open a shop again.[85] In similar fashion, a local woman, Mary Sharkey, who built an oven and hired a baker, was threatened with eviction unless she destroyed her oven and dismissed her baker. She complied. Holland quoted the parish priest as saying: 'There is only one shop allowed in the village'. The same applied in Bunbeg, where 'competition is not tolerated'.

A section of Holland's third article dealt with the collection of taxes, a controversial issue because tenants were expected to pay extra rates for the posting of special police in the district following the disappearance and killing of sheep. What made it an even more touchy subject for Hill was the refusal by one of his long-serving bailiffs to collect the police rate from families in Tullaghobegley. Hugh McBride, who had been in George's service since 1838, considered the people too poor to pay. His defiance resulted in his dismissal in March 1857.[86] Hill's agent appealed to the Donegal stipendiary magistrate, Daniel Cruise, for help and he authorised the head constable to act as collector, accompanied by a substantial squad

---

83 *The Ulsterman*, 13 Jan 1857.

84 'The state of Donegal', *Northern Whig*, 26 Dec 1857; 'Lord Leitrim and his tenantry', *Londonderry Sentinel*, 18 Dec 1857; 'Lord Leitrim's ejectments', *Derry Journal*, 6 Jan 1858.

85 *Destitution*: 2735-40. Cf Ó Gallchobhair (1962): 28.

86 Ibid. 450.

of policemen.[87] According to Holland, the rate was collected at bayonet point as officers 'marched from cabin to cabin, seizing this man's horse, that poor fellow's sheep, the other one's solitary cow'.

Hill was upset enough by Holland's articles to send one of them, to the Dublin Castle administrator, Thomas Larcom. In his accompanying note, he said he had been 'assured that it is libellous'.[88] If he took legal advice, he did not act on it. He would have been on firm ground should he have chosen to go to law over Holland's confident claim that he was trying to convert his Catholic tenants to Protestantism and competing in that effort with the Dunlewey owner, Mrs Jane Russell.[89] This allegation appears to have been wide of the mark, at least in Hill's case, although his wife, Louisa, was certainly committed to conversion.[90] Hill's church, St Patrick's in Bunbeg, was built to serve the Protestant workers, shepherds and tradesmen he brought to the area; and it was far too tiny to accommodate more than 50 people. By contrast, Mrs Russell's church was huge, designed to be an impressive memorial to her husband whose body she interred in a vault beneath the floor.[91] She was eager to convert local people to Protestantism but her efforts were, it would seem, slight.[92]

There is an intriguing postscript to Holland's visit to Gweedore at the end of 1857. By his own account, he spent time at Hill's 'fancy hotel', recording that he found it 'not a very bad hotel at all'. He addressed his article to tourists, imagining them enjoying a light supper and 'a genial glass of punch' before continuing: 'When you come down to breakfast, the visitor's book will be on the table before you. Straightway you will seize a pen, and inscribe on the white page ... your admiration at everything – not forgetting his lordship, the punch, or the pretty barmaid.'

Was it a coincidence that the single discordant note inscribed in the Gweedore Hotel visitors' book, dated 8 December 1857 – on the

---

87 Cf *Londonderry Sentinel*, 7 Sept 1857.

88 N.L.I. MS 7632. Hill to Larcom,10 March 1858. Cf. 'Mockery of Justice', *The Ulsterman*, 8 March 1858.

89 Her husband, James, died 2 Sept 1848, two years after acquiring the property from James Dombrain. See Chapter 6.

90 Hillan (2011): 131.

91 *Ireland's Own*, 15 Feb 2019. The church, which has been a ruin since the 1950s, is known as 'Donegal's Taj Mahal'. www.irelandsown.ie/the-old-church-of-dunlewey-the-donegal-taj-mahal.

92 Maguire (1920): 265-6; Ó Gallchobhair (1962): 28.

concluding day of Holland's visit – was a critical poem by a person who signed himself 'Shaun'? It began:

For sheep destruction, landlord rule and comfort 'rich and rare',
Gweedore is famed through Erin's isle, this notebook doth declare.
But tenant slaves are crouching here, beneath their tyrant's sway,
And grimly curse the hour their moors became the Scotchman's prey.

And though the traveller must confess, Lord George Hill has striven well
To make his stay right pleasant here, at this, his own hotel.
Yet truth will urge the candid man to speak his feelings free
And cry against the power he wields against his tenantry ...[93]

There were two further clues to it being Holland's work. The letter D in 'December' at the head of the poem had a distinctive curlicue which was very similar to the D in 'Denis' in his signature appended to the front page of the first edition of the newspaper he launched seven months later.[94] Secondly, in the poem's (partly legible) second stanza, there are references to 'the sweet lassie' who served him his 'warm punch'. These lines echoed mentions in his newspaper articles of 'the pretty barmaid' and a 'genial glass of punch'. The boldness in criticising his host is entirely in keeping with Holland's confrontational character, and, in fairness to Hill, he must be commended for not having excised it.

---

93 An anonymous contributor to the visitors' book later claimed the poem's author was a 'Billy Williams', but Holland is a far more likely candidate.
94 *The Irishman*, 17 July 1858; VB2, 7 Dec 1857, p43j.

10

THE POWER OF PUBLICITY

The newspaper is the chronicle of civilisation, the common reservoir into which every stream pours its living waters, and at which every man may come and drink – Edward Bulwer-Lytton[1]

Although Denis Holland did not single-handedly change the conversation about landlordism in west Donegal, his eye-witness contribution played a crucial part in what happened next. It bolstered the determination of the priests to press their case. It helped to put the landlords on the back foot. It aroused the interest of other writers.[2] It alerted an editor in Dublin to there being a story in the north-west worthy of investigation. And it caught the attention of several MPs, thereby hastening Westminster's decision to act.

Hyperbole, journalism's trademark trait, worked. Holland's flagrant use of it helped to transform the way in which the press covered events in the county. The plight of Gweedore's tenantry had previously been portrayed as a battle between manipulative priests and misunderstood landlords. This was no longer tenable as newspapers inched towards the heart of the matter: it was about the ownership of land, about the nature of landlordism, about the rights of the people who lived and worked on that land. The people, as represented by their priests, were, even if unconsciously at this point, crying out against the system itself.

Holland, more polemicist than politician, did not seek to forge a press consensus. In spite of it not being entirely true, he presented *The Ulsterman* as the lone champion of Gweedore's downtrodden tenants. Attack was his default position. He dismissed the *Belfast Mercury* as a 'miserable organ'

---

1 'Diffusion of newspaper knowledge', *The Odd Fellows' Magazine*, April 1839
2 Perraud (1863) accepted Holland's work as truth-telling.

and condemned the *Banner of Ulster*, which had accused his paper of 'sectarianism and Popish intolerance', as the 'hot and eulogistic champion of the landlords'.[3] Given that the *Banner* had a record of campaigning for tenant-right, it was a gratuitous insult. Similarly, his accusation that the *Londonderry Standard*'s support for tenants was contingent on them being Presbyterians rather than Catholics was unfair and understandably outraged its editor, James MacKnight. 'It is a foul calumny', he wrote. 'The manifest object is to place the Presbyterian advocates of tenant-right before the public in the attitude of narrow, bigoted, denominational partisans, who overlook injustice till it has reached their own sectarian household... Every reader of our journal knows that this is a sheer fiction.'[4] As proof of his paper's impartiality, he took the priests' side over the official rejection of their petition, calling it a 'technical irregularity'.[5]

The *Derry Journal* did not wish to be left behind. Having previously been cautious in its criticism of landlords, only occasionally daring to publish anonymous letters, its editorials now began to echo both Holland's forthright language and his certainty. It also took the opportunity to sling some mud at the city's stalwart Protestant title by referring to the *Londonderry Sentinel* as 'the unscrupulous organ of landlordism'.[6] The *Journal* recognised that Holland's descriptions of poverty among the people of Gweedore corresponded with those of the priests. Soon, the petition organised by the three clerics – John Doherty, Hugh McFadden and James McFadden – was boosted when seven more of their number agreed to sign.[7]

Published in the form of an appeal to 'Countrymen and Fellow Christians', it alleged that the people 'down in the bogs and glens' of Gweedore and Cloughaneely were living in squalor and misery.[8] 'Harsh and tyrannical' landlords were accused of depriving their tenants – 'innocent Celts' – of mountain pastures, which they had enjoyed the use of 'from time immemorial', in order to benefit from renting the land to

---

3 *The Ulsterman*, 4 Jan 1857.
4 *Londonderry Standard*, 31 Dec 1857.
5 *Londonderry Standard*, 14 Jan 1858.
6 *Derry Journal*, 23 Dec 1857.
7 They were Hugh McFadden (Raphoe), Daniel McGee (Bunbeg), John O'Donnell (Dungloe), John Flanagan (Ramelton), Bernard McMonagle (Dunfanaghy), John McGroarty (Cashelmore) and Hugh Cullen (Carrigart). But two others, Joseph McGhee and Pat Gallagher, did not sign: *Longford Journal*, 25 March 1858.
8 *Londonderry Standard*, 4 Feb 1858; *The Ulsterman*, 5 Feb 1858; *The Tablet*, 6 Feb 1858; *Derry Journal*, 10 Feb 1858; *Freeman's Journal*, 12 Feb 1858; *Catholic Telegraph*, 13 Feb 1858.

'Scotch and English graziers'. The consequent reduction in the already poverty-stricken tenants' income left them 'bare-footed' and 'perishing of hunger and nakedness in their damp and comfortless cabins'. It was noticeable that much of the detail echoed allegations in the anonymous letters sent to newspapers two years before. There were also similarities in style and substance, suggesting that 'A Gweedore Man' and 'A Gweedore Tenant' may well have taken holy orders.

The fact that one of the organisers was the Cloughaneely curate, Hugh McFadden, was hugely significant because he had greeted George's reforms enthusiastically back in 1843.[9] At that time, he had signed a report extolling 'the great benefits which his lordship has conferred upon this extensive district' and had praised, in particular, 'the neat and comfortable cottages' with their 'well-ventilated rooms' and 'comfortable' beds.[10] Had everything gone backwards over the course of fifteen years?

From January 1858, events speeded up as each side tried to wrestle the initiative from the other. The priests went on the offensive by campaigning for an inquiry into conditions on the estates of Lord George and his neighbours. They staged relief fund meetings in towns where a 'heart-rending statement' was read out.[11] It was published throughout Ireland, England and Scotland, and in papers in Britain's other colonies, often under the unequivocal headline: 'Destitution in Donegal'.[12] It secured coverage in America too.[13] As a result, money flowed into what was soon being called 'the Gweedore Fund', which took on a life of its own.[14] Subscribers ranged from named individuals giving £20 to less wealthy, anonymous, donors: 10s from 'a young lady' in Dungarvan, 5s from 'a friend to the poor' in Glasgow, and a shilling from 'a Catholic' in Bristol.[15] Contributions were also sent to the bishop, Patrick McGettigan, who was sceptical about the priests' initiative but thought it politic to announce that he had passed the

---

9 See Chapter 5.

10 *Londonderry Sentinel*, 16 Sept 1843.

11 *Armagh Guardian*, 12 Feb 1858.

12 All 1858: *Dublin Evening Post*, 16 Feb; *Tipperary Free Press*, 16 Feb; *Kilkenny Journal*, 17 Feb; *Newry Examiner*, 17 Feb; *Southern Reporter & Cork Commercial Courier*, 17 Feb; *Morning Chronicle*, 18 Feb; *Inverness Courier*, 18 Feb; *Dublin Evening Post*, 18 Feb; *Wexford People*, 20 Feb; *Glasgow Free Press*, 20 Feb; *Home News for India, China and the Colonies*, 25 Feb.

13 *The Pilot*, 17 April 1858.

14 *Weekly Freeman's Journal*, 27 Feb 1858; *Cork Examiner*, 1 March 1858; *Derry Journal*, 3 March 1858.

15 *The Tablet*, 27 Feb 1858.

money to the fund in a letter to the *Derry Journal* in which he registered his concern at the people's 'heavy burthen of persecution and misery'.[16] He had been outmanoeuvred by John Doherty, the Gweedore priest he had attempted to silence by transferring him to Carrigart.

The landlords responded with a tactic designed to deflect government interest. They staged an 'independent' inquiry by the poor law commissioners (in effect, themselves). They chose 'a public servant of great experience and ability', poor law inspector Richard Hamilton, to conduct it.[17] His 'witnesses' were landlords, their agents and bailiffs, plus the stipendiary magistrate who was a regular visitor to their houses.[18] The inquiry was applauded by the Dunfanaghy Poor Law Union's board of guardians, of which Hamilton was a member, as was Hill. There was no attempt to conceal that this would be a stitch-up. Even before Hamilton started his 'investigation', the board issued a statement describing the priests' destitution claims as 'wholly false and without any foundation'.[19] Yet, none of the priests were examined. After just twelve days, Hamilton presented his report which, inevitably, found 'the condition of the peasantry in Gweedore to be far better at present than at any time since the period of the famine'. There was no evidence of destitution.

Hamilton's vindication of the landlords was greeted by supportive newspapers, several of which gleefully reported that the priests' appeal was based on 'wholly false' statements.[20] According to the *Tyrone Constitution*, the priests had set out to frustrate Hill's attempt to turn his mountains 'to profitable account' and gullible people were being fooled into answering the call for charity. Money is being sent 'from all quarters', it said, from 'distant localities, where the donors can have no knowledge of the circumstances'.[21] Another paper expressed the landlords' frustration at the negative publicity: 'It is astounding that such a story that was concocted at Gweedore could get belief even for a single day.'[22] Unsurprisingly, an Orange Order paper named after Hill's family title, the *Downshire Protestant*, fulminated against the

---

16 *Derry Journal*, 31 March 1858.
17 *Hansard* 22 April 1858, vol 149 col 1531.
18 *The Ulsterman*, 19 March 1858.
19 *Dublin Evening Mail*, 22 Feb 1858; *Belfast News-Letter*, 23 Feb 1858.
20 Ibid.
21 *Tyrone Constitution*, 5 March 1858.
22 *Warder & Dublin Weekly Mail*, 6 March 1858.

priests for their 'wilful misrepresentation' and 'foul falsehoods'.[23] The headline over the *Belfast News-Letter*'s editorial made its position crystal clear: 'The Gweedore Humbug'.[24]

MacKnight at the *Londonderry Standard* was wholly unconvinced by Hamilton's clean bill of health for the landlords. In calling for a government investigation, he argued: 'Never were Russians serfs worse treated than are Queen Victoria's free subjects at this moment in the wilds of Donegal', a description of the region borrowed from Holland.[25] MacKnight followed up by giving considerable space to the priests to rebut what they called a 'one-sided and false' report.[26] Their forensic dissection of the evidence accepted by Hamilton illustrated the partiality of all fourteen witnesses. His report also failed to stem the public's sympathetic response to the appeal for funds. Denials of distress achieved comparatively little traction, quite possibly because the horrors of the hunger years were still fresh in the public's memory. In an attempt to settle the matter, the *Dublin Evening Post*'s editor, W.A. Conway, dispatched a reporter 'of long experience' to Gweedore 'with instructions to make the most careful and searching investigation'. James Williams was soon walking in Denis Holland's footsteps.[27]

According to his article, he found examples of 'profound' destitution in the 'fifteen or twenty houses' he visited.[28] He wrote: 'I entered one on all-fours, through a hole in the wall, and I there found an aged matron ... seated before a fire on the hearth ... There was no window nor aperture to admit the light of day, save the hole by which I entered ... In this hovel, unfit for the habitation of a single human creature, there were seven persons.' In another house, he inquired about the food: 'They exhibited a metal pot which contained the meal for the family. This was chopped or pounded potatoes in pulp, and with this pulp reheated, and with some sea-weed which they exhibited in a wooden vessel, called noggin, they made up their dinner and supper in one meal.' He reported speaking to 'a police official' who 'asserted that there was no worse part of Donegal than what I had seen; he may be

---

23 *Downshire Protestant*, 12 March 1858.
24 *Belfast News-Letter*, 15 March 1858.
25 *Londonderry Standard*, 14 Jan 1858.
26 *Londonderry Standard*, 1 April 1858.
27 Williams stayed at the Gweedore Hotel, noting: 'Everything good of its kind'. VB, 10 March 1858.
28 *Dublin Evening Post*, 16 March 1858.

right or wrong; but this is certain, that human misery could scarcely be greater than what I have witnessed in Derrybeg'.

Williams's report was warmly welcomed by Holland on the grounds that 'the *Evening Post* is a journal which even the landlords cannot accuse of being violent or fierce. It is known to be a cautious, moderate, prudent organ of respectable Whiggery'. He argued that it was written by someone without a 'motive for concealing the truth, or exaggerating what he saw', prompting Holland to conclude triumphantly: 'Does anybody now believe for a moment that the Editor of *The Ulsterman* exaggerated … in his faithful pictures of landlord wrong and tenant misery in the wilds of Donegal? God be thanked. Truth is great and it will prevail.'[29]

Its greatest value was its timing because its publication coincided with the release of Hamilton's report, sowing yet more confusion over whether or not people were living in destitution. For outsiders, such as MPs in Westminster, it was impossible to ascertain the truth from conflicting newspaper reports. Had a collective of ten priests really lied? Had the landlords collectively lied? If so, had poor law inspector Hamilton conspired in their lies? Had two journalists, Denis Holland and James Williams, been guilty of fabricating their eye-witness accounts?

As politicians in Ireland and England began to show interest in what was happening in Donegal, the people of Gweedore were dismayed by the postponement of a trial for the twenty-one men and one woman – almost all from Hill's estate – on charges of stealing or destroying sheep. Prosecutors were unable to produce enough evidence for the case to go ahead, and the judge refused to grant bail, consigning them to many more months in jail.[30] There was also anger at the harsh sentences handed down to a father and son, James and Charles Doherty, who were convicted of receiving stolen sheep. The son got six years' penal servitude and the father 15 months.[31]

Hill and his fellow landlords seemed unable, or unwilling, to recognise the gravity of the situation. The tenantry had several concerns. They were unhappy about the scale of their rents. They resented the arrival of non-native shepherds on land they regarded as their own domain. They were upset at the imprisonment of so many men – heads of families whose income was vital to their households – and alarmed at the prospect of

---

29 *The Ulsterman*, 19 March 1858.
30 'Charges of maiming and destroying sheep', *Armagh Guardian*, 12 March 1858. Four of the accused, Thomas McBride, Neal Gallagher, Patrick Coyle and Hugh Gallagher, were released soon after due to inadequate evidence.
31 *Longford Journal*, 20 March 1858.

lengthy jail sentences should they eventually be convicted on the word of informers granted immunity from prosecution. Their communities appeared to be under existential threat, which was just the kind of situation likely to generate militant action from ribbonmen or their close cousins, the mollies (Molly Maguires). A residual respect for Hill, given his stance during the hunger years, may have stayed their hand on his estates. But that respect was also tempered by wistful memories of life before his 'improvements' of twenty years' before.

For the first time in their history, the people of Gweedore were the beneficiaries of a somewhat positive press, and not just within Ireland. The mainstream pro-government Protestant newspapers remained sceptical, of course, but their normal hostility towards the rebellious peasantry was muted by the reports of well-attended public meetings in support of the tenants and the increasing level of donations to the Gweedore fund from around the world. A further factor was the portrayal of Hamilton's investigation as hopelessly biased, which moved a Liberal MP, John Bagwell, to demand the setting up of a parliamentary select committee to inquire into the alleged destitution in Donegal.[32] His call was supported by another Liberal, Sharman Crawford, with whom Holland had campaigned for tenant-right years before.[33]

Even politicians who did not believe the priests accepted that a select committee inquiry was the only rational way to resolve the conflicting testimonies. They included Lord Naas, then serving his second term as the Chief Secretary for Ireland.[34] Sir Edmund Hayes, the Donegal MP, also backed the idea on the grounds that it would exonerate Lord George, a 'nobleman', he said, who 'had not evicted a single person'.[35] Hill might have wished for a better champion. Hayes, who lived in Drumboe Castle, Stranorlar, had determined to be on the wrong side of history. He had voted against every parliamentary reform bill, had funded one of the clubs dedicated to denying Catholics political rights and had sought to retain the levying of church tithes.[36] With conservatives such as Naas and Hayes on one side and liberals such as Crawford and Bagwell on the other, a large enough number of less

32 *Londonderry Standard*, 1 April 1858.
33 *Belfast Morning News*, 14 April 1858.
34 *Hansard*, 22 April 1858, para 1529.
35 *Morning Post*, 23 April 1858.
36 www.historyofparliamentonline.org/volume/1820-1832/member/hayes-sir-edmund-1806-1860.

committed MPs were persuaded to vote for the inquiry. Westminster's honourable members were on the verge of getting acquainted with the reality of life in a faraway place of which they knew little.

Soon after the vote, tension eased a little on Hill's estates when thirteen of his tenants, who had spent some eight months in Lifford jail awaiting trial, were granted bail despite the Crown's insistence that they should remain in custody.[37]

Both Hill and Holland had other, more personal, matters on their minds ahead of the select committee inquiry. Holland had fallen in love with William Watson's second daughter, Ellen, and they married in Belfast in June 1858.[38] A month later, Holland took his bride to live in Dublin and, in a dramatic move funded by his father-in-law, decided to close *The Ulsterman* and, in its place, launch *The Irishman*.[39] His choice of title did not only indicate that he was seeking a nation-wide audience; it was a tribute to Mitchel's short-lived *United Irishman* of a decade before. In his farewell to his Ulster readers, Holland said he was disengaging from 'Belfast's miserable municipal broils' and, in his prospectus for *The Irishman*, he wrote of 'knitting Ulster more closely to the rest of Ireland' by making 'Donegal and Derry as familiar in national politics as Cork and Clare'. His central message was that nationalists should fight not with the sword but 'with the tongue of the teacher and the pen of the journalist'.

His appreciation for armed rebellion was not dimmed, however. Significantly, he used *The Ulsterman* presses to print an English translation of a sympathetic biography, by a French writer, of Robert Emmet, the Irish patriot executed in 1803 for his attempt to revive the United Irish rebellion.[40] Holland explained that he published the book 'because no one else would. In England, publishers refused the work, lest this eulogy of a young Irish martyr should injure the 'cordial alliance'. In Dublin, those whose trade is printing and publishing feared the risk, with the petty trader's timidity – some, too, would not offend "the Castle". In this emergency, I undertook the risk, that so good a book should not be lost to the Irish public.'[41]

---

37 *Dublin Evening Post*, 6 May 1858.
38 *Northern Whig*, 4 June 1858. They were married in St Malachy's, Belfast on 2 June 1858.
39 The titles overlapped for six months. Last issue of *The Ulsterman*, 31 Jan 1859. First issue of *The Irishman*, 17 July 1858.
40 *Robert Emmet* by Countess Louise d'Haussonville, translated by John P. Leonard (original, Paris: M. Lévy Frères, 1858).
41 'A word from the publisher'. Preface to *The Ulsterman* edition: https://archive.org/details/robertemmet00haus/page/n5/mode/2up.

By far the most memorable passage in his prospectus illustrated that his continuing concern was for 'the peasantry of Ireland, the strength and flower of those who toil and sweat upon this island'. As an editor, he wrote, it was for him 'to expose their wrongs and struggle for redress'.

By contrast, Hill's major concern was for his eldest son, Arthur, who was taking part in one of the bloodiest episodes in the history of British imperialism: the Indian Rebellion. Hill had lacked the funds to buy Arthur entry into either the cavalry or infantry, but family connections came to the rescue. Through a recommendation by his niece's husband, Alexander Hood, a colonel in the Royal Scots Fusiliers, Arthur secured a commission as an ensign in the 3rd battalion of the Rifle Brigade (the Prince Consort's Own).[42] Hill's brother, Atty, also provided Arthur with a quarterly allowance of £25.[43] Arthur saw action during the relief of the sieges of Cawnpore and Lucknow, during which, according to his detailed journals, he had several brushes with death.[44] He wrote letters to his step-mother, Louisa, and his sister, Norah, about his exploits, such as his 'narrow escape from an ambush' on the way to Cawnpore.[45]

Norah, at twenty-two, was contemplating her wedding. As the daughter of a fifth son of a marquess she had become engaged to the fifth son of a viscount. Captain the Honourable Somerset Richard Hamilton Augusta Ward was the youngest son of the third Viscount Bangor of Castle Ward in County Down. Ward had joined the 72nd infantry regiment when he was seventeen, and fought in the Crimean War. Two years later, he went to India where he met Arthur, the beginning of a long-lasting friendship. Although there is no record of how and when Ward met Norah, the connection was clear because the Bangors were friendly with the Downshires. It says much about the parlous state of Hill's finances that their wedding in Dublin was funded by his brother, Marcus.[46] Hill accepted a loan of £450, at 5 per cent interest.[47]

Proof that the Ward and Hill families had grown close emerged in a letter sent to Hill by his youngest son. Two months after his ninth birthday in June 1858, George Marcus Wandsbeck was spending time in Dublin with

---

42   *The Globe*, 24 Oct 1855. Davis (2021a): 19.
43   Davis (2020c): 36.
44   Davis (2021a): 22.
45   January 1858, Hillan (2011): chapter 6.
46   *Dublin Evening Mail*, 27 April 1859.
47   LGH's Memorandum Book. He recorded paying off the debt in April 1862. Davis (2021a): 20.

his mother, Louisa, while Hill was in London ahead of his appearance before the select committee. The letter, written from 24 Merrion Square South over a period of three days, was addressed to 'The Lord G Hill, 25 South Street, Grosvenor Square, London'. Sadly, the opening word, a name, is indecipherable:

> My dearest Papsy, [?] is going to Lord Bangor's yacht to sail. Mama & I have been driving about. We went to see Mrs Dobbs & found she was gone to Paris & then we went to Mrs Reilly & she was not at home. In the afternoon Mama Gogo and I went to the Viceregal Lodge. Mama wrote your names down. The thorns were lovely and sweet. The grass was not cut. Lady Bangor went early this morning to Castle Ward. Mr Sproule is going on the 24th to London. Please write soon. I hope you will come back soon. There are 2 kittens & a cat. Goodbye my dearest Papsy I am your very affect(ionat)e & duti(fu)l child. G.M.W. Hill[48]

This letter from a loving son may well have given Hill heart as he prepared for an interrogation about his record as a landlord and allegations that his tenants were living in destitution.

---

48 Letter by courtesy of Jean Chippindale, Lord George's great great granddaughter.

11

FACTS AND FICTIONS

As soon as the land of any country has all become private property, the landlords, like all other men, love to reap where they have never sowed, and demand a rent even for its natural produce – Adam Smith[1]

There is destitution in Gweedore. There is no destitution in Gweedore. The people have never been so badly off. The people have never been so well off. The people live in hovels and exist on potatoes and seaweed. The people have clean cottages and enjoy good diets. The tenants of Lord George Hill have been treated very badly. The tenants of Lord George Hill have been treated very fairly. Landlords have abused the ancient rights of native people by barring them from mountain grazing land. Landlords have exercised the inalienable rights granted to them through their legal ownership of land. Rents have been raised to unacceptable levels that the people cannot afford. Rent rises have been restrained and the people have paid them on time.

The House of Commons select committee, sitting in London, was required to decide what was fact and what was fiction in faraway Donegal. Were the landlords and their retinues of bailiffs, agents and sub-agents telling the truth? If so, surely it meant that the tenants and their priestly representatives were telling lies? What weight, if any, should be given to the evidence of outsiders whose testimonies largely supported those of the priests? Answering these questions would have tested an impartial panel of judges. But the nine members of the Gweedore Committee were anything but impartial.

---

1 *The Wealth of Nations* (1776), Book 1, chapter 6.

Most were Conservatives, and with only one exception, all were Protestant and substantial landowners. At least four of them were well known to Hill. Conway Richard Dobbs owned a large estate in Down adjacent to the Downshire estates. In 1832, he had succeeded Hill as MP for Carrickfergus, standing as a Tory and enjoying the support of Hill's brother, Lord Downshire. Sir Edmund Hayes was the MP for Donegal, a landlord, and a declared admirer of Hill's reforms. Sir William Somerville, Ireland's chief secretary during the hunger years from 1847-52, owned a substantial acreage of Meath. He had been married, until her death in 1843, to Lady Maria Conyngham, who had attended balls with Hill in the 1820s and 30s.[2] Her brother, the second Marquess Conyngham, was the unloved absentee landlord of estates that bordered Hill's. Lord Naas (later the sixth Earl of Mayo) owned some 7,800 acres in Mayo, Kildare and Meath, and succeeded Somerville as Irish chief secretary. He had taken Hill's side in parliamentary speeches during the debates leading up to the committee's appointment.

Of the others, two had large estates in Ireland. Rickard Deasy, a lawyer from County Cork, held the legal rank of third serjeant-at-law.[3] John Bagwell, the committee chairman, had an extensive landholding in Tipperary. In his youth, he was regarded as 'a Tory of the first water'.[4] But, by 1856, he was being described as 'a Liberal gentleman' in the ranks of 'the more advanced Whigs'.[5] Two more were land-owning gentry based in England. Sir John Yarde-Buller's family had property in south Devon and Staffordshire. Philip Wykeham Martin, born and raised in Leeds Castle, Kent, was elected in Rochester as a Liberal. The ninth member, the lone Catholic, was John Francis Maguire, founder in 1841 of the *Cork Examiner*. A strong supporter of tenant rights, he had won his Dungarvan parliamentary seat as an independent. Maguire also knew Denis Holland well, having been his first employer and as organiser of Cork's Historical and Literary Society.[6]

Most of the evidence the committee heard over a series of sittings in June 1858 was predictable. Witnesses stuck to their scripts by repeating accounts they had made in the months before. The landlords, John Obins

---

2 *Morning Post*, 20 June 1832. She married Somerville in December 1832.

3 A lucrative post, it was regarded as a stepping stone to becoming attorney-general, which he achieved in 1860.

4 *St James's Chronicle*, 27 May 1851.

5 *The Globe*, 19 Aug 1856; *The Times*, 16 Feb 1857.

6 *Cork Examiner*, 31 Oct 1849, 21 Nov 1849. See Chapter 6.

Woodhouse, Wybrants Olphert, the Rev. Alexander Nixon and Hill, along with men on their payroll, told of the benevolent treatment given to their tenants. The priests told of the tenants' miserable conditions, as did the five visitors to the district: Holland, the Dublin journalist James Williams, and three tenant-right activists, lawyer Thomas Neilson Underwood, Sharman Crawford and his son, James.

How upsetting must it have been for Lord George, a man convinced he had done right by his tenants? There was an especial interest when he was examined because of his fame as Ireland's 'improving landlord' and author of the best-selling *Facts from Gweedore*. Now in his fifty-seventh year, with twenty years' experience as a landlord, he was the hero to some and villain to others. Everyone was eager to hear what had he to say about the state of his tenantry. The committee record shows that Hill's name was mentioned 370 times, more than any other individual. His examination, which took place over two days, was one of the longest, involving 312 questions during an inquisition dominated by two members: Maguire (145 questions) and Dobbs (114).[7]

Most of the soft early questioning by Dobbs enabled George to repeat what readers had learned in *Facts*. He told of the poor state of the tenantry at the time he acquired the estates and read Patrick McKye's 1837 petition into the record. He related his various building works (the corn store, harbour, school-house, church, etc).[8] Largely irrelevant questions enabled Hill to paint the now familiar portrait of himself as a kindly landlord. His rents were fair. His 'improvements' had been welcomed. Tenants appreciated his annual awards for their work and the improved condition of their houses. Next to his 'comfortable' and admirable hotel was his 'model farm', which was, supposedly, a source of wonder to his tenants.[9] His shops were a major resource for the good of the people. His encouragement of stocking-making by the women had proved profitable for them and their families.

Some questions exposed the committee members' bias in favour of the noble lord:

---

7 Collectively, Naas, Hayes, Deasy, Wykeham-Martin and Yarde-Buller asked a total of 52 questions. Somerville asked none.
8 *Destitution*: 6632-57.
9 Ibid. 6750.

Dobbs: Did you, in point of fact, expend the whole of 13 years' income that you had received from that property, in the improvement of it?[10]

Hayes: Your object has been always to foster the people, and to make them independent through their own resources?[11]

Naas: 'Did you find that the people were really grateful for the trouble which you took in giving them those stockings to manufacture?[12]

Asked about his abolition of the rundale system and the reorganisation of his tenants' farms, Hill said:

> The greatest pains were taken by the surveyor, my agent, and myself, to see that justice was done to each individual; the tenants were all called upon to assist in dividing the land, and nothing was done without their full consent and approbation, and they were given time to talk over and think over the different farms and divisions, and if anyone had any complaint to make the surveyor returned to the ground, my agent returned to the ground, and I returned to the ground, and we endeavoured to give the fullest justice to all; and they have expressed themselves frequently as being perfectly satisfied.[13]

When Hill failed to give specific answers, he was rarely pressed. Asked about the level of rent increases, he replied: 'I have no statistics in reference to that'.[14] The committee simply let it pass. Oddly, he was not obliged to provide figures about his overall income. No-one inquired whether he was making a profit and, if so, how much.

Maguire alone was persistent and occasionally penetrating. His line of questioning rattled Hill, who felt as if he was appearing in court. 'I am here before the public on my trial', he said at one point, 'and I wish the public to know the whole truth'.[15] He also sought leniency, complaining that 'of late years my health has not been very strong'. In addition, he told the committee his 'very able and excellent agent', Francis Forster, was 'lying dangerously ill' in hospital in Brighton.[16]

There were moments of tetchiness when being critical of his critics. He was especially sharp about his former bailiff, Hugh McBride, explaining that he had dismissed him 'because I considered him an unfaithful servant'.[17] According to Hill, it was McBride's duty to discover the

---

10 Ibid. 6679.
11 Ibid. 6769.
12 Ibid. 6866.
13 Ibid. 6660.
14 Ibid. 6819.
15 Ibid. 6934.
16 Ibid. 6761. Forster died 14 Sept 1858, aged 59. *Dublin Daily Express*, 6 October 1858.
17 Ibid. 6754.

perpetrators of the sheep outrages, and his failure to do so showed 'he had not my interest at heart'.[18] This was a rare glimpse of steel cloaked by the benign image Hill sought to convey in *Facts* and in the press. He was determined to get his way and showed no sympathy for the man who questioned his decision, even though McBride had worked faithfully for him for seventeen years. He also contested the bailiff's claim that he took land to build his hotel without paying for it.[19]

Just as revealing was his attitude towards his tenants, disingenuously suggesting they were able to exercise free will:

> **Maguire**: Would you be surprised that they [the tenants] could be anything else but miserable and wretched, considering that they squat down on those cuts which are let to them in a state of nature, and are compelled to make every improvement for their occupation?[20]

> **Hill**: I do not compel them to do anything … and without fear I will say they are in far better circumstances than they were then, even after having paid the taxes which their own misconduct has put them under.

Much was both concealed and disclosed in his answer, helping to provide an insight into the conundrum about whether Hill's goodness, or badness, as a landlord. Note first that misery is a relative term. To say that his tenants were living in 'far better circumstances' than in 1837 did not mean that they were no longer in a miserable state. They could, as Maguire implied, simply have moved from extreme misery to moderate misery. Anyway, what does a state of misery mean? There appears to have been a commonsensical, if rigid, working definition of what constituted destitution: to have nothing (without possessions, without income, without a house). Therefore, in the literal sense, the description by priests and journalists of west Donegal's tenantry being destitute may have been inaccurate. However, it did not negate the argument that the people were living in extremely straitened circumstances.

Then there was Hill's belief that all of his tenants were obliged to pay for the 'misconduct'. Did it not occur to him that there would be resentment among those who were entirely innocent? Should all of his 3,000 tenants be made to pay the extra police tax because a minority acted against the shepherds? It is no wonder that his imposition of collective responsibility would result in the waning of his assumed popularity.

18 Ibid. 6880-1.
19 Ibid. 2794, 6683.
20 Ibid. 6921.

Most significant of all were the underlying assumptions contained in his answer to Maguire; firstly, about the role and power of a landlord; secondly, about the perception of that role and power by his tenants. Even if it were accepted that Hill and his fellow landlords had treated their tenantry well, it was patently obvious that the tenants did not view it as so. They were aware they were not masters of their own fate. Their lives were circumscribed by what their landlords decided on their behalf. In that sense, the difference between good and bad landlords – between Hill and Conyngham, say, or Hill and Olphert – could be considered marginal. There cannot be any doubt that Hill had behaved much better, incomparably better, towards his tenants than other landlords. As he rightly reiterated in his evidence, no-one on his estates died from starvation during The Great Hunger.[21] But it was significant that his exertions on his tenants' behalf during those terrible years, including his waiving of a year's rent,[22] did not appear to have an enduring effect on their opinions of him.

Hill was wrong-footed when Maguire asked him if he kept his tenants 'under perpetual notice to quit'. He began by saying he did not. Then he hedged a little by saying he had 'found it necessary to put the whole of the tenantry under notices to quit for a certain number of years' because 'there were troublesome subjects in each townland'. He had lifted the notices after 'things went on so well', but reimposed them due to 'the sheep outrages' and 'only for the purpose of keeping the disorderly in some kind of order'. Maguire, unimpressed with the dissembling, asked his question again: 'They are under notice to quit at the present moment, are they not?' Hill, pushed to give a one-word reply, grudgingly said: 'Yes'.[23]

Exchanges over emigration were also enlightening. In order to demonstrate that living conditions in Gweedore were satisfactory, Hill asserted that few of his tenants emigrated and some even returned after going abroad.[24] Maguire, clearly well briefed by the priests, named a succession of people who had emigrated, almost all of whom Hill did not know, or know about.[25] As Maguire's questioning became more persistent, Hill's answers grew unhelpfully evasive. Maguire: 'Are there 260 police in the district?' Hill: 'I do not know'. Maguire: 'Is there not a large force in that district?' Hill: 'There is'.[26]

21 Ibid. 6693.
22 Ibid. 6777.
23 Ibid. 6929-30.
24 Ibid. 6753.
25 Ibid. 6871-79.
26 Ibid. 6884-5.

Hill was at his most defensive when dealing with mountain grazing rights. He asserted that 'sufficient' land was granted to the tenants while 'the remainder ... was allotted to me as landlord'.[27] He categorically denied that his tenants had ever been allowed to run their cattle on mountain land and, when they had done so, he said he had fined them for trespass, or impounded their animals.[28] He claimed that his tenants did not seem unduly upset when he first let land to James Huggup in 1855. It was almost two years later when the threats to shepherds and the killing of sheep began. These 'outrages committed by the tenants' were the reason, according to Hill, that he stayed away from Gweedore for a year and made only a fleeting visit in the following year.[29] He thought 'it was their duty to discover the perpetrators of those outrages', telling them he 'would not come amongst them unless they behaved themselves better'.[30] Clearly, some did not behave because they posted notices at his hotel 'threatening my agent, and threatening all gentlemen who should attend there'.[31] He also received a letter threatening his life unless he 'did justice' to his tenants.[32]

When Holland was called to give evidence, there was no hint of defensiveness. He repeated his eye-witness accounts from his visits, beginning with the poor conditions he found on the estates of Nixon and Olphert. Then he dealt with questions about the 'abominably wretched' cabins he saw on Hill's land.[33] Coaxed by Maguire into describing one particular house, he said:

It was a single chamber; there was a little wall of turf made at one end of it; a kind of screen about five feet high and four feet in length; inside that was a little mountain cow. By the fire, a man was seated in very ragged clothing; he had no coat on, and the rest of his clothing was very ragged; he had a sickly child in his arms, and there was a pot over the fire containing sea weed and other stuff ... it was very offensive-looking ... opposite him was seated another child on a little turf heap; the fire was made of damp turf, it smoked very much, and seemed to give out but little heat; there was a deal table, and that was all the furniture I noticed ... There was a quantity of some kind of rags tied up in a bundle in one corner, which answered as a sort of seat or couch, and, I suppose, was a bed at night.[34]

---

27 Ibid. 6660.
28 Ibid. 6800-11.
29 Ibid. 6699.
30 Ibid. 6762.
31 Ibid. 6763.
32 Ibid. 6764-5.
33 Ibid. 2436.
34 Ibid. 2445.

He told of the tenants' difficulty in paying rents and rates. In order to do so, some went to Scotland at harvest time to earn money while their 'women and children begged along the roads'.[35] His picture of life in Gweedore was the polar opposite of Hill's. He saw no evidence of a better farming system. He thought the tenantry looked thin and wretched. But he was 'astonished to see the people exhibit so much intelligence in the midst of so much physical destitution'.[36] Holland calmly ignored the fact that he was repeatedly asked similar questions by different members of the committee. Bagwell, the chairman, was less inclined to put up with the repetitiveness, and he stepped in to elicit Holland's overall assessment: 'From your inspection of that district during the 10 days, and from ocular demonstration, you were led to believe that the people were in a very destitute state?' Holland replied: 'Extremely destitute'.[37]

Other eye-witness accounts, from Sharman Crawford and Neilson Underwood, complemented Holland's account. But the majority of the committee were unmoved by the weight of evidence which pointed towards destitution. Their short report, written by Yarde-Buller, chose to accept the semantic distinction advanced by Olphert: there was 'poverty' among the people of west Donegal but no 'destitution'.[38] Accordingly, the report stated that, although the tenants were 'very needy', destitution 'did not, and does not, exist'. As for their poverty, it was 'not attributable to the landlords'. Turning to the tenants' complaints about the letting of land for sheep-grazing, the committee found that 'an erroneous opinion exists in the minds of the people as to their rights over the mountains'.[39]

Maguire's lengthy minority report, replete with history and context, was completely at odds with Yarde-Buller's short, dismissive statement. He wrote of the people having 'endured many ... grievous privations ... and wide-spread distress'. He conceded that the priests' allegations had been exaggerated, but they were motivated by 'strong feelings and lively sympathy' because of witnessing 'great suffering ... exceptional even in Ireland'. He pointed to the tenants' 'squalid' houses and inadequate diets. He believed the people's poverty had been compounded by the abolition of free commonage and the requirement to pay police tax when it was

---

35 Ibid. 2462, 2507.
36 Ibid. 2469.
37 Ibid. 2531.
38 Ibid. 4821. Yarde-Buller's report, as amended by Deasy, was adopted by the committee majority.
39 *The Ulsterman*, 19 July 1858.

most likely that sheep had been stolen by outsiders. 'It appears beyond dispute', he wrote, 'that there was a general absence of the substantial comforts which tenants ought to enjoy in any well-regulated state of society'. The facts of distress were 'proved' by 'trustworthy strangers' such as Holland, Underwood and Crawford.[40]

Irish press reaction to the reports was predictably split on religious and political lines. The Ascendancy papers greeted the majority viewpoint. For one Dublin paper it confirmed 'to the very letter our views respecting the outrageously false statements' by the priests.[41] Another praised the 'enlightened and impartial tribunal'.[42] In Ulster, the Presbyterian *Banner of Ulster* argued that the committee, in finding the allegations of destitution to be 'totally false and unfounded', had 'given the Donegal priests a lesson they will not soon forget'.[43] The *Ballyshannon Herald*, the paper closest to Gweedore, hailed the exposure of 'one of the most flagrant impostures of modern times' and believed the committee had vindicated 'Lord G. Hill' for his 'exalted philanthropy'.[44] The *Downshire Protestant*, in triumphalist mode, published the lyrics of a song deriding the 'shameless' priests.[45] The *Belfast Mercury* concentrated its fire on Maguire by accusing him of playing 'first fiddle for the priests'.[46] Nationalist-minded papers hailed Maguire's opinion as 'a fair resumé of the evidence'.[47] According to the *Freeman's Journal*, the committee had tried, but failed, 'to butter up the landlords of Donegal, and to censure the Catholic clergy'.[48] The *Dublin Weekly Nation* scorned the report of a 'partial, packed and prejudiced' committee which had ignored 'the terrible reality' witnessed by Underwood and Crawford.[49]

Maguire's own paper shrugged aside the majority report as unsurprising given that the majority of the committee 'would see with landlord eyes, hear with landlord ears, and judge with the intellects of the landed

---

40 Bagwell's support for the majority report earned him a severe rebuke: *Dublin Evening Mail*, 11 Aug 1858; *The Tablet*, 14 Aug 1858.
41 *Dublin Evening Mail*, 16 July 1858.
42 *Dublin Daily Express*, 26 July 1858 . Cf. *Kilkenny Moderator*, 17 July 1858; *Kerry Evening Post*, 17 July 1858; *Cork Constitution*, 20 July 1858.
43 *Banner of Ulster*, 15 July 1858.
44 *Ballyshannon Herald*, 23 July 1858.
45 *Downshire Protestant*, 23 July 1858.
46 *Belfast Mercury*, 20 July 1858.
47 *Tuam Herald*, 17 July 1858. Cf. *Tipperary Free Press*, 16 July 1858; *Meath People*, 17 July 1858.
48 *Freeman's Journal*, 14 July 1858.
49 *Dublin Weekly Nation*, 31 July 1858.

aristocracy'.[50] Holland's paper agreed: 'The sham inquiry has done its work'. It had 'whitewashed the landlords'.[51] However, 'we were prepared for this ... We expect no justice for the tenantry of Ireland from the hostile parliament of England.' He made a similar point the following week: 'We foresaw that ... the committee would be disposed to give a verdict in favour of the witnesses who occupied the highest social position'.[52]

Despite the landlords' claim that they had been exonerated, they adopted an extraordinary, and cynical, plan to reinforce their supposed victory. They offered their tenants a financial incentive to sign statements applauding the committee's decision and regretting the sheep 'outrages'. Holland received an anonymous letter, signed by 'one of Lord Hill's tenants', which alleged that he and his neighbours had been pressured into signing the documents. Holland decided to investigate and claimed to have discovered 'a plot' between the landlords and Dublin Castle: tenants would be relieved from paying the hated police tax in return for disavowing the evidence presented on their behalf to the parliamentary committee. They would be required to sign a memorial to the Viceroy, Lord Eglinton, 'to express our most unfeigned regret and entire disapprobation of the late barbarous outrages that have been perpetrated in this part of the country, and show our firm determination to suppress ... such disgraceful proceedings for the future'.[53]

According to Holland's anonymous source, Hill summoned representatives of his tenants to his hotel to tell them they could avoid paying their taxes if they signed a petition denying that they had lived in a state of 'distress'. All of them were under notice to quit and agreed to sign. Holland remarked: 'I could not blame them. I could only grieve at their slavery'.[54]

Unlike most editors, Holland refused to let the Gweedore issue rest. He began by giving considerable space to the priests to respond to the committee.[55] He followed up by accusing Hill of 'lording it over these poor north-western Celts, and writing impudent puffs of himself' in order to win 'a reputation as a model landlord'.[56] Instead, his was a 'patriarchal Arcadia' promoted by 'a lying book, and lying newspaper puffs' which had been

---

50 *Cork Examiner*, 14 July 1858.
51 *The Ulsterman*, 16 July 1858.
52 *The Ulsterman*, 23 July 1858.
53 *The Ulsterman*, 12 Nov 1858. The idea may have been prompted by the publication of a 'congratulatory address' presented to Wybrants Olphert by his tenants: *Belfast Morning News*, 26 July 1858; *Ballyshannon Herald*, 6 Aug 1858.
54 Ibid.
55 *The Ulsterman*, 21 Aug 1858.
56 *The Ulsterman*, 15 Sept 1858.

designed to fool the public. He was particularly upset at Hill's claim to have encouraged women to make stockings, arguing that the practice had long predated Hill's arrival. 'For ages the peasantry of the Donegal Wilds have spun, and woven, and fashioned their own garments of their own native wool, and made large supplies of socks and stockings, too, for what we may call the 'foreign' market.' The terrier journalist gnawed still further at the bone by revisiting Gweedore in autumn 'to ascertain how far the prospects of the harvest would lead one to hope for a change in the condition of the people during the coming winter'. After talking to them about 'their grievances, their wrongs, and the many crushing oppressions they had suffered', he wondered how they could subsist on their crops. It convinced him that the cause of their misery was 'landlord rule and British law'.[57]

The timing of Holland's visit was significant because it occurred two weeks after the attempted murder of one of the landlords who had given evidence to the committee. The Rev. Alexander Brown Nixon of Falcarragh, one of Hill's nearest neighbours and a fellow magistrate, was attacked while being driven home from Sunday service. Three men dressed in women's clothes stopped his coach, enabling one of them to shoot Nixon in the face at point blank range. He sustained severe injuries to his mouth and jaw.[58] It was established that the trio, immediately designated in the press as Ribbonmen, were from outside the district. However, it was assumed they had acted on behalf of Nixon's tenants who were under notice to pay rent increases.[59]

A report in Holland's paper noted that Nixon was unpopular even before the dispute over grazing rights: 'That the landlordism of Mr Nixon is execrated by his tenantry there is no doubt ... and while no man can palliate the crime of murder (from the thought of which we shrink with horror), it would be well for the landlords of Donegal to reflect on the sad and painful truth that a maddened, outraged peasant is not likely to prove such a nice moralist as those who have few of the wrongs and sufferings of mankind to bear.'[60] Elsewhere, there was considerable sympathy for Nixon, whose injuries robbed him of the ability to speak. Hill was at the meeting of magistrates who offered a

---

57 *The Ulsterman*, 12 Nov 1858.
58 *Derry Journal*, 27 Oct 1858; *Dublin Evening Packet*, 28 Oct 1858; *Dublin Daily Express*, 28 Oct 1858.
59 N.L.I. Larcom papers, MS 7,633.
60 *The Ulsterman*, 29 Oct 1858. Cf. McFadden (1889): 101.

£500 reward to capture the killers.[61] They were never found.[62] Nixon moved away, never setting foot again on his Donegal estate.[63]

As Hill tried to come to terms with his tenants' hostility, he pursued other money-making avenues. In company with James Dombrain, he set up a copper mining operation in Mayo.[64] He became a director of a land investment company set up to acquire encumbered estates.[65] And he joined several other Donegal landlords to build a Derry-to-Letterkenny railway line.[66] There were other interests too, such as his antiquarian hobby. He presented a collection of ancient bronze pins to the Royal Irish Academy, telling its cataloguer, William Wilde, that they had been found amid the Gweedore sand dunes.[67] Hill had previously given the Academy the bones of an Irish elk, extinct for at least 8,000 years, which were found in a bog near his Ramelton home.[68] Hill and Wilde were also leading subscribers to a fund for the widow of John Hogan, the celebrated sculptor of church effigies and an admired marble statue of Daniel O'Connell.[69]

But these were no more than distractions. The parliamentary inquiry, the shooting of Nixon and the growing popularity of papers professing a nationalist or Catholic agenda alarmed Hill and his fellow Ulster landlords. Their concern was echoed by their peer group across Ireland, where violent incidents against landlords, their bailiffs and properties were not uncommon. 'The state of the country has been such, for a considerable time past, to excite the most serious apprehensions, especially among the holders of property in land', observed one Ascendancy paper, which ascribed 'Ribbon propaganda' and the

---

61 *The Sun*, 4 Nov 1858.

62 In February 1861, twelve men were accused of attempting to murder Nixon and of murdering James Murray, a shepherd on Adair's Glenveagh estate. The informer who named them proved unreliable and all were discharged without trial. *Morning Chronicle*, 15 Feb 1861; *Belfast Morning News*, 16 Feb 1861.

63 *Freeman's Journal*, 1 Aug 1881. Nixon died, aged 78, in March 1882: *Belfast News-Letter*, 28 March 1882.

64 *Mayo Constitution*, 23 March 1858; *Dublin Evening Packet*, 28 Sept 1858; *Freeman's Journal*, 28 Sept 1858.

65 *London Evening Standard*, 4 June 1858; *Derry Journal*, 22 Sept 1858

66 *Londonderry Standard*, 10 Nov 1859.

67 Wilde, William R., 'Remarks on Donations Presented', *Proceedings of the Royal Irish Academy* (1836-1869), Vol. 7 (1857–1861).

68 Kinahan, G.H., 'Additional List of Megalithic and Other Ancient Structures, Barony of Kilmacrenan, County Donegal', *The Journal of the Royal Historical and Archaeological Association of Ireland*, Fourth Series, Vol. 9, No. 81 (Oct 1889 – Jan 1890).

69 *Saunders's News-Letter*, 19 April 1858; *Dublin Evening Mail*, 21 April 1858.

consequent unrest to 'those lying tales of famine'.[70] It was time, thought Hill and his nephew, the Marquess of Downshire, to go on the offensive. Along with James Naper, owner of a 180,000-acre estate in Meath, they issued a circular calling 'landed gentry' to a Dublin meeting to discuss the need for parliamentary action 'for the better protection of life and property in this country'. It was, as the nationalist *Freeman's Journal* pointed out, a thinly-veiled demand for yet another coercion law.[71] For Holland's *Irishman*, it was nothing less than a 'war against the Irish people' not seen since 'the days of Cromwell'.[72] And Holland took the opportunity to castigate Hill for 'a new despotism' in spite of being 'lord paramount, judge, grand-juror, landlord in hapless Guidore, master of the model hotel, of the model shop, of the model farms, ribbons of bog and marsh, from which these starving Celts are flying [to Australia]'.

Hill will not have been surprised by this attack from Holland; more surprising was his failure to obtain overwhelming support from fellow landlords. Several refused to attend, some going public to say so.[73] His major arguments were that agrarian criminals, such as the Ribbon societies, were enjoying impunity because too many jurors were drawn from 'the lower classes' while too many 'incompetent' magistrates lacked the necessary education for the task. He thought entrants to the police force should be vetted and then paid well. Licences for pubs, where Ribbon conspiracies are 'concocted', should be restricted. As a liberal sop, and as reinforcement of his 'improving landlord' status, he added: 'While we are anxious to see the laws repressing crime made more effective, we are not unmindful of the necessity of improving the social condition and habits of the humbler classes. The improvement of the dwellings of the labouring population and of the small farmers of Ireland are matters of vital importance.'[74]

Six months later, with Hill's coercion initiative having come to nothing, Holland wrote a lengthy article which viewed the sheep dispute from the perspective of west Donegal's tenantry. It was a typical Holland tirade, repeating arguments he had made frequently for almost two years, but it included some interesting new information about Hill's attempt to prevent

---

70 *Dublin Evening Packet*, 11 Jan 1859.
71 *Freeman's Journal*, 13, 15 Jan 1859.
72 *The Irishman*, 15 Jan 1859.
73 *Manchester Guardian*, 19 Jan 1859; *The Times*, 20, 24 Jan 1859. 'I know of no present circumstances which call for such measures', Marquess of Clanricarde, *The Irishman*, 29 Jan 1859. Also, the Earl of Granard.
74 *The Irishman*, 15 Jan 1859. Cf. *The Times*, 14 Jan 1859.

the disappearance and destruction of sheep. He had recruited 'two or three men' from each Gweedore townland to comprise a force of ninety-four and constituted them as special constables to protect the sheep. Should an animal be killed they would be expected to pay for the losses. All went well until several sheep were declared by their Scottish owner to be missing. He was preparing to take legal action when twenty of the beasts were found by the regular police. Holland concluded: 'If the constabulary had not found them, this man would have deposed on oath that they were maliciously destroyed, and the Grand Jury would have granted him warrants to recover their price from the poor starving peasants of the district'.[75]

Not that Holland, a consistent champion of the Irish language, had any faith in the courts anyway, especially if witnesses wished to use their native tongue. He discovered instances of judges and lawyers insulting and belittling people who were unable to give evidence in English. He viewed this as a 'conspiracy' by stipendiaries 'to extirpate the glorious old language of our sires' and 'the last sweet relic of our nationality, the glorious musical tongue of the Gaedhel'.[76]

In the case of the missing sheep, Holland's suspicion that Scottish shepherds were making unscrupulous demands for compensation for lost sheep was borne out in subsequent court cases, where juries often rejected their claims.[77] Although Holland could not bring himself to say it, Hill's ploy to have the people police themselves can be seen as shrewd and effective. At a time when Donegal was regarded as one of the worst counties for agrarian crime, Gweedore was relatively peaceful.[78] But Hill's failed demand for coercion legislation placed him firmly in the Ascendancy camp; he had, as it were, come home. A Whig no longer, he was avowedly a Tory.

Holland, in sensing this hardening of stance, referred to him as 'Lord George Hill of Guidore notoriety' and dismissed his initiative as a 'most insolent and atrocious proposal'.[79] To add to Hill's embarrassment, Holland's attack coincided with the departure of 'the first batch' of Gweedore emigrants to Australia. Some 280 people, 'chiefly young men aged from eighteen to twenty-five', but also including older men, their wives and children, were seen off at Derry railway station by several priests who had first taken up their cause, including Fathers James

75 'The Horse-leech in Donegal', *The Irishman*, 30 July 1859.
76 'Extirpating the language of Ireland', *The Irishman*, 13 Aug 1859.
77 *The Irishman*, 11 Aug 1860.
78 See Vaughan (1983): 25. S.P.O. Irish Crimes Records, 1848-93.
79 'War against the Irish people – a landlord conspiracy', *The Irishman*, 15 Jan 1859.

McFadden and John Doherty. According a *Derry Journal* report, they were due to sail to Sydney from Birkenhead. And two more batches, each of 300 people, were set to follow.[80] 'We are not anxious to re-open the painful subject of Gweedore destitution', commented the paper, 'but we cannot omit the opportunity of pointing to this strangely eloquent commentary on the opulence said to exist in the backward districts of the County Donegal ... Surely, it was not a plenitude of prosperity that led ... these poor people to leave their birthplace?'[81] Hill came in for special mention as one the proprietors who believe that making 'men and women retire [from their land] to make room for cows and sheep' amounts to 'improvement'. Referring to Hill's coercion manifesto, 'which has made the noble lord famous during the last fortnight', it indicated what he and his peers really thought of 'the rights of the human occupier'.

The mass emigration from Gweedore was largely ignored by the mainstream Dublin press.[82] So, Hill may well have taken heart from a measure of newspaper praise for his coercion ambitions. One paper backed him by urging the eradication of 'the Ribbon hydra' and its 'reign of terror' in west Donegal, which had 'banished such a model resident as Lord George Hill'.[83] There was no reign of terror, as a London paper correctly remarked: 'The evil is not quite so formidable as some of them would represent it'.[84] Nor was Hill banished. For a short while he may have travelled less often from Ramelton to Gweedore. Even though there was no genuine threat to his life, the district continued to be unruly, with instances of petty crimes and yet more instances of sheep being killed or stolen.[85]

It was possible, however, that one particular sequence of incidents did disturb him. It began with the arrival of a new neighbour, a wealthy businessman from Queen's County (County Laois) named John George Adair, who bought several tracts of land that were amalgamated into a giant estate centred on Derryveagh.[86] Adair was soon in dispute with tenants who objected to him hunting across land they regarded as their exclusive domain.

---

80 'The Gweedore Emigrants', *Derry Journal*, 26 Jan 1859.
81 'The Gweedore Exodus', *Derry Journal*, 26 Jan 1859.
82 In America, it was widely reported. Cf. *The Pilot*, 5 May 1860, 15 Feb 1862.
83 *Warder & Dublin Weekly Mail*, 15 Jan 1859.
84 *London Evening Standard*, 17 Jan 1859.
85 *Ballyshannon Herald*, 7 Jan, 11 March, 18 March 1859; *Belfast Morning News*, 26 July 1859.
86 According to Adair, in evidence to House of Lords select committee, his estate totalled 60,000 acres. *Evening Freeman*, 30 April 1860. Vaughan (1983) states that the Derryveagh estate was 11,602 acres.

Even more unpopular was his decision to follow Hill's example by importing sheep and employing two Scottish shepherds. Matters came to a head when one of them, James Murray, was murdered, his skull crushed by a rock.[87]

The crime remained unsolved, but Adair was convinced (without a shred of evidence) that his tenants were involved and, five months after the murder, he ordered the eviction of all 244 (including 159 children) from his land.[88] Bailiffs accompanied by a large police force, 'to protect the Adair crowbar brigade', tumbled the houses of 47 families.[89] Even some of Adair's 'warmest friends' regarded this 'terrible infliction' as disproportionate.[90] *The Irishman* carried a letter accusing 'West-British rags' of taking Adair's side,[91] yet most newspapers, including mainstream titles, were critical of the evictions.[92] Holland, unsurprisingly, was quick to make the case against 'the great ruling prince of Glenveagh'.[93] For once, he found himself among the majority. There was little sympathy for Adair after politicians read the harrowing reports of innocent people forced from their houses, and even less when it was realised that the tenants were almost certainly innocent.[94] By far the most damning condemnation was delivered by another Irish landlord, Lord Palmerston, who said of Adair: 'A man's mind must, indeed, be very much distorted who can fancy it a real justification for sweeping away a whole population that he thought they ought to give evidence against a murderer, when probably they knew no more about the deed than he did himself'.[95]

If Hill was troubled by Adair's actions, he kept his counsel, saying nothing in public about the matter. But the fact that Adair was able to 'stand aloft in the Grand Jury box, as much a member as Lord George Hill' did not escape the notice of the *Derry Journal*, which considered Adair's presence as inappropriate.[96] No matter. Landlords, good or bad, well-meaning or pitiless, titled or commoner, stood together to run the local administration and dispense the law.

---

87 *Ballyshannon Herald*, 23 Nov 1860. Cf Vaughan, op. cit. 22.

88 'Wholesale depopulation at Glenveagh', *Ballyshannon Herald*, 19 April 1861. Figures from Vaughan (1983): 11.

89 'The Adair clearance in Glenveagh', *The Irishman*, 13 April, 1861.

90 *London Evening Standard* and *Morning Herald* (London), 11 April 1861.

91 Letter dated 1 May from 'An Observer' in Letterkenny, *The Irishman*, 11 May 1861.

92 Critics included see *Dublin Evening Post*, 11 April 1861; *Londonderry Standard*, 2 May 1861; *Banner of Ulster*, 13 April 1861. Among his defenders were *Dublin Daily Express*, 10 April 1861; *Belfast News-Letter*, 17 April 1861; *Belfast Mercury*, 12 April 1861.

93 'Homeless,' *The Irishman*, 13 April 1861.

94 *Hansard*, Commons 24 June 1861.

95 *Hansard*, Commons, 2 July 1861.

96 *Derry Journal*, 15 July 1863.

12

FLANNEL AND FENIANS

This Irish county bears an evil name,
And Bloomfield's district stands the worst in fame,
For agitation, discord, threats, waylayings,
Fears and suspicions, plottings and betrayings;
Beasts kill'd and maim'd, infernal fires at night,
Red murder stalking free in full daylight.
That landlords and their tenants lived as foes
He knew, as one a truth by hearsay knows.
– William Allingham[1]

The Derryveagh evictions, which were to become an enduring symbol of landlord cruelty, did not noticeably stimulate greater hostility at the time towards landlords within Donegal. Tenant farmers in 1860 were diverted by the need to cope with successive years of 'deficient harvests'.[2] As a result, a reporter from the Dublin-based conservative newspaper, *Saunders's News-Letter*, thought 'the condition of the small farmers' to be 'very low' across Donegal. Yet, in Gweedore, he found 'no cry of extreme of distress'.[3] As with so many past visitors, he registered his delight with Lord George's 'well conducted' hotel and was impressed with his land reclamation. Of Hill's tenants, he wrote: 'Some individuals living along the sea shore may be in want of food a month or two before the next harvest, but the great majority ... will not suffer severely'.[4]

'In want of food for a month or two!' What a sly euphemism for hunger. And how large was that minority who were due to suffer from a

---

1 *Laurence Bloomfield in Ireland*, chapter two.
2 Coulter (1862): 315.
3 Ibid. 322.
4 Ibid. 322-3.

period of starvation? It was a superficial piece of reporting. No names of tenants. No interviews with them. No detail of their conditions. Just the acceptance of an assurance from unnamed sources that, in the long run, all would be well. Hill must have been relieved that he was not visited by journalists who were willing to get their hands dirty by entering tenants' homes, such as Denis Holland and James Williams.

Indeed, Hill began to exhibit a renewed confidence. His embarrassment at being required to appear before the parliamentary inquiry eventually passed. Vindicated by its 'official' outcome, he continued to let out land to shepherds; he felt able to increase rents, albeit marginally; he improved the marketing and sale of his tenants' knitted goods. He even decided to acquire yet more land. In spite of his supposed financial constraints, he managed to find £2,620 to pay an absent Scottish clergyman to acquire a townland of 1,500 acres adjacent to Bunbeg, Knockastoller.[5] The deal, which gave him fishery rights, meant his Gweedore estate now totalled 24,284 acres.

During this period of heightened activity, Hill was involved in a variety of initiatives. He had nets removed from the River Clady to boost angling and subscribed to a lobby group aimed at amending the fishery laws to outlaw the use of all fixed nets.[6] He threw his weight behind a proposed bill to fund the drainage of Irish land.[7] He chaired the Galway-based Iodine and Marine Salts Company which was pioneering a new process to extract iodine from seaweed.[8] He also made sure his annual shows, in which his tenants competed for awards for their agricultural output or manufacture of tweeds and flannels, received favourable newspaper coverage.[9] Meanwhile, journalists continued to praise Hill's other form of flannel, his propaganda, as if they were revealing his abolition-of-rundale story for the first time.[10]

Not all the publicity was positive. A Scottish-based Catholic newspaper referred to 'the sainted Lord George Hill of starved Gweedore notoriety ... where, if a sheep strays from its mountain path, the inhabitants are taxed

---

5 Memo Book, op cit, 1862. In addition, he paid legal fees of £152.40. Cf. McFadden (1889): 32.

6 Field, 26 July 1862; Freeman's Journal, 7 Nov 1862; Dublin Daily Express, 17 Feb 1863.

7 Dublin Daily Express, 23 April 1862.

8 Dublin Evening Mail, 14,16 Feb 1863; Cork Examiner, 23 Dec 1863.

9 Londonderry Sentinel, 15 Sept 1863; Derry Journal, 17 Sept 1864.

10 Cork Constitution, 13 March 1862.

for the loss of the mutton they never tasted'.[11] Of his exhibition of 'charming' Donegal-knitted stockings, it observed: 'You would easily know by the look of them that the fingers that wrought them were small and thin' due to 'a peculiar kind of marine diet'.

A more penetrating appraisal of Hill's efforts came from a journalist with background knowledge of the area. Robert Arthur Wilson, who had been born in Falcarragh, was dispatched to Gweedore by his Belfast editor. His article, despite being laced with patronising guff about the 'primitive warm-hearted' inhabitants, was a rare attempt to see beyond the chorus of praise accorded to Hill.[12] This was no Holland-like diatribe: he chose the scalpel rather than the bludgeon. Delicately maintaining his distance from Lord George – 'said to be a good landlord' – he concentrated on the conditions he found, the scarcity of arable land, the oddity of isolated cottages perched among the rocks, and the hardship involved in collecting seaweed. He concluded that the people's 'breathing misery is not life'.

Wilson was moved to ask: 'How do they exist at all?' Then he answered his own question: 'Some of them go to the harvest in Scotland and England; some them make kelp; some of them get work at roads; and some of them catch fish in the season'. He ventured to suggest that the rebellion over the 'sheep question' was a direct result of the lack of arable land. Using the highland pastures had been the only way for the tenants to make a profit from their cattle. Anxious to be fair, he wrote: 'It is easy to blame the people; it is easy to blame the landlords ... but what is to be done when there is not enough of cultivated ground to sustain the population?' His solution: 'The problem might be solved ... if someone with capital would employ the people to break in the waste land'. Yet he did not seem to find it relevant to point out that it was the landlords who were the local capitalists. Nor did he explore why tenants were reluctant to reclaim land because improving their holdings resulted in demands for a higher rent.

Wilson had, however, stumbled on a major problem facing Irish landlords whose best hope of increasing profits was to cultivate more land. Many of those who did have capital (probably a minority anyway) felt they were making enough money and saw no good reason to spend it on land reclamation. Many who favoured reclamation didn't have sufficient funds. Hill, who was pressing the government to underwrite drainage schemes,

---

11 *Glasgow Free Press*, 4 June 1864.
12 'The Land of the Fomorians', by R.A.W, *Belfast Morning News*, 28, 29 Sept 1863.

might well have claimed he was in the latter cohort. Then his tenants might well have countered: if you are so keen to reclaim waste land on your estate, why spend £2,620 to acquire more uncultivated land?

Articles and commentaries critical of Hill made little difference to the glowing reputation he continued to enjoy, particularly in England. During a parliamentary debate on distress in Ireland, Sir Robert Peel, sixteen years after his late father had commended Lord George, did the same. He quoted a letter he had received from Hill in which he wrote that 'although great distress existed, there had been an immense improvement in Donegal, and that the people in these poor districts were all of them paying their rents'. This encouraged Peel to argue that that the state of Ireland 'was sound and satisfactory'.[13] Hill continued to be useful to Westminster politicians who wanted the English to believe all was well across the Irish sea.

Dublin Castle also saw virtue in being associated with Hill's good works. During a tour of Ulster, the Viceroy, Lord Carlisle, stayed at both Ballyare and 'the far-famed Gweedore Hotel'.[14] His visit to Ballyare House did not go entirely as he wished. In a letter a friend, he said the avenue to the house was too narrow to take his carriage and the absence of a recognisable front door was odd. Of the evening's entertainment, songs delivered by Hill's daughters, Norah and Cassandra, he wrote: 'They are near being Muses, Sybills, Sirens, but stop just a little short of these'.[15] He was buoyed the next day by his trip to Gweedore, where, according to newspaper reports, he witnessed – from an open carriage – 'the excellence of the crops and the sanitary condition of the people'.[16] He was also pleased with his accommodation.[17] Carlisle's tour was reported to have received acclamation from people of all classes' who 'forgot Derryveagh evictions, tenant-right demonstrations, Orange processions and prosecutions, famine cries, and education questions, and thought only of the presence among them of the genial, kind, accomplished, and popular representative of their gracious Queen'.[18] As for Lord George, according to the writer, he 'has shown that there is, after all, a way of reaching and winning the Celtic heart, even by the Saxon and the Protestant'. One of Carlisle's successors as Lord Lieutenant, the Marquess of Abercorn,

---

13 *The Times*, 21 Feb 1862; *Daily News*, 22 Feb 1862.

14 *Belfast Morning News*, 17 June 1863; *The Times*, 18 June 1863.

15 N.L.I. MS 40, 028/6 Lord Carlisle to Lady Campbell, 21 June 1863.

16 *Banner of Ulster*, 20 June 1863.

17 VB 2:166, 14 June 1863.

18 *Cork Constitution*, 23 June 1863, citing the *Daily Express*; *The Times*, 22 June 1863.

travelled across from his own 15,000-acre estate in Tyrone, Baronscourt, to Gweedore. He professed himself 'much pleased' with his trip to Bunbeg before moving on to stay with Wybrants Olphert in Falcarragh.[19]

Among the Ascendancy milieu and its acolytes, these vice-regal visits were probably viewed as feathers in Lord George's cap. What they did illustrate was a pronounced period of calm and relative peace in Donegal. So much so that Hill felt confident enough to stage an event in Gweedore to celebrate the marriage of Queen Victoria's eldest son. He had Bunbeg illuminated and provided tea and cake for the local children.[20] And it was an outwardly relaxed Hill who began to introduce his children to a social life they rarely glimpsed from Ballyare, taking Augustus to a Dublin Castle ball on the week of his twenty-fifth birthday and accompanying 22-year-old Cassandra to Hillsborough Castle for a night of amateur dramatics.[21]

By far the most intriguing visit to the Gweedore Hotel in this period was made by a poet born in nearby Ballyshannon, William Allingham, who signed the visitors' book without adding any comment or verse.[22] Two months' later, the first instalment of Allingham's most famous poem, *Laurence Bloomfield in Ireland,* was published.[23] The lengthy, overtly political work sympathised with poor tenant farmers and criticised their landlords, often harshly, with the exception of the central character. Instead, he is portrayed as developing into a kindly, reforming landlord who lives in harmony with his tenants after settling them on new farms. It is therefore entirely plausible to suggest that Allingham based Bloomfield, at least in part, on Hill. According to Allingham, landlordism, of itself, was not the problem. Neither was the Ascendancy. What mattered was the quality and character of individual landlords. His poem suggests that reforming landlords would negate Fenian revolution. Hill could not have agreed more.

The Irishman's successful launch in 1858, and its subsequent early years, were a tribute to Denis Holland's vision and energy. His paper secured a large enough audience to attract advertisers, with ads filling the front and back pages. Its distinctive format, using three wide columns, proved as easy for readers to negotiate as the more usual six-column layout. In editorial terms, it offered widespread international news, detailed coverage of Westminster politics, hard-hitting leading

19 *Dublin Evening Mail*, 14 Sept 1868. VB 2:302, 11 Sept 1868.
20 Rejoicings at Gweedore', *Londonderry Sentinel*, 20 March 1863.
21 *Dublin Daily Express*, 5 March 1864; *Belfast News-Letter*, 27 Oct 1864.
22 VB, 2:147, 22 Sept 1862.
23 Published serially in twelve parts in *Fraser's Magazine* between 1862-4.

articles, lengthy idiosyncratic essays and (mostly second-rate) poetry. Among its contributors were the talented Young Irelander John Edward Pigot (later to help found the National Gallery of Ireland), Michael Whitty (founder, owner and editor of the *Liverpool Daily Post*) and, from Paris, John Mitchel. Holland ensured that the paper played a significant role in the Irish nationalist debate.[24]

His own nationalistic commitment shone through much of the material. What set him apart from so many fellow nationalists was his concern for the welfare and interests of the agrarian poor, including strong support for the Irish language. It led him to take up causes other politicians of his stripe did not appear to notice. One outstanding example was his essay, 'Recreation for the peasantry', which advocated the revival of the Gaelic sport of hurling and, significantly, called for it to be efficiently organised.[25] He imagined 'a system of rural parish clubs' which might also have beneficial 'educational purposes'. His ideas anticipated the structures adopted sixteen years later, in 1884, by the founders of the GAA.[26]

Holland's output was prodigious. Apart from writing for, and editing, the paper, he regularly gave lectures, made speeches and attended political meetings.[27] He even found time to write a novel, *Ulic O'Donnell*, an unexceptional rags-to-riches tale which drew on details from his Gweedore visits.[28] For his newspaper contributions, he adopted several pseudonyms, most usually *Allua*, a name taken from the poem *Gougane Barra*, written by his Cork relative, Jeremiah Joseph Callanan.[29] Holland wrote continually about the plight of the agricultural poor, arguing that 'the mass of our peasantry ... are left to starve' while food is shipped off to England; reminding readers of the destitution inquiry, and the plight of 'the suffering poor of Gweedore'.[30] His workload, involving long hours at his Dublin newspaper office, must have placed a strain on his marriage. He had little editorial assistance to help fill *The Irishman*'s pages and

---

24 McNicholas (2007a): 238. It became Mitchel's 'favoured outlet', Kelly (2009).

25 *The Irishman*, 2 October 1858.

26 De Burca (1980): 4; de Burca (1968): 41-2.

27 'Gregory the Seventh, or the Pope in the Olden Times', Denis Holland lecture, *Belfast Morning News*, 1 February 1860; St Patrick's Day toast, Rotunda, Dublin, *Cork Examiner*, 22 March 1861.

28 It was serially published in an Irish-American newspaper, *The Pilot*. First instalment: Vol 24, No 42, 19 Oct 1861.

29 See Chapter 6. Holland's other pseudonyms: Lamhdearg, Otho, Le Reveur, Abhonmor, or, simply H.

30 *The Irishman*, 5 Oct 1861; 28 Dec 1861; 25 Jan 1862; 31 May 1862.

occasionally his lack of attention to content led to errors. Also, as had long been the case, he could not be induced to take any interest in the paper's commercial affairs. Together, these oversights were to prove disastrous. Extra pressure came as a result of his outspokenness on the platform and his pursuit of a feud with Alexander M. Sullivan, editor of centrist nationalist title, *The Nation*.

Holland's problems began in spring 1861 with the republication, in company with a couple of other papers, of a news item from the *Dundalk Democrat*. It told how William Jones Armstrong, landlord, magistrate and deputy lord lieutenant for the county of Armagh, had mistreated his tenants.[31] It was utterly false. Once aware of its error, *The Irishman* issued an abject apology for the 'great injustice done to Mr Armstrong' and offered a mealy-mouthed explanation: 'It crept into our own columns among the ordinary items of news'.[32] But Armstrong pursued his libel actions and other offending titles, such as the *Dundalk Democrat* and *Freeman's Journal*, settled ahead of a trial.[33] Holland refused to do so. He told the court that, on the day the item was published, 'a gentleman named Siggarson' was in charge of the paper because he was away.[34] He suggested Armstrong should be satisfied with the apology and the £5 he had paid into court. The jury disagreed, awarding Armstrong damages of £50 and, crucially, ordering Holland to pay all the legal costs.[35] This was devastating for Holland's finances and he responded by attacking all involved – Armstrong, the judge, the jury – on the grounds that all of them were Protestant and guilty of anti-Catholic bias.[36]

Holland may have felt better for venting his spleen. It did not affect the financial reality, however. He was obliged, once more, to borrow money from his father-in-law, William Watson, who was also concerned about the future of his daughter, now a mother of two, including a boy born just nine months' before. As security, Holland made over the property of *The Irishman* to Watson.[37] One of Watson's first discoveries was the parlous state of the paper's accounts. It appeared that the man responsible for them,

---

31 'The crowbar in the County Armagh,' *The Irishman*, 6 April 1861.
32 *The Irishman*, 25 May 1861.
33 *Belfast News-Letter*, 15 July 1861.
34 George Sigerson, physician, poet, writer (1836-1925). *Belfast News-Letter*, 26 July 1861.
35 *Belfast Morning News*, 26 July 1861.
36 *The Irishman*, 27 July, 3 Aug 1861. *Armagh Guardian*, 2 Aug 1861.
37 *Dublin Weekly Nation*, 9 August 1862.

Richard Pigott, was either incompetent or a thief.[38] He was dismissed. It is doubtful if Holland was unduly worried about that turn of events. As long as he could edit his paper and was able to write as he wished, then all was well. His mind was on politics, as both journalist and activist.

Holland's major political initiative involved two of his former tenant-right campaigners, Thomas Neilson Underwood and Samuel MacEvatt. Together, in March 1861, they were among the founders of the National Brotherhood of St Patrick, a 'debating society' with a strong nationalist ethos and regarded as 'a cultural-political body that advocated Irish independence'.[39] At the launch meeting, Holland appeared to support physical force by saying: 'All means are good, and holy, and blessed of Heaven by which you can achieve the independence of your country'.[40] The NBSP had a set of 'rules' but, as one critic remarked, its 'openness' was 'opaque in the extreme'.[41] Its objects, said another writer, 'would have puzzled the Sphinx to tell. The members themselves did not know, or at least they pretended not to know.'[42] Despite having no definitive programme, it gained traction through mentions in *The Irishman*, and, in Britain, through coverage in the *Universal News*. Holland also travelled to England to promote the Brotherhood.[43] In public, it maintained an arms-length link to the clandestine Fenian organisation, the Irish Republican Brotherhood. That separation was also clear in private, as became evident during preparations for the funeral of Terence Bellew MacManus, a Young Irelander who had died in exile in San Francisco after escaping from Van Diemen's Land.[44]

Holland was quick to seize on the likely benefits of turning MacManus's funeral in Dublin into an NBSP 'event'. To that end, he set up a committee ahead of MacManus's body being repatriated from America to Ireland.[45] 'We did our work exceedingly well', Holland wrote years later, '[but] another committee came in and overpowered us.'[46] He claimed that he 'approved silently' of the takeover by 'John O'Mahony's

38 Donovan (1904): 40-43; O'Connor (1889): 5-7.
39 McNicholas (2007a): 314. Clarke (1926): 114.
40 *Wexford People*, 8 Sept 1877.
41 Ibid. 206. Rules: *The Irishman*, 17 Aug 1861.
42 Donovan (1904): 82.
43 *The Irishman*, 20 July 1861.
44 Pigott (1882): 114.
45 *Cork Examiner*, 5 June 1861; *Dundalk Democrat*, 13 July 1861; *Penny Despatch and Irish Weekly Newspaper*, 9 Nov 1861.
46 Article in New York *Irish People*. Extract in *Flag of Ireland*, 19 June 1869

disciples, the Fenians' despite them having 'robbed me of the credit of a noble, national undertaking'. Holland's voice can certainly be heard in the address 'to the people of Ireland' extolling MacManus's patriotism.[47] On the day itself, Holland, was identified by newspapers as one of the leading mourners among the vast throng.[48] He was full of admiration for Mahony's arrangements: 'The Fenians have done this and they have done well ... Honour to whom honour is due'.[49]

So where did it place Holland in relation to Fenianism? He always made it difficult to divine exactly where he stood on the Irish nationalist spectrum by flirting with the Fenians' organisation, the Irish Republican Brotherhood, without becoming a member.[50] As a result, some leading Fenians remained sceptical about his loyalty to the cause. We have to think of Holland as a fringe Fenian who, only on occasion, revealed his intellectual support for physical force. 'Every man entering the national struggle', he said in an 1861 speech, 'should learn the use of arms'.[51] He was surely aware that the NBSP was close in spirit to the IRB, into which it was eventually absorbed. It was also the case that, under Holland, *The Irishman* provided a platform for the IRB to defend itself against post-O'Connell constitutional nationalists, such as Sullivan.[52]

And it was Sullivan who featured, centre stage, in the drama that terminated Holland's editorship. The other main character was a Fenian, Jeremiah O'Donovan Rossa, founder of a secret 'literary club' in Cork, the Phoenix Society, whose nationalist aims were virtually identical to those of the IRB (into which it was assimilated). The society's existence emerged in newspapers, including *The Irishman*, in November 1858.[53] The following month, Rossa and fourteen of his alleged Phoenix comrades were arrested for membership of an illegal body.[54] During a court appearance it emerged they had been betrayed by an informer, Daniel Sullivan (nicknamed Goulah).[55] But Rossa believed *The Nation*'s

---

47 *Dublin Weekly Nation*, 24 Aug 1861.
48 *Cork Examiner*, 16 Sept 1861; *The Irishman*, 21 Sept 1861; *Dublin Evening News*, 25 Sept 1861.
49 *Flag of Ireland*, 19 June 1869.
50 O'Leary (1896) Vol 2:103n.
51 Reported by *Cork Examiner*, 22 March 1861.
52 Andrews (2014): 189.
53 *The Irishman, Longford Journal, Southern Reporter & Cork Commercial Courier*, 20 Nov 1858.
54 *Dublin Daily Express*, 10 Dec 1858.
55 *Cork Examiner*, 24 Dec 1858.

Sullivan (no relation) was guilty of exhorting the government to act against the Phoenix Society. Sullivan, close to the Catholic hierarchy, also made much of the fact that senior clergy had criticised Phoenix.[56]

Rossa, who spent seven months in jail for conspiracy, did not go public with this allegation until writing a letter to *The Irishman* in April 1862 in which he accused Sullivan of 'the betrayal of the Phoenix prisoners'.[57] He continued: 'Your paper was the first to proclaim openly that a secret society did exist in Ireland'. Rossa then coupled Sullivan's name with that of the Goulah, stigmatising the editor as an informer.[58] Sullivan, outraged at the slur, responded by suing Holland (rather than Rossa) for libel in the hope of securing £3,000 in damages.

While awaiting the opening of the trial, Holland delivered a well-received lecture on the life and times of Wolfe Tone.[59] His apparent lack of concern about the outcome of the case rested on his certainty that the Rossa letter amounted to fair comment. But his senior barrister was not content to rely on that defence alone. During his cross-examination of Sullivan he sought to show how Sullivan's political aims, including his support for action to oust Britain from Ireland, were similar to those held by both *The Irishman* and the Phoenix Society. In other words, his reputation was no different from Holland's or Rossa's. The jury took less than forty-five minutes to return a nuanced verdict, finding that Sullivan had been libeled but awarding him a risible sixpence in damages.[60] 'This', concluded *The Irishman*, 'is understood to be a triumph for the defendant'.[61] In fact, it was anything but a triumph for Holland because he was obliged to pick up all the legal costs.

Holland, writing as *Allua*, took the opportunity to pour scorn on Sullivan for 'prosecuting a brother journalist for libel' and for using 'Her Majesty's Court' to do so.[62] Accepting that he must pay the costs, he called Sullivan 'a pseudo nationalist', and wrote: 'What is the paying of some £250 to the 'deep damnation' of having been plaintiff in that most disgraceful libel action?'[63] The answer was not to Holland's liking or

---

56 McNicholas (2007a): 221.
57 *The Irishman*, 26 April 1862. For Rossa's release, see *Cork Examiner*, 27 July 1859; *Wexford Independent*, 30 July 1859.
58 See *The Pilot*, 11 Jan 1873.
59 *Freeman's Journal*, 27 May 1862.
60 *Weekly Freeman's Journal*, 21 June 1862.
61 *The Irishman*, 21 June 1862.
62 Ibid.
63 *The Irishman*, 28 June 1862.

benefit. He was forced once more to look to his father-in-law, but Watson was losing patience. His temper was not improved when Sullivan sued him, as Holland's guarantor, for his legal costs of £137 13s 8d.[64] Watson had had enough and decided *The Irishman* must be sold.

Holland looked to the National Brotherhood of St Patrick to acquire the paper and its branches set about raising the necessary funds. It came to nothing.[65] Instead, Watson opened negotiations in autumn 1862 with P.J. Smyth, a wealthy Young Irelander who had helped John Mitchel escape from Van Diemen's Land.[66] The deal was sealed the following April, with Smyth and Holland announcing the change in short, separate items in *The Irishman*.[67] Smyth wrote of Holland as 'our friend' and 'an honourable man' who had laboured 'under circumstances of peculiar difficulty'. Holland referred to 'private and personal' reasons for departing. Privately, the NBSP lamented the loss of 'their' paper in the belief that, in its new incarnation, it would 'crush' the Brotherhood.[68] Holland cannot have been happy about the loss. Nor were others. '*The Irishman*, unassociated with the name of Holland, is a nonentity', said a Glasgow paper.[69] As for the Ascendancy press, it was delighted by the change of ownership with several papers reporting that they now expected 'considerable moderation' in the 'tone and temper' of the 'journal of extreme Roman Catholic ultramontanism'.[70]

These events strained Holland's relationship with Watson, probably to breaking point. They must also have affected his marriage to Watson's daughter, Ellen. By spring 1863, the couple had two boys, aged two and four, but he did not allow family life, nor his disappointment at losing his paper, to stifle his enthusiasm for provoking public controversy. As talks between Watson and Smyth neared their conclusion, Holland delivered a speech at a well-attended St Patrick's day dinner in Dublin's Rotunda which attracted considerable press hostility. He contended that he was sick of Ireland being cast as a nation of saints and martyrs; it was more important to wage war against the current problem of starvation. In a

64 *Dublin Daily Express*, 4 Nov 1862.
65 NBSP circular to members, 1 April 1863.
66 Dictionary of Irish Biography.
67 *The Irishman*, 4 April 1863.
68 NBSP circular, op cit. Comerford (1985): 97.
69 *Glasgow Free Press*, 11 April 1863.
70 *Northern Whig*, 6 April 1863; *Dublin Daily Express*, 7 April 1863; *Londonderry Sentinel*, 7 April 1863.

memorable phrase, he declared he didn't want to be a martyr because he preferred bread and butter and beef. *The Nation*, edited, of course, by Sullivan, chose to cast 'the disgraceful speech' in the most negative way, accusing Holland of sneering at the memory of saints and those who had sacrificed their lives for Ireland. Its weekend issue carried a letter calling Holland 'impious, irreligious and anti-Catholic'.[71] The criticism rankled with Holland. Six years later, he wrote of being 'attacked in a most brutal way' and that 'every word I uttered [was] misrepresented'.[72]

It was the last formal speech given by Holland in Ireland. Some five months after making it and stepping away, reluctantly, from the editor's chair at *The Irishman*, he followed the path taken by so many Irish nationalists of the period by leaving the country of his birth. His departure was widely lamented when he travelled to London, supposedly alone. From there, he generously wished his successor well.[73]

71 *Evening Freeman*, 18 March 1863; *Dublin Daily Express*, 18 March 1863; *The Nation*, 18 March 1863; *Dublin Weekly Nation*, 21 March 1863.

72 *The Emerald*, 6 Nov 1869.

73 *The Irishman*, 2 May 1863.

13

A TALE OF TWO EXILES

*Sacred to the memory of Lord George Hill. A self-denying Christian, he
devoted his life and fortune to civilize Gweedore and raise its people to
a higher social and moral level*
– Plaque on wall of St Patrick's Church, Bunbeg

In 1864, Lord George Hill and Denis Holland had optimistic, if very
different, hopes for the future. Hill, born in London, was thriving in
Donegal. Holland, born in Cork, was writing (and conspiring) in London.
The landlord and the journalist were going about their business in their
separate spheres, spurred on by the hope that all would work out to their
advantage. In his self-imposed exile, Holland continued to agitate for
Irish independence, remaining as resolute as ever. He had not stopped
dreaming of the union being repealed and still entertained hopes of a
full-throated insurgency. Smarting from the loss of his newspaper, he
was determined to become an editor once more. Through the National
Brotherhood of St Patrick (NBSP), he had an easy entrée to London-
based nationalists who were keen to publicise their cause among the ever-
growing Irish populations in cities across Britain.

Before Holland's arrival, an obsessive London-based Fenian activist,
Thomas Hayes, had been raising money in the expectation of launching
a paper. He and his comrades offered a warm welcome to Holland. After
all, here was an NBSP founder, an experienced editor with a proven
record of promoting militant nationalism and a man who had no truck
with *The Nation*, a paper Fenians disdained. All seemed set fair for
him. On visits to Brotherhood branches, he was greeted as a 'a true

and devoted patriot' and a 'tried and talented friend'.[1] In September 1863, he was listed among the group that founded a newspaper, the *Irish Liberator*.[2] It meant that he could take up where he had left off at *The Irishman*, fusing class warfare with revolutionary nationalism while urging readers to join the NBSP and, by extension, the Irish Republican Brotherhood (IRB). In one issue, he wrote: 'There is not a young Irishman of national feeling ... between the ages of sixteen and thirty-five whose principles are not those of the National Brotherhood, and who is not a rebel at heart and a revolutionist in purpose'.[3]

This kind of exhortation to action should have pleased Hayes, but within months of the *Liberator*'s launch, he was complaining about Holland. 'We are not satisfied [with] our editor', he wrote to the NBSP organiser in Dublin, J. P. McDonnell. 'Mr Holland is not the man we thought he was'.[4] This did not immediately affect Holland's position, nor his status within the wider Fenian movement. He was much missed in Dublin by the IRB's leader, James Stephens, who did not trust the post-Holland *Irishman* to act for the movement. As a consequence, he launched his own title, the *Irish People* – secretly funded by the Fenian Brotherhood in America – and recruited Holland as its London correspondent.[5] At the same time, under a variety of pseudonyms, he went on writing for *The Irishman*.

Holland at thirty-seven, alone in London and estranged from his family, was a very different man from the teenage campaigner for abstinence. 'Tee-total, Holland was not', observed a fellow journalist and IRB member, Joseph Clarke.[6] In his view, Holland was a 'scholar of the easy way of living and imbibing', describing him as 'a cheerful Bohemian ... with a fine head, flowing brown beard, small delicate white hands and excellent manners'. By his own account, Holland frequented the pubs of Fleet Street, but drink was not always the central reason for his visits to the area. He regularly attended the Cogers debating society, of which Dickens – whom he admired and sought to emulate – was a member.[7] His penchant for public speaking continued: he addressed the 1864 St Patrick's Day festival in London, reiterating one of his favourite themes:

---

1 *United Irishman*, 15 Aug 1863. Cf. *The Irishman*, Aug 8,15, 22 1863.
2 Bell (1967): 261-2 Company registered 21 Sep 1863.
3 *Irish Liberator,* 21 Nov 1863. Cf McNicholas (2007): 273.
4 Hayes to MacDonnell, 29 March 1864. NAI, FB/C6/E22/n.9.
5 First issue of *The Irish People* dated 28 Nov 1863.
6 Clarke (1925): 25, 38. Cf McNicholas (2007a): 235, 290.
7 *The Emerald*, 26 Feb 1870. Held at Discussion Hall, Shoe Lane, off Fleet Street.

'The fate of Ireland rests in the hands of Irishmen. Nothing great was ever done for the country that the people did not do for themselves'.[8]

Clarke, while appreciating Holland's 'charm of manner and skill as a raconteur', was not impressed with his intellect, considering him to be 'a facile writer … without any depth of thought or purpose'.[9] Yet there was no complaint about his editorial work for the *Liberator*. As expected, its publication drew criticism from the more centrist Irish newspaper editors who feared this 'disseminator of disaffection' with its 'articles of the most vehement character' had been 'sent to spread sedition … among the Irish'.[10] There was more to the paper than politics. Despite Holland's acquired lack of abstinence, he devoted space to the London Catholic Teetotal Union. He also gave a favourable review to a biography of his former temperance mentor, Father Mathew, written by his one-time Cork editor, John Francis Maguire.[11] Holland revealed his own move away from being teetotal by urging readers to avoid 'over-indulgence in alcoholic drinks'. Hayes, meanwhile, asked McDonnell to look out for an 'honest sober man' to replace Holland.[12]

McDonnell did not act with any haste, nor did he seem unduly concerned about allegations of Holland's fondness for drink. Hayes therefore redoubled his efforts. First, he registered his surprise that Holland should be working as a columnist for the *Irish People*. Then he complained that Holland was 'a bad turncoat' for attending a dinner during which Queen Victoria was toasted.[13] Another unnamed complainant to McDonnell saw Holland as an unacceptable 'literary nationalist'.[14] The behind-the-scenes pressure eventually told. Early in 1864, Holland was deposed in favour of a man he genuinely admired, David Bell, a Presbyterian minister and tenant right campaigner, whom he lauded for giving 'a stirring speech … stressing the potential power of the Irish around the world'.[15]

---

8 *Dublin Weekly Nation*, 2 April 1864.

9 Clarke (1925): 38; Pigott (1882):79.

10 *Cork Constitution*, 3 Nov 1863; *Newry Telegraph*, 5 March 1864. Cf. *Warder and Dublin Weekly Mail*, 31 Oct 1863; *Wexford People*, 27 Feb 1864; *Birmingham Daily Post*, 10 Nov 1863.

11 *Irish Liberator*, 21 Nov 1863. Mathew died in 1856. *Father Mathew: A Biography* by J.F.Maguire (London: Longman, Roberts & Green, 1863).

12 Hayes to McDonnell, 4 Nov 1863. Fenian briefs C6 E20 N69.

13 Hayes to McDonnell, 29 March 1864. NAI, FB/C6/E22/n.9.

14 Anonymous to McDonnell, 13 April 1864.

15 *Irish Liberator,* 5 Dec 1863. Bell survived only to 3 June, also falling foul of Thomas Hayes.

An underlying complaint about Holland among Fenians was his supposedly lukewarm attitude to the use of physical force. In fact, his attitude, as had long been the case, was one of ambivalence. It was what consigned him to the periphery of the IRB. Yet he cannot have been other than aware that the NBSP was a feeder organisation for the IRB, and therefore made him a tacit supporter of physical force. Although he did not embrace membership himself, he didn't prevent others from joining and even appeared to encourage them to do so.

Almost nothing is known of Holland's life over the following three years in London, where he appears to have spent many evenings at the theatre and afternoons in taverns.[16] He avoided official scrutiny by keeping his distance from Fenian conspirators, many of whom were arrested. Nevertheless, his support for the cause was evident in the scores of articles and essays he contributed to *The Irishman*, and elsewhere, usually under the pseudonym Allua or, simply, D.H. (and sometimes Celt). Many of them were either quasi-Fenian calls to arms or, at the least, trenchant demands for breaking the link between Britain and Ireland: 'No people are satisfied with any rule but their own; and no rule, but self-rule, can be just or wholesome'.[17]

His articles were salted with sarcasm. When Ireland's census figures were published in 1861, showing a population decline of a million in ten years, he wrote about the thousands of acres 'converted from the fruit-bearing farms of honest Irish peasants into the wide waste pastures of fat brutes, for the English market', part of the 'diabolically ingenious operations of our English enemy … to root out the Irishrie'.[18] After men were arrested in Dublin on charges of high treason and treason-felony, Holland called them 'offences which England is constantly creating for Ireland'.[19] Despite being in London, he managed to expose the existence of a secret Orange society in Ulster. Investing his story with more than a hint of journalistic hype, he told of documents that 'fell into our hands whilst travelling in England'.[20] He claimed that the organisation, 'The Magnanimous and Invincible Order of Black Knights', was designed to circumvent laws precluding oath-taking

16 See his 'Men Whom I Have Known' series in *The Emerald*.

17 *The Irishman*, 24 Feb 1866.

18 'Decennial return of the legalised extirpation of the Irishrie', *The Irishman*, 20 July, 1861. Cf. 'What they call Irish prosperity' *The Irishman*, 17 Aug 1861.

19 *The Irishman*, 18 Nov 1865.

20 'The Black Knights – a singular revelation – Secret Conspiracy', *The Irishman*, 4, 11 Oct 1862.

by the Orange Order. Although the order of black brethren may have been in existence for many years, it had remained unknown and Holland had therefore landed a genuine scoop.[21]

Just as fascinating was Holland's series of articles in spring 1866 about physiognomy, the pseudo-science of assessing character through a person's facial characteristics. He was concerned about the publication of photographs of Fenian prisoners and what they represented to the public or, more pertinently, what he feared the authorities wished them to represent. Aware that the images of the 'conspirators' were meant to indicate Irish savagery, he wrote that as 'a laborious student of this science ... I can discover no evidence of villainy in this panorama of faces'. Instead, he chose to 'read' the portraits in a positive fashion, calling them men who were 'kindly, amiable, good'.[22] In further articles, he sought to undermine the supposed intention to portray the photographed prisoners as scoundrels.[23]

These lengthy pieces were an excellent example of both Holland's intellectual curiosity and his wit. A very different feature of his writing talents occurred towards the end of the year when he began to compose serial fiction for a new Dublin magazine, The Shamrock.[24] Launched as a companion to The Irishman, it was grandly billed as a journal of Irish history, literature, arts and science. As a penny weekly, it was known more prosaically as 'a story paper'. Holland's undistinguished first effort, 'Pardoned yet Guiltless', ran to fourteen instalments. Sadly, having failed to win an audience for a previous novel, it whetted his appetite for the genre.[25] A first-rate journalist was on his way to becoming a second-rate writer of romantic fiction. He was not to be the Irish Dickens.

It also heralded the final phase of his life. Evidently, he 'dragged along in London without heart'[26] and, at the end of 1867, for reasons he did not explain to his Irish readers, he left London for New York. There, he was greeted warmly by a Boston-based newspaper popular with the ever-increasing expatriate Irish community as 'our distinguished countryman'.[27]

21 See McClelland, Aitken, 'The Origin of the Imperial Grand Black Chapter of the British Commonwealth', The Journal of the Royal Society of Antiquaries of Ireland, Vol. 98, No. 2 (1968):193.

22 'A gallery of Irish faces: A study of the portraits in The Irishman', The Irishman, 7 April 1866. See Mac Suibhne and Martin (2005).

23 'A gallery of Irish faces', parts two and three, 28 April, 5 May 1866. Cf. 10 Aug 1867

24 First issue dated 6 Oct 1866.

25 Ulic O'Donnell, published 1860. See Chapter 12.

26 Joseph Clarke, The Pilot, 11 Jan 1873

27 The Pilot, 14 Dec 1867.

Back in Ireland, the distinguished Englishman, Lord George Hill, was enjoying a tranquil existence. We have pen portraits of him during this period from two young men who lived in Ramelton. One, Samuel Bayne, regularly saw him on Sundays driving his carriage into town from Ballyare to attend church and sometimes he stopped to talk. He described him as 'a charming man and an Irish (sic) gentleman of the old school'.[28] He thought Hill was poor, believing 'he used a plain hemp rope for his leader, as he could not afford leather traces'.[29] Another, Stephen Gwynn, a friend of Hill's daughter, Cassandra, considered Hill to be 'a very pattern of gentleness and courtesy, short, white-haired and white-bearded, always dressed in grey Gweedore frieze ... never clad in anything else'.[30]

It was a time of relative peace in Donegal. As a grand jury member, he was present at the spring assizes in 1863 when the presiding judge announced that a mere fifty offences, few of them serious, had been reported by the county's police over the previous seven months.[31] There were merely faint echoes of the 'sheep outrage' that had undermined his status. In the worst of the very occasional outbreaks of misbehaviour, two of his tenants were sentenced to three months' hard labour.[32] Ribbonism appeared to have been quelled and when Fenianism dominated newspaper headlines in the following years, it gained little or no traction in the county.

Hill watched from the calm of Gweedore in August 1866 as scores of arrests took place in Dublin after the suspension of *habeas corpus* due to 'the Fenian conspiracy'.[33] However, in Donegal, almost every man arrested as a suspected Fenian was quickly released for lack of evidence.[34] The *Derry Journal* thought the government was 'making quite too much of this Fenian craze'.[35] And the *Londonderry Sentinel*, something of a public relations pamphlet for Hill's enterprises, felt confident enough to urge tourists to visit his Gweedore Hotel on the grounds that Fenian threats from America were no more than 'mere words'.[36] Hill refurbished and enlarged the hotel, marketing it more aggressively by placing adverts in newspapers that extolled its virtues,

28 Bayne (2016): 12.
29 Ibid.13.
30 Gwynn (1903): 142, 78.
31 The Hon Justice Hayes, *Ballyshannon Herald*, 13 March 1863.
32 *Londonderry Sentinel*, 8 March 1864; *Derry Journal*, 9 March 1864.
33 *Evening Freeman*, 3 Aug 1866.
34 *Derry Journal*, 18 Sept, 11 Oct 1865.
35 *Derry Journal*, 27 Sept 1865.
36 *Londonderry Sentinel*, 17 Aug 1866.

along with those of the couple who managed it.[37] He also regularly released lists of its guests, including titled visitors, to lure tourists.[38]

In some ways, Hill's life in his late sixties resembled that of his younger years. He found time between his Gweedore 'duties' – such as organising annual shows of his tenants' produce[39] – to mix with 'fashionable people' in Dublin, often attending balls and parties, although rarely by himself.[40] If he was not accompanied by his wife, Louisa, then he took his unmarried daughter, Cassandra, or his youngest sons, Augustus and George, both of whom were also unmarried. He was often at functions hosted by the Lords Lieutenant.[41] When the Marquess of Abercorn was given the role, he and Cassandra greeted him and his daughters at the Gweedore Hotel.[42] He maintained his close links with his Downshire relatives. As grand-uncle to the fourth marquess, he and Louisa attended the extravagant coming-of-age celebrations for his son at Hillsborough Castle, which included a torch-lit procession, fireworks display and music played by a military band.[43] They were also guests at the wedding of the marquess's daughter, Lady Alice Hill, to the Conservative politician, Lord Kenlis.[44] A year later, following the death of the marquess, Hill was among the chief mourners at his funeral.[45]

There were signs that Hill's attachment to the Church of Ireland, which had always been strong, deepened further in these years. Aside from his regular attendance at services, he was an enthusiastic member of the Derry and Raphoe diocesan council, which he represented at the general synod. As a patron of the Protestant Orphan Society, he took a keen interest in its work, and attended its key meetings.[46] He also served on the financial committee of the Church of Ireland home mission, which existed to 'spread the gospel', and was a committee member of the Irish Evangelisation

---

37 *Londonderry Sentinel*, 7 June, 21 Oct 1873.
38 *Derry Journal*, 29 July, 1865, 4 Aug 1866; *Londonderry Sentinel*, 14 Aug 1868, 11 Oct 1870.
39 *Derry Journal*, 17 Sept 1864.
40 *Dublin Evening Post*, 26 May 1864. Cf. *Ballyshannon Herald*, 2 Sept 1864; *Londonderry Sentinel*, 13 June 1871, 24 Sept 1878.
41 *Dublin Evening Post*, 5 March 1864; 18 Feb 1865; 4 Feb 1867.
42 *Morning Post*, 16 Sept 1868.
43 *Dublin Evening Post*, 12 Jan 1866; *Belfast News-Letter*, 8 Jan 1866; *Illustrated London News*, 20 Jan 1866.
44 *The Times*, 11 Oct 1867; *Dublin Evening Mail*, 12 Oct 1867.
45 *The Times*, 14 Aug 1868.
46 *Londonderry Sentinel*, 9 May 1865.

Society.[47] Even more significant was Hill's backing for the so-called 'Protestant Declaration', a petition signed by virtually every Irish peer opposed to Gladstone's proposal to disestablish the Church of Ireland.[48] The prime minister's intention was clear. 'So long as that establishment lives', he told MPs, 'painful and bitter memories of Ascendancy can never be effaced'.[49] In response, the Ascendancy's 2,300-word petition, published at full length in the majority of Irish newspapers, sought to unite Anglicans and Presbyterians by raising the fear of the Pope supplanting the British monarch as 'the supreme ruler in Ireland'.

Its authors saw disestablishment as 'a perfidious violation of the union between England and Ireland' and, in a clause with particular relevance to landlords such as Lord George, the document contended that it would enable Catholic priests and a 'disaffected portion of the peasantry' to overturn 'all the rights of landed property'. This argument was developed by an English newspaper which viewed disestablishment as the precursor to land reform, citing Hill's opposition to sub-divided holdings in its argument against any extension of tenant right.[50] Ahead of the parliamentary debate, Hill attended the Derry diocesan synod, during which it was argued that without the Ascendency there would be a power vacuum in Ireland.[51] He was chosen by that meeting to be its representative at a Dublin conference of senior clergy and laity where, predictably, delegates resolved to oppose disestablishment.[52] It was to no avail. The Liberal majority in the Commons overcame objections from Conservatives and the Lords to pass the Irish Church Act, later regarded as 'an event of the highest significance in the history of nineteenth century Ireland'.[53]

Hill's allegiance to Protestantism also led him into controversial areas, such as his unwise decision to subscribe to a book of poetry by Robert Young, whose 'Orange doggerel' was widely condemned for its sectarian content.[54] Young's 'seditious and licentious songs' were said to breathe 'slaughter, carnage, murder, and bloodshed on a grand scale'.[55] In his

---

47 *Dublin Evening Mail*, 5 Sept 1871; *Witness* (Belfast), 19 April 1878.

48 *The Times*, 18 March 1869; *Southern Reporter and Cork Commercial Courier*, 22 March 1869.

49 *Hansard*, 1 March 1869.

50 *Yorkshire Post,* 14 Sept 1869.

51 *Manchester Courier*, 30 March 1869.

52 *Evening Freeman*, 13 April 1869.

53 Comerford in Vaughan (1989): 443.

54 *Kilkenny Journal*, 21 Nov 1866 https://www.dib.ie/biography/young-robert-a9177.

55 *Dublin Evening Post*, 30 March 1867.

London column for *The Irishman*, Denis Holland took the opportunity to poke fun at Young's titled subscribers, contending that they had been 'grossly deceived' into supporting a man 'employed all his life in the vicious task of inflaming the evil passions of low Orangemen'.[56]

This incident, a relatively trivial error of judgement when set against examples of Hill's largely liberal social and religious record, was much more significant than he, and those who hymned his achievements, seemed to realise. It was but one illustration of the way in which, no matter how hard he strove to be different from his peers, he was not able to distance himself from them. Despite widespread loathing for landlords such as Lord Leitrim and John George Adair, Hill was tainted by association, administering justice alongside them as a member of the grand jury and mixing with them socially. He appeared oblivious to his tenants' anti-English and, by extension, anti-monarchical, sentiments by speaking at a public event arranged to celebrate the Prince of Wales's recovery from typhoid fever.[57] Attended by only thirty titled landowners and their acolytes, it was billed as a spontaneous show of respect by 'the people of Donegal'. That prompted the *Derry Journal* to call it a farce, enhancing its attack by pointing out that Leitrim was 'engaged in the congenial occupation' of a court action to challenge the rights of his tenants.[58]

As for Adair, in January 1873, the Lord Lieutenant (Earl Spencer), was 'pleased to appoint' as Donegal's high sheriff the landlord responsible for evicting 244 tenants twelve years before.[59] Hill, who had been high sheriff in 1845, and the rest of the county's land-owners, did not register any surprise let alone protest. When Adair convened meetings, such as one about the need for the government to acquire the Irish railway network, they all attended.[60] There were also uneasy reminders for Hill that the image of the 'improved' Gweedore he wished to project did not always find favour, even among those who might have been expected to support him. When Edward Senior, the Poor Law Commissioner, was questioned by a parliamentary committee considering taxation in Ireland, one remark must have pained Hill. Senior described Ulster as the most prosperous part of country, with the exception of the western districts

56 *The Irishman*, 30 March 1867.
57 *Northern Whig*, 2 March 1872; *Londonderry Sentinel*, March 1872.
58 *Derry Journal*, 4 March 1872. Cf. *Londonderry Sentinel*, 5 March 1872.
59 *Freeman's Journal*, 22 Jan 1873.
60 *Londonderry Sentinel*, 13 March 1873.

where he 'had seen more misery in the neighbourhood of Lord George Hill's property … than he had seen in the south or west of Ireland'.[61]

Nor could Hill draw much comfort from an article in a respected Scottish quarterly which explored 'untenable theories' about 'the Irish question'.[62] That question concerned the dispute over land ownership and the nature of the relationship between owners and tenants. Its anonymous writer sought to explain the historical reasons for the development of the rundale system within Donegal as 'clan colonisation' which, over time, had created 'evils' of subdivision. Tenants, it argued, were supposedly 'not averse to change when an alteration was proposed which would define their holdings'.[63] Hostility to changes arose because they were generally instituted by new proprietors, such as Hill. The author, in highlighting Hill's clash with Holland, appeared to sympathise with the latter, referring to him as an 'authority' and citing several paragraphs from his 1857 trip to Donegal. Much shorter shrift was given to Hill, merely noting in passing the 'narrative of his ameliorations'.

Hill could count on considerable support from the mainstream press, his fellow landlords and, of course, members of his church.[64] William Walsh, dean of Cashel and canon of Dublin's Christ Church Cathedral, delivered lectures over a number of years lauding Hill's 'exertions' in Gweedore. He told how the poor peasantry had prospered because Lord George, having 'lived amongst the people for many years … had succeeded in effecting wonderful improvements'.[65] These 'improvements' were forever being discovered by journalists who, despite acknowledging that the reforms were 'matters of history' and 'rendered famous over the kingdom', wrote as if telling the story of 'the great benefactor' for the first time. Their findings reiterated in almost every detail the reports published by admirers more than thirty years before, all of them highly influenced by Hill's *Facts from Gweedore*. Some felt the need to embellish the truth, such as the writer for the country magazine, Land and Water. 'It is no exaggeration', he wrote, before doing just that, 'to say Lord George found the place a savage

---

61 *Dublin Evening Post*, 28 June 1864.
62 'Literature of the Land Question in Ireland', *North British Review* Vol 51 (Oct 1870). The *Review* had been acquired the year before by a liberal Catholic owner, Lord Acton. Cf *North British Agriculturalist*, 3 Nov 1869.
63 Ibid.
64 Inter alia, see *Irish Times*, 21, 27 May 1875, *Irish Times*; *Belfast News-Letter*, 27 July 1876.
65 'Donegal and its legends', *Londonderry Sentinel*, 10 May 1873, 11 Jan 1877.

wilderness, inhabited by savage tribes'.[66] Another, who registered surprise that 'so many of the people' in west Donegal spoke Irish and knew 'scarcely a word of English', lavished praise on Hill's beneficence.[67]

Journalists also revelled in endlessly repeating one of the least believable 'facts' in *Facts*: the claim that on an unnamed Donegal island a horse was owned by three men who each undertook to shoe one foot, rendering the animal useless because there was no-one to shoe the fourth foot.[68] Anti-Irish politicians, such as Charles Buxton, MP for East Surrey, enjoyed telling this tall tale. He liked to conclude his version by saying the horse was always lame ... 'just like the Irish people'.[69] An Irish joke was conceived, albeit at one remove, courtesy of Lord George Hill.

Entirely unexpected official praise for Hill arrived via Dr Robert Baker, one the Crown's inspectors of factories, who went beyond his normal industrial remit to comment on the effect of Hill's agricultural reforms. In an otherwise routine report to parliament on factory conditions, he devoted a lengthy passage to the Gweedore improvements. He believed they deserved attention as 'the beginning of good things for Ireland', which should set a standard for other landlords to replicate.[70] Baker, following the now familiar precedent, drew on Hill's *Facts* to tell the history of the transformation from pre-1838 misery to modern contentment. Seven hundred acres of waste land have been reclaimed, he reported, and tenants were benefiting from the resulting quantity and quality of produce. They were enjoying better conditions, with good houses, and a healthy income from the marketing of their knitted socks and the making of frieze and flannel. If Hill's example were followed, he wrote, 'the tide of emigration would flow back again to the neglected hills and valleys'.

Publication of the report prompted the *Derry Journal* to carry a leading article, repeating Baker's findings and calling Hill 'a model Donegal landlord'. Given its strong nationalist leanings, it was a surprising intervention on Hill's behalf.[71] The paper praised him for 'the immense benefits which he has, in a quiet and unostentatious way, conferred upon the

---

66 'Through the Donegal Highlands', republished by *Londonderry Sentinel*, 21 Oct 1873.
67 'Two hundred miles and more through the Wilds of Donegal', by Drummond Grant, *Coleraine Chronicle*, 3 Aug 1872.
68 *Facts*, 3: 18-19.
69 *East Surrey Advertiser*, 17 Oct 1868.
70 *Irish Times*, 19 May 1875.
71 'Donegal landlordism – the Gweedore property', *Derry Journal*, 21 May 1875.

people in one of what was the poorest and most backward districts of the county'. It claimed that 'the kindliest relations' now exist between Hill and his tenants in contrast to some of 'his brother land owners in the county'.

This accolade was too much for Father John Doherty to bear. The 'obnoxious priest', as Hill had once termed him, returned to the fray with a letter to the *Journal*, running to almost 1,700 words, in which he contested the paper's (and Baker's) portrayal of Gweedore.[72] He accepted that he always found Hill 'kind and obliging, urbane and courteous' but felt sick *ad nauseam* on reading 'the hypocritical cant of model landlordism and improvements'. He took issue with every 'fact' and reiterated tenants' complaints about the deprivation of mountain pastures and the dispute over sheep farming. He scorned the claim that Hill had been responsible for the reclamation of land, arguing that he had extracted money from tenants who carried out the work. Something rang hollow in Doherty's diatribe, however. It dealt with the past rather than the present.

Both he and Hill were aware that change was in the air. A new direction of travel had been evident since the passing of Gladstone's Land Act in 1870. It gave tenants increased security of tenure and some rights to compensation. Despite being watered down, it amounted to a tentative first step towards constraining the powers of landlordism and challenging the supremacy of the Ascendancy. During the parliamentary debate, Hill may have taken heart from favourable references to his Gweedore reforms, but he could surely see history was moving against him and his class.[73] He would also have been aware of the reform's sceptical Irish and English critics, who regarded it as a 'sham', a view shared by Doherty and echoed from his American bolthole by Denis Holland. He realised that tenants would still face the peril of eviction and one of the results, large-scale emigration, was evident in the thousands he witnessed arriving every month in New York. Yet more land reform was required.

There were some pleasant diverting moments for Hill. He presented Dublin zoo with a peregrine falcon found by one of his tenants.[74] He took pleasure in the farm around his home in Ramelton, entering cattle into agricultural shows and occasionally winning prizes.[75] It was a

72 *Derry Journal*, 26 May 1875.
73 *The Times*, 15 June 1870.
74 *Londonderry Sentinel*, 28 Oct 1870.
75 *Londonderry Sentinel*, 7 Aug 1873, 2 Aug 1877; *Dublin Daily Express*, 19 Aug 1875, 2 Aug 1877.

venture in which his wife and youngest daughter, Cassandra, took a close interest. His eldest son's marriage was also a welcome distraction. In February 1871, 33-year-old Arthur married Helen Trench, a daughter of the Protestant Archbishop of Dublin, Richard Chenevix Trench, who conducted the wedding ceremony at Dublin's St Patrick's Cathedral.[76] They spent their honeymoon at Sopwell Hall in Tipperary, the seat of Helen's uncle, Baron Ashtown.[77] Arthur, a soldier with the Rifle Brigade since his youth, achieved the rank of captain three years before the wedding, and was known thereafter as Captain Arthur Hill.[78] He retired on half pay for a while and then sold his commission in 1873.[79] Aware that he would inherit Gweedore and Ballyare, he decided against settling in Donegal, choosing to live on the other side of Ulster, in Strangford, County Down, near his sister, Norah, and her husband, Somerset Ward. His friendship with Ward, forged in India, grew closer still.

Denis Holland arrived in New York with a scoop. Two weeks before, it had been reported that Colonel Thomas Kelly, the Fenian Brotherhood's chief organiser in Ireland, had been arrested on the City of Paris steamer in Queenstown (Cobh, County Cork) harbour. Holland, who happened to be on board, was able to reveal to the Boston newspaper, *The Pilot*, that police had arrested the wrong man. Kelly was free and on his way to America.[80] It secured Holland a warm welcome to his new home. And he was soon in business. Within weeks of his arrival he was helping to launch and edit a weekly 'literary journal', *The Emerald*. He contributed a story to the first issue and several more in the following two years.[81] These tales, a mixture of historical fiction, romance, violence and nostalgia, usually had an undisguised nationalist theme, as did his novel, *Donal Dun O'Byrne*, which was published in 1869.[82] It was a melodramatic story of the United Irishmen rebellion which drew heavily on the memoirs of one

---

76 *Freeman's Journal*, 17 Feb 1871.
77 *Leitrim Journal*, 25 Feb 1871.
78 *Daily News*, 20 May 1868.
79 *Evening Freeman*, 14 July 1869; *The Star,* 1 July 1873.
80 *The Pilot*, 14 Dec 1867.
81 'Frank McDermody or murder will out', *The Emerald*, 8 Feb 1868; 'The Irish Legion in France', 9 May 1868; 'The Doctor and the Ghost', 6 June 1868; 'Allen Durrow, or The Blacksmith's Dumb Pupil', 22 May 1869; 'Evil Days and Future Joys', 6 Nov 1869. In the same period, he wrote 'The Spaniard's Dollars: A Tale of Glencolumkille'. See *The Pilot*, 21 Nov 1903.
82 In Glasgow by Cameron & Ferguson. *The Pilot*, 28 Aug 1869.

of its participants, Myles Byrne.[83] It was popular enough to be reprinted occasionally in the following years and at least one critic considered it 'worthy of study by every Irish advocate of armed force as a means of deliverance from alien oppression'.[84] His most interesting contributions to the paper were a series of pen portraits under the title 'Men whom I have known'.[85] Most of them were politicians, including Daniel O'Connell, Sharman Crawford, William Smith O'Brien, Isaac Butt and his boyhood friend, Joe Brennan. Where he had previously been harsh, in these articles he was kindness itself, indulging in a sort of nostalgic revisionism.

So, O'Connell was 'one of the greatest Irishmen that ever lived … the greatest man of the age', a 'physical and intellectual giant' with 'an extraordinary graciousness of manner'.[86] However, he did not feel able to forgive the 'Head Pacificator', as he called him, for his willingness 'to emasculate the warlike manhood of Ireland by his astounding doctrine that "no political amelioration was worth the shedding of a single drop of blood"'.[87] Even Palmerston, an Irish landlord, was remembered as 'remarkable', 'heroic' and a 'genius'.[88] Amid Holland's overblown prose and excessive emotionalism, there were savage barbs to appreciate. Of Castlereagh, he wrote that 'after cutting the throat of Irish liberty [he] cut his own carotid artery'. [89] Lord John Russell was an 'aristocratic cur'.[90] Prince Albert was a 'cunning bargainer and chafferer' whose 'great exhibition' was 'a monstrous sham'.[91]

But *The Emerald*, as with Holland's previous enterprises, did not last for long, publishing its final issue in August 1870. It failed, according to *The Pilot*, because its illustrations were 'mediocre' in contrast to 'its literary contributions', especially those by Holland.[92] Within a month, the ever-optimistic journalist was writing stories for yet another short-lived title, *The Sunburst*, which advocated Irish nationalism and

---

83 Byrne (1780-1862) published three volumes of *Memoirs* in 1863.

84 *A Catholic catalogue embracing a library of approved books* (Dublin: MH Gill & Son, 1921).

85 *The Emerald*, from 21 Aug 1869 to 12 March 1870.

86 *The Emerald*, 28 Aug 1869.

87 *The Emerald*, 18 Dec 1869.

88 *The Emerald*, 5 Feb 1870.

89 *The Emerald*, 19 Feb 1870.

90 *The Emerald*, 28 Aug 1869.

91 *The Emerald*, 26 Feb 1870.

92 *The Pilot*, 13 Aug 1870.

temperance.[93] His own teetotal days were long behind him and there were hints by his acquaintances that Holland, living alone in Brooklyn on meagre earnings from his writing, was over-fond of drink.

Desperate to earn money, he contributed articles to another new title, the *Celtic Weekly*, and posted off several serialised tales to his former paper in Dublin, *The Shamrock*.[94] By this time, there was concern among his friends about his state of mind. One found him 'a broken, heart-weary man' and a misanthrope.[95] They rallied round to buy him a ticket on a ship to Ireland, but he didn't turn up for the sailing.[96] Destitute, depressed and drinking, Holland, aged just forty-six, was old before his time.[97] On 14 December 1872, he died, according to a newspaper report, 'sitting in a chair in his bedroom' at his apartment in Brooklyn.[98] The cause of his death was not reported.

His funeral, on Christmas Eve, was attended by a swathe of New York's Irish journalistic and political community. Among the mourners were leading Fenian activists such as John Devoy, John Locke and James McDermott along with the editors of the *Brooklyn Eagle*, the *Irish Democrat* and the *Irish People*. These papers told of his brilliant past career, his talent and his patriotism. There was no attempt to conceal his sad, final years. He 'pined for the green fields and sunny vales of Ireland ... missed old friends and old associates ... and drooped like a caged bird', said one, adding that he went 'through life in a dreamy, mechanical sort of way'.[99] The longest and most detailed obituary was carried in a Boston paper, *The Pilot*, because its New York correspondent, Joseph Clarke, knew Holland well, having first met him in London in 1861.[100] Then, Holland had been 'the picture of hope and manhood ... a man of information and anecdote, which he had the faculty of imparting with fluency and point'. In American

93 *The Pilot*, 3 Sept 1870.

94 Among them were 'MacMahon of Thomond, or The Fortunes of an Exile' (20 May 1871); 'The Country and the Town: A Tale of Common Life in Ireland' (19 Aug 1871); 'Love or Justice, or The Father and the Judge' (18 May 1872).

95 *The Pilot*, 28 Dec 1872. First issue of *Celtic Weekly* on 2 March 1872 contained Holland's story, 'Bessie Moran's Dream: A Tale of War'.

96 *The Pilot*, 23 March 1872, 11 Jan 1873.

97 Reprint from New York's *Sunday Democrat and Weekly Catholic Advocate*, in *The Irishman*, 4 January 1873.

98 Ibid.

99 *Sunday Democrat and weekly Catholic Advocate*, 23 Dec 1872.

100 *The Pilot*, 11 Jan 1873.

exile, however, he became 'a broken, melancholy, aimless man'. Clarke wrote: 'He died as sadly as the last years of his life. In a cold, lonely chamber in Brooklyn, without a soul of his kindred near him'.

Clarke recalled Holland's 'bold' journalism in Belfast and Dublin in the face of 'all the anti-Irishisms of the English press'. He also acknowledged that Holland was the 'greatest impulse' behind the National Brotherhood of St Patrick, which he recognised as 'a step-stone to the Irish Revolutionary Brotherhood'. In other words, Holland should be seen as a Fenian. This was a singular view. Within Ireland, where newspaper reports registered profound shock at Holland's death, there were no overt references to his link to Fenianism. 'An honest man has passed away in exile', said his old title, *The Irishman*, in a report starkly headlined: 'Denis Holland is dead!'[101] His death was widely reported in newspapers across Ireland, from Belfast to Wexford, and from Dublin to Limerick. All of them preferred to remember his journalism rather than his politics. 'He was a fluent and graceful writer, and was highly respected by his professional brethren', said one.[102] 'Mr Holland was a brilliant and trenchant litterateur', said another.[103] A third, in his home city, observed that he was 'well known to most Irish journalists for literary abilities of a decidedly high order'.[104]

A lengthy appraisal of his career in *The Irishman* recalled his work at *The Ulsterman* on behalf of the north's 'oppressed tenants and the then shackled Catholics'. His journey 'into the wilds' had led him to write articles later published in a book, *The Landlord in Donegal*, which, it said, 'still forms, a work of great value to the historical investigator. Its exposure, at once accurate and caustic, of the despotism of the mountain landlords, who fancied themselves safe in their obscurity, had a wider influence than he could have hoped, and proved, perhaps, of more importance than ever he was aware'.[105]

---

101 *The Irishman*, 4 Jan 1873.
102 *Belfast Telegraph*, 2 Jan 1873.
103 *Freeman's Journal*, 1 Jan 1873.
104 *Cork Daily Herald*, 31 Dec 1872.
105 'In Memoriam', *The Irishman*, 4 Jan 1873.

14

DEATH, DISCORD AND DEFEAT

'Fame is a vapour; popularity an accident; riches take wings; the only earthly certainty is oblivion' – Horace Greeley[1]

'Even in the rush of European events, the circumstances of the murder of the Earl of Leitrim and of his two ill-starred companions give it an importance of the first magnitude. An act of open civil war could not have created more consternation and horror ...'[2]

Those opening sentences to a Dublin newspaper report on the killing of Lord George Hill's neighbour in 1878 framed the way in which the incident would be regarded ever after, not simply as an extraordinary crime, which it was, but as an attack on landlordism itself, which it was not. The report rightly conveyed the predominant public reaction to the killings in Britain and across most of Ireland. Within Donegal, however, there were many people who had little, if any, sympathy for the third Lord Leitrim. He was a notorious figure, known for his ruthless treatment of tenants, for being litigious, and for picking quarrels, including one with a Lord Lieutenant (Earl of Carlisle).

Leitrim's overall intentions, the modernising of agricultural production and the creation of an orderly society, were not dissimilar to those of Hill. In that sense, it has been argued that Leitrim was misunderstood, suggesting that his high-handed confrontational style, amplified by later myth, cloaked a more mundane truth about his reformist agenda.[3] Critical contemporaneous press coverage implied otherwise. Even in newspapers regarded as friendly towards the Ascendancy, his actions and statements

---

1 Harriet Beecher Stowe, *Men of Our Times: Leading Patriots of The Day* (New York: JD Denison, 1868): 304.
2 *Freeman's Journal*, 4 April 1878.
3 See Malcomson (2009).

attracted hostility. Clearly, he made no effort to build a sympathetic public profile. Such was the antipathy towards him, he attracted censure from the so-called 'unscrupulous organ of landlordism',[4] the *Londonderry Sentinel*, which registered its 'unqualified protest against Lord Leitrim's arbitrary conduct towards his tenantry'.[5]

Hill's friendship with the Leitrim family, the Clements, dated back to his days as dance partner to Leitrim's sister.[6] He also dealt with Leitrim during his time as comptroller of the Lord Lieutenant's household in the early 1830s. Once he became a Donegal landlord it was natural that the men would see a lot of each other. They were similar in age, their homes were not too far apart, and both served on the county's grand jury. Hill followed Leitrim's lead in offering annual prizes to diligent tenants. Despite his own ruthless dealings with his tenants and his opposition to the concept and practice of tenant right, Leitrim appreciated Hill's 'superior management'.[7] In fact, Hill was said to be Leitrim's 'biggest friend' in Donegal and was appointed as an executor of his will.[8] At the time of the murder, the two men had not met for a considerable time, as Hill explained in a letter to Leitrim's nephew and successor to the title. 'Of late years', he wrote, 'he has always said he could not come to see us because he had so much business'.[9]

Unsurprisingly, Hill was badly shaken by the manner of Leitrim's death, which was a bloody affair.[10] He was ambushed by three men – Michael McElwee, Nial Shiels and Michael Heraghty – as he travelled from his house in Carrigart along Mulroy Bay towards Milford. His driver and clerk were shot dead; Leitrim, only wounded in the hail of bullets, was clubbed to death with a rifle butt. McElwee was a Ribbonman, the other two were Fenians, as was the supposed organiser of the assassination, Mandy Callaghan.[11] However, the reason for attack was as much personal as political. Callaghan had lost a lengthy court case with Leitrim and all four men were related to people who believed they had been ill-treated at some time by Leitrim.[12] Heraghty, who was arrested and died in Lifford

---

4 *Derry Journal*, 23 Dec 1857.

5 *Londonderry Sentinel*, 18 Dec 1857. See also 15 Jan 1858 and 16 Oct 1863.

6 See Chapter 1.

7 Malcomson (2009): 271.

8 Ibid. This was Leitrim's 1859 will. He was not an executor of the final 1875 will.

9 Ibid. Letter to R.B. Clements, Warrens Papers NLI MS 33,849

10 Hillan (2011): 187.

11 MacSuibhne & Dickson (2000): 25; Malcomson (2009): 186, 190.

12 *Freeman's Journal*, 4 April 1878.

jail of typhus, was never convicted of the murder.[13] McElwee and Shiels remained free, despite being named in a police report two years later.[14]

Following the attack, the district was proclaimed under the Peace Preservation Act.[15] Yet Hill himself, and most of his fellow Donegal landlords, despite their outrage, were not unduly unnerved by the murder. Perhaps they saw it in context as being a specific act against an eccentric member of their 'club' rather than an assault on landlordism. They were more exercised by the failure of the police to bring the assassins to justice. It did not appear to affect Hill's routine over the following months. He travelled fairly regularly between Gweedore and Ballyare, where, in late summer, his farm boasted an unusually heavy crop of oats.[16] In September, soon after attending a military ball in Letterkenny, he was buoyed by the display of a banner at his annual show in Bunbeg proclaiming: 'Long live Lord and Lady Hill'.[17] He was also pleased about his eldest son, Arthur, securing a lucrative post as inspector of Ireland's prisons.[18]

Hill's own finances, never flush, were strained. Reports by people who met him in his seventies are suggestive of an elderly man living in a sort of genteel poverty.[19] Unlike Leitrim, renowned for his canny accounting, Hill had always been improvident, hence the need for occasional loans from his brothers, Atty and Marcus. Clearly, there was no similarity between his existence and that of his Gweedore tenants. He did not live hand to mouth. But, compared to those of his own class, he was hard up. Belatedly, in taking stock of the situation for many of his hard-pressed tenants, he came to recognise that Gweedore could not sustain an ever-increasing population. In so doing, he accepted that there might be virtues in emigration. He had previously set his face against it, viewing it at the personal level as 'punishment' and, on the wider political scale, as 'national suicide'.[20] But there is evidence, albeit anecdotal, to suggest he helped some of his tenants to settle in New Zealand.[21]

---

13 Thousands turned up at his funeral in national colours, Murphy (1980): 476.

14 Malcomson (2009): 190. A monument erected in 1960 near the men's homes in Fanad stated that 'by their heroism' McElwee, Shiels and Heraghty 'ended the tyranny of landlordism'.

15 Murphy (1981): 419.

16 *Londonderry Sentinel*, 13 Aug 1878.

17 *Londonderry Sentinel*, 3 Sept 1878; *Derry Journal*, 4 Sept 1878; *Londonderry Sentinel*, 24 Sept 1878.

18 *Irish Times*, 10 Sept 1878. Six years later, his annual salary was reported to be £600. *Freeman's Journal*, 16 Sept 1884.

19 Gwynn (1903); Bayne (2016).

20 *Facts*: 56.

21 See Hillan (2011): n52 citing Kay Carter at www.ancestry.com/boards/surnames.hill/4160.

Maybe his change of mind was also a recognition that the Ireland he knew, the Ireland of union with Britain, the Ireland of the Ascendancy, the Ireland of landlordism, was under threat. He could not know it was on the threshold of its final stage of its union with Britain, but he was able to see that landlordism was at the centre of increasing political agitation. His tenantry were now being championed not only by priests but by the emergent, articulate Irish political class. It would have been no surprise to Denis Holland, dead for almost seven years at this point, because he had envisioned that opposition to British rule would eventually manifest itself over the question of land ownership. His belief in a nationalism built around a campaign for the rights of Ireland's rural poor was on the verge of being realised. Hill, by contrast, eschewed this kind of macro political view. Instead, by illustrating the value of small-scale, personal, pro-active proprietorship, he had hoped to influence his more aggressive peers to follow suit. At the same time, he could neither disguise that he was one of them, nor did he seek to distance himself from them, as his friendship with Leitrim showed. Annoyingly, he left no record of his innermost thoughts about his failure to convince others of his policy.

At the beginning of 1879, Hill's 36-year-old daughter, Cassandra, took to the stage at a concert to inaugurate Ramelton's town hall and delighted the audience by singing, in Irish, the haunting air An Chúilfhionn (The Coolin).[22] Hill, who had contributed to the building of the hall, did not attend. A month on from his 77th birthday his health was failing; he had difficulty breathing. Despite that, a week or so after the concert, he felt well enough to make the arduous trip to Bunbeg to visit the school he had founded and funded.[23] Forty-five years' on from seeing Gweedore for the first time, this proved to be his final visit. On 31 March, Cassandra sent her brother, Arthur, a telegram, urging him to come to Ballyare. She and their step-mother, Louisa, were aware that Hill would not recover from his severe lung complaint.[24] Arthur was on hand on 6 April, along with his brothers and sisters, to witness Hill draw his last breath.[25]

---

22 *Derry Journal*, 15 Jan 1879. Hillan (2018).

23 *Londonderry Sentinel*, 28 Jan 1879.

24 Davis (2020d) 31 March 1879. Louisa must have informed her sister, Lizzy, who wrote to her son that Hill 'is dangerously ill of congested lungs and they say his recovery is … hopeless'. Hillan (2011): 185 and n43.

25 Arthur recorded in his journal that on 'Palm Sunday, at about 12 o'clock, our dear Father passed away', Davis (2020d), 6 April 1879. The death certificate stated that he died of 'senile decay and congestion of the lungs', death register No 4, 9 Donegal Ancestry, Ramelton.

Press coverage of his death in Ireland was muted; in England, it was almost non-existent. *The Times* accorded him one paragraph; the *Daily Telegraph*'s paragraph was even shorter, while *The Guardian* didn't mention his passing at all.[26] Irish newspaper tributes to the 'venerable Lord George Hill' were overwhelmingly kind, if brief, a recognition perhaps of him having reached a 'ripe old age'. Greater emphasis was placed on his kinship with his ancestral family, noting, for example, that he was 'great uncle to the present Marquess of Downshire', rather than detailing his own career. Among the most prominent obituaries were those in Ulster. It was natural that the *Londonderry Sentinel* should give him a great send-off, reminding its readers that his lordship had 'overcome the prejudices' of his tenants 'to be regarded as one of the best landlords in Donegal'. He had transformed a wilderness into 'a fairly productive, if not fertile district' by reclaiming land and had established manufactures for the benefit of the peasantry.[27] He was, said the *Belfast Weekly News*, 'one the purest and most devoted of Irish patriots' whose 'eminently useful life amid the wilds of Donegal was a romance'. He had 'sacrificed his ease and fortune to provide civilisation, industry and enlightenment in the rude but lovely region he made his adopted home. He was one of the best of landlords, and by all classes greatly esteemed.'[28]

One of the most generous tributes was carried by the nationalist *Derry Journal*, which said his death would 'cause a general feeling of regret' among his tenants because 'Lord George was a kind and generous landlord'. In Gweedore, it said, he had 'laboured earnestly to promote the prosperity of the people, introducing manufactures, solely intended for their benefit ... Among the best traits of Lord George's character – and he had few bad ones – was his earnest anxiety to promote the social condition and general welfare of the working classes.'[29] For many Dublin-based papers, it appeared that the landlord renowned for his agricultural and social 'improvements', a man perpetually celebrated in print down the years, had been largely forgotten. One typical report, missing his main landlordly contribution by a mile, stated: 'The deceased nobleman was chiefly known in connection with the Gweedore Hotel, which he established for the convenience of tourists in the Donegal Highlands'.[30]

26 *The Times*, 11 April, 1879; *Daily Telegraph*, 12 April, 1879. See also *The Globe*, 8 April, 1879.
27 *Londonderry Sentinel*, 8 April 1879.
28 *Belfast Weekly News*, 19 April, 1879. See also *Dublin Evening Mail*, 8 April 1879.
29 *Derry Journal*, 9 April 1879.
30 *Freeman's Journal*, 8 April 1879; *The Irishman*, 12 April 1879.

Over the years, Lord George Hill's name had regularly featured in headlines in England. Now, only the most avid newspaper reader would have located reports of his death. Politicians who had once lined up to praise Hill's sterling efforts as an improving Irish landlord were silent. It was as though he had served his purpose during a former period when the shoring up of landlordism was in Britain's political interest. A new reality meant that it had become largely irrelevant in Westminster whether Irish landlords were good or bad. Gladstone, who was determined to end the Ascendancy's grip on Ireland, was the key political figure and on the verge of forming his second administration.

In Ireland, beyond Ulster, there were only sparing references to Lord George's demise. Oddest of all was the fact that his funeral went unreported. A Ramelton neighbour, Sir James Stewart, happened to die one week after Hill and his burial, attended by 400 people in 38 carriages, got top billing in the *Londonderry Sentinel*.[31] By contrast, Lord George's interment alongside his first wife, Cass, in Letterkenny's Conwal Church of Ireland cemetery, was not mentioned. Instead, a eulogy delivered days later by the Church of Ireland rector in Gweedore, Hugh Carson, was reported in full.[32] He reiterated the view that Hill had bought his estates not 'as a profitable investment' but 'with the express purpose of reclaiming a waste … improving and elevating a tenantry whose civilisation was, it is said, not far above central Africa's'. He spoke in similar terms of Hill's transformation of the district where 'the mud-hut in the wilderness gave place to the stone cottage'. Underlining Hill's paternalism, he supposedly spoke of his tenants as 'his children'. Surely Hill would have blushed as the panegyric continued: 'He was good to the poor … but he never talked of his goodness, nor cared to trumpet it. He did good simply because it was his nature.' There was a wider message as well: 'Other landlords … guided by the light of his example, will learn that property has its duties as well as its rights'.[33]

It is highly unlikely that 'other landlords' were moved by Carson's plea because they were dealing with unwelcome realities, as Hill's son was about to discover. It was the least propitious time to become a landlord. Firstly, the west of Ireland was suffering from a new famine. It was nothing like as severe as the Great Hunger, and, although it did not

---

31 *Londonderry Sentinel*, 19 April 1879.
32 *Londonderry Sentinel*, 15 April 1879.
33 Ibid.

affect Donegal as badly as some other counties, there were many, many cases of destitution.[34] Emigration increased. Secondly, 1879 marked the formation of the Irish National Land League, an organisation dedicated to the abolition of landlordism. Thirdly, parliament was discussing the introduction of a new land law, enacted in 1881, to provide tenant farmers with rights that had the effect of depriving landlords of their rights. For Captain Arthur Blundell George Sandys Hill, there was also a fourth unfavourable factor: he was an absentee landlord, living some 200 miles from Gweedore in Bray, County Wicklow, who viewed his Donegal estate 'purely as a business'.[35]

Then there was his character. He lacked his father's tact in his dealings with the tenants and shared none of his father's intense interest in Gweedore or, indeed, in the Irish people. His privately expressed reaction to the killing of Lord Leitrim was revealing. He noted succinctly in his journal: 'wretched Irish people'.[36] This withering reference was not an isolated example of his sense of difference from 'the Irish'. Born in England, spending months at a time as a child in England, and after years as a British army officer, his was a wholly English, and Protestant, sensibility. He viewed the Catholic tenants for whom he was now responsible as a people apart, foreigners, as it were, in their own country.

According to his father's will, he inherited an estate valued at 'under £7,000'.[37] This included the land in Gweedore, the property in Ramelton, including its farm, plus unspecified effects in England. It did not make Arthur rich, nor even comfortable by his class's standards. He became reliant for regular (and handsome) income on his post as prisons' inspector. Almost immediately, with tenants demanding rent decreases, he became embroiled in a legal case, a hangover from the past that pointed to the problematic relationship he would have with his tenants in the future. It concerned a long-running dispute over Gweedore's sandbanks.

In the late 1850s, after tenants complained to Lord George that their land was being ruined by sand blowing in from the shore, he had paid for bent grass to be planted to stabilise the dunes. Eventually, the scheme worked. Sand stopped drifting inland and the bent, having grown strong, could be harvested, and sold, for roof-thatching. According to Hill's

---

34 'Kilmacrenan extraordinary presentment sessions', *Derry Journal*, 1 March 1880.
35 Hillan (2011): 212.
36 Davis (2020d) 11 April 1878.
37 *Morning Post*, 23 Aug 1879.

lawyers, taking account of costs for planting and security (observers were employed to prevent damage to the dunes and theft of the bent), it proved profitable. In February 1879, sales realised their greatest annual profit. But all did not go smoothly because there were continual disputes over tenants allowing their cattle to wander across the sand hills. In the course of sixteen years, on some fifty occasions, fines were imposed for trespass.

Magistrates sitting at Bunbeg were told that the largest incursion of cattle occurred two months after Lord George's death. As a result, his son had twenty-four tenants charged with trespass. Even before the hearing, one of them, Bryan McBride, was imprisoned for a fortnight. That upset his neighbours and, with their parish priest's help, they managed to hire a lawyer to argue that the sandbanks had always been regarded by tenants as common land. The resident magistrate found it impossible to decide the issue and, to Hill's dismay and the tenants' delight, he dismissed the case.[38]

Hill also served notice that he would not be bound by a sentimental attachment to his father's enthusiasms. He closed the Bunbeg school, of which Lord George was inordinately proud, having visited it three months before his death.[39] The prosecution of tenants and the school cost-cutting were signs of things to come, and mark the beginning of public confusion about Arthur's regime and that of his father. It is clear that some of the mud which has been attached to Lord George Hill's name over the course of the 130 years should have been directed only at his son. Whatever misgivings people may have about the reign of Hill *père*, there cannot be a shadow of doubt that compared to Hill *fils* he was a much more admirable and adroit landlord. This is not to say that Arthur inherited estates and tenants in as perfect a state as his father's publicity would have had people believe. We have to keep in mind that poverty is a relative term and the living conditions for many people in Gweedore remained anything but desirable. This reality would turn Arthur's inheritance into a poisoned chalice.

It wasn't too long before he found that his father's 'obnoxious priest', John Doherty, had been replaced by a turbulent priest all of his own. And Father James McFadden would provide a far greater challenge than his predecessor. During the Land War, many Catholic clergy acted as spokesmen and advisers to their parishioners but the priests' power

38 *Derry Journal*, 29 Aug, 26 Sept 1879; *Londonderry Sentinel*, 25 Sept 1879.
39 *Derry Journal*, 9 Jan 1880.

in Donegal was recognised as exceptional.[40] And none more so than McFadden's. Within months of Hill assuming responsibility for the Gweedore estate, he discovered just how wily an opponent he had when tenants sought a substantial reduction in their rents because of a poor harvest. Eight of them sent a letter to Hill which found its way on to the front page of the *Derry Journal*. 'In this our hour of trial', they wrote, 'we ask you for relief ... by abatement of our rents'. McFadden and his curate appended a note saying: 'We approve this course which they have adopted, and we earnestly pray that their appeal shall not be unavailing'.[41] Hill's reply, also carried by the paper, argued that a general rent reduction was out of the question; but if his agent found individual cases of hardship he would alleviate their suffering by offering them employment. Hill must have been astonished to see this private exchange of letters in print. McFadden had slyly scored his first propaganda victory.

Within a fortnight, he scored a second with a long letter to the Dublin-based nationalist paper, the *Freeman's Journal*, which began: 'The darkest page in the past history of Gweedore does not contain a parallel in wretchedness and misery to the scene which I witnessed today'.[42] He told of a 'multitude of applicants' from among the estate's tenants for a portion of the £14 he had been sent by charitable donors, including his bishop. The hyperbolic McFadden had thrown down the gauntlet. Unlike Doherty, who had no support from his bishop, McFadden was able to count on backing from the church hierarchy: his uncle, Daniel McGettigan, was Archbishop of Armagh, primate of all Ireland.

Born in Carrigart, some twenty-five miles north of Gweedore, McFadden had arrived as the parish priest of Tullaghobegley in 1875, aged thirty-two. Initially, he and Lord George enjoyed a warily cordial relationship because both men shared an interest in stamping out illicit distillation. McFadden formed a branch of the Temperance League, which was praised by Hill but unpopular with many of the priest's new parishioners. He was very organised and busy, often involved in fund-raising on behalf of various Catholic charities. It earned him praise for being a 'zealous priest' with 'indefatigable energy'.[43] In spite of his opposition to the making of poteen and an authoritarian style, he

---

40 Murphy, D, 'Land War in Donegal', *Donegal Annual* p476.
41 *Derry Journal*, 31 Dec 1879.
42 *Freeman's Journal*, 10 Jan 1880.
43 *Derry Journal*, 16 Oct 1878.

gradually won the respect of his flock. His prestige increased in the summer of 1880 when a flash flood deluged the Gweedore church during a service. Water burst through the doors, filling the chapel in minutes to a depth of twelve feet. Five people were drowned and one hundred were injured.[44] McFadden was reported to have climbed atop the altar, telling people 'to keep cool' before he and others broke through a window, enabling people, including himself, to clamber out to safety.[45]

'The Gweedore catastrophe', as it became known, raised McFadden's public profile. He had already won over local sceptics by securing relief for families suffering from famine distress.[46] In that, he was supported by Gweedore's Protestant minister, Hugh Carson, a significant ally as McFadden sought to convince landlords of their responsibilities towards their beleaguered tenants.[47] By far the biggest step taken by McFadden was to join the Land League, the organisation that unified the two nationalist wings – the constitutional led by Charles Stewart Parnell MP and the physical-force led by the former IRB member Michael Davitt. Holland would have been delighted that land had, at last, become the central issue in the agitation for political change. He would have recognised that underlying the League's call for tenant rights and rent control was an attempt to create conditions, and support, for the formation of an Irish state.

McFadden, who quickly assumed control of the League's Gweedore chapter, chaired a League rally in Derrybeg in January 1881, winning cheers from the large crowd by telling them it was their 'duty' to 'bring about the entire abolition of a system that has steeped the nation in poverty and shame'.[48] He urged 'the men of Cloghaneely and Gweedore to ... exhaust all constitutional means to raise yourselves from the depths of slavery and degradation into which you have been plunged by landlordism'. He appeared intent on forcing a confrontation with Hill. Meanwhile, reports emerged about tenants' conditions that were eerily reminiscent of claims made in 1857 and, even more alarmingly, prior to Lord George's elimination of rundale. 'I was sorry to hear that the process of subdivision was going forward on Captain Hill's and other estates', wrote James Hack Tuke, the English Quaker philanthropist regarded as an impartial observer.[49]

44 *Irish Times*, 18, 20 Aug 1880.
45 *Belfast Morning News*, 18 Aug 1880.
46 *Derry Journal*, 4 Feb 1880.
47 Carson would later say he held no brief for Captain Hill, *Northern Whig*, 28 Jan 1890.
48 *Derry Journal*, 5,17 Jan 1881.
49 Tuke (1880). 'The Irish land question', *The Times*, 30 Sept 1880.

Hearing was not seeing. Tuke, who enjoyed 'a sound working friendship' with McFadden,[50] may have been relying on the priest for his information. Could conditions really have changed so dramatically in the months since the son took over from his father? Had famine bitten so hard? Were matters worse than Lord George had previously led the world to believe? Was McFadden exaggerating in order to make a political point? Twenty-two years on from the 1858 parliamentary inquiry, the same questions about Gweedore were being asked all over again. Who could one believe?

Throughout the spring of 1881, a lively debate was hosted by the editors of the *Derry Journal* and the *Londonderry Sentinel* as Hill and McFadden, joined by an anonymous 'Gweedore correspondent', wrote letters back and forward attacking each other's views about the state of Gweedore.[51] Although their argument ostensibly concerned new rent demands, much of the correspondence recalled past disputes, including interpretations of evidence given to the parliamentary select committee. The old argument about grazing rights also got a renewed airing. Lord George was dead; the debate over his decisions was very much alive. There had been no honeymoon period for Arthur Hill because McFadden, a committed and clever opponent, was quick to sense that the new landlord lacked his father's *noblesse oblige*.

Knowing of the people's rising anger, McFadden also understood that a lengthy period of calm in the final decade of Lord George's life had passed for ever. Unlike Hill, he grasped the significance of a refusal by tenants living on the Rev. Alexander Nixon's estate in neighbouring Falcarragh to accept rent increases. They announced that they wouldn't pay 'pending a settlement of the land question'. In other words, a decision by the Land Court.[52] This statement transformed a local rent dispute into a broader political issue, and McFadden, unlike Hill, read the runes. The central concern of people living in Ascendancy Ireland was not the amount of rent they had to pay but the very fact they had to pay anything at all.

Therefore, McFadden wasn't surprised at the tenants' refusal to accede to Hill's rent demands. Nor was he much surprised when Hill responded by issuing notices for eviction to people he regarded as 'ruffians'.[53]

---

50 Beattie (2016): 39.

51 *Derry Journal*, 28 March, 22, 29 April 1881; *Londonderry Sentinel*, 29 March, 12 April 1881.

52 *Ulster Examiner & Northern Star*, 4 Jan 1881.

53 Davis (2020d), 26 May 1881.

What shocked both men was the violence that exploded when a process server arrived in Gweedore, escorted by thirty Royal Irish Constabulary (RIC) officers, to serve the writs. McFadden was unable to calm the huge crowd, composed mostly of women, which gathered to prevent writs being served. They stoned the police, who were forced to take shelter in their barracks.[54] Seventeen women and five men were later convicted on riot charges and given prison sentences.[55]

Even with the introduction of the Land Commission and Land Courts following the 1881 legislation, Hill and his fellow landlords did not seem to realise that history was moving inexorably against them. As a consequence, Hill stumbled from crisis to crisis over the following years. He issued fifty-four eviction notices just before Christmas 1881.[56] As inspector of prisons, it was surely unwise of him to visit Derry jail and (allegedly) abuse several of his tenants who were serving time for failing to pay their rents.[57] Another of his questionable decisions was to appoint his brother-in-law, Somerset Ward, as his agent. As old soldiers, both were jointly schooled in wartime military discipline and viewed anyone who was not British as 'the natives'.[58] Although unused to the concept of compromise, finances did force some early retreats. Hill first decided to offload the Gweedore Hotel.[59] Then he closed down the farm at Ballyare. All the stock, plus crops, horses and farm implements, were auctioned off – in the name of Lady George Hill – and realised £600.[60] He also put the 'commodious' Ballyare House itself up for sale, with its mill and '200 acres of rich land'.[61] The fearful residents, his step-mother Louisa and sister Cassandra, who were living under the shadow of eviction, must have been relieved when months passed without any offers. At intervals, Hill would alarm them by raising the possibility of a sale.[62]

The English press had been consistent in its support for Lord George, as had English visitors to Donegal. Now, publicity for his son's regime turned negative. One of the first examples came in letters to influential London-based newspapers by the social reformer Alice Hart. Following

54 *Ulster Echo*, 21 May 1881; *The Times*, 23 May 1881.
55 *The Times*, 16 June 1881. See Murphy (1981): 479.
56 *The Times*, 15 Dec 1881.
57 *Derry Journal*, 2 June 1882.
58 Hillan (2011): 158.
59 *Manchester Courier*, 17 Nov 1883.
60 *Derry Journal*, 15, 18 Dec 1882; Davis (2020d), 28 Dec 1882.
61 *Derry Journal*, 12 Jan 1883; Field, 20 Jan 1883; *Irish Times*, 25 Jan 1883.
62 Hillan (2011): 198, 212-3, 215-6, 226.

a trip to Gweedore, she wrote of Captain Hill's tenants being 'reduced to the lowest ebb of poverty'.[63] She complained that he had 'sent his bailiff to collect rents and to serve ejectment processes' to 'hundreds of his wretched tenantry' suffering from hunger. 'Poverty and misery' in Gweedore, she wrote, 'are enough to make the most stony-hearted weep'. In a detailed eye-witness account, differing little from the Denis Holland's report twenty-five years before, she told of the pitiful conditions of single-roomed houses with hardly any furniture or cooking utensils, inhabited by people in rags. In calling for contributions to a Donegal Famine Fund, she concluded with a rhetorical question that gave no comfort to Hill: 'Can we judge them coldly and harshly if ... they are even driven into acts of lawlessness?'

The following year, an unnamed visitor who stayed at the Gweedore Hotel to enjoy the fishing, spent enough time away from the river to notice that 'the experiment' by the 'chivalrous' Lord George Hill with 'motives purely philanthropic ... to turn a desert in the direction of a paradise ... can hardly be said to have succeeded, seeing the present state of the district'.[64] It was 'hopelessly overcrowded', he wrote, and 'after very considerable emigration, it is simply unfit for human habitation'. He evidently made intimate inquiries because he was able to report that 'on Captain Hill's estate there are not half a dozen tenants who pay the £4 of rent which renders them liable to rating. All the rest are practically paupers, their average rents being under £1, many being as low as 10 shillings'. Like Mrs Hart, he thought 'the interiors of the hovels ... are miserable in the extreme. There is nothing that can be called furniture; the bed clothing is wretched; the animals, where any are kept, live in one end of the cabin'. And, like James Hack Tuke, he claimed that the rundale system 'seems to have survived Lord G. Hill's reforms'.

Another intervention came from Mary Power Lalor, the philanthropist who owned an estate in County Tipperary. In early 1883, at the request of the Catholic bishop of Raphoe, Michael Logue, she began to raise money to help Donegal's starving children, specifically those in Gweedore and Glencolumkille.[65] The fact that there were children in such need in Gweedore supported the views of Hart, Tuke and The Times's correspondent

---

63 'The starving peasants of Donegal', *Daily Chronicle*, 8 June 1883; 'An appeal for a starving population', *The Times*, 3 July 1883. See *Hansard*, HC Deb 5 July 1883 vol. 281, cc. 551–78.
64 *The Times*, 1 Sept 1884.
65 *Dublin Daily Express*, 9 Feb 1883; *Freeman's Journal*, 10, 28 Feb, 1883; *Tablet*, 3 March 1883.

about conditions in the district.[66] Power Lalor also provided seed potatoes because people had been so hungry and needy they had eaten their own stocks. Oddly, during a week-long trip to Donegal, she did not go to Gweedore.[67] But her fund-raising efforts earned her considerable praise.[68] By contrast, Hill, owner of the largest estates in west Donegal, was subjected to relentless criticism. It did not change his mind. Against the background of a negative press, and in the face of McFadden's continuing hostility, he pursued recalcitrant tenants to issue eviction notices.[69]

In response, under McFadden's guidance, they pursued Hill by taking him to the Land Court to argue that their rents were too high and therefore unfair. The sub-commissioners were impressed with the arguments of the majority, granting them reductions of up to 37 per cent (compared to the 20 per cent average across Ireland), while a minority had their rents slightly increased.[70] Mountain grazing rights were also restored. 'All lying and swearing to it', Hill noted angrily in his journal, naming McFadden and the solicitor who argued the tenants' case, James O'Doherty, as the major culprits.[71] The court's ruling was, of course, a severe financial blow to the unhappy landlord.

Hill's poor relations with his tenants worsened considerably when he issued eviction notices for non-payment of rent in August 1886.[72] A force of almost two hundred policemen accompanied the sub-sheriff to carry out the 'cruel proceedings'.[73] The nationalist press was heavily critical.[74] In the course of the month, there were sixty-seven evictions, of whom thirty-one were readmitted as 'caretakers'.[75] To put this in perspective, during Lord George's time, despite the issuing of many eviction notices, none had led to an eviction. In ploughing new ground, his son was sowing discord, which soon attracted attention in parliament. Politicians' comments in this period about Hill marked the beginning of misunderstandings about father and son. A speech by Thomas Sexton, a Belfast MP, illustrates the point. During a debate on the inability of Irish tenant farmers to pay their

---

66 'The Starving Children of Donegal', *The Irish Monthly*, Vol. 11, No. 118, April 1883.
67 'A Six Days' Trip in the Donegal Highlands', *The Irish Monthly*, Vol 11, No 119, May 1883.
68 *Dublin Weekly News*, 7 April 1883; *Derry Journal*, 11 April 1883.
69 *Derry Journal*, 21 Jan 1884; 'Landlordism again!', *Dublin Weekly News*, 26 Jan 1884.
70 *Derry Journal*, 11 June, 10 Aug 1884; *Belfast News-Letter*, 1 Aug 1885; *Londonderry Sentinel*, 8 Aug 1885.
71 Davis (2020d), 6 June 1884.
72 *Freeman's Journal*, 9, 12 Aug, 1886.
73 *Freeman's Journal*, 13, 14 Aug 1886.
74 *Flag of Ireland, Dublin Weekly Nation, Dublin Weekly News*, 14 Aug 1886.
75 *The Times*, parliamentary report, 23 Aug 1886.

rents, he spoke up for the people of Gweedore, calling it 'that wretched spot where the tenants by a labour worse than penal servitude have made some soil on the face of the rock'.[76] He went on to accuse Hill of threatening tenants and of trying to prevent them making their case in the Land Court. Sexton continued: 'Captain Hill, the landlord, or rather his father, some 40 years ago, broke up the communities in the villages, put an end to the pastoral life of the people [and] took from them the only thing that was of any value – the common right of grazing'.

The conflation of the regimes of father and son stung Hill's agent, Somerset Ward, to defend Lord George in a letter to *The Times*. He had acquired land in Gweedore, he wrote, 'not as a commercial speculation, but for the purpose of endeavouring to improve the condition of the people. During 40 years he spent his time and income almost entirely for this one object, and the state of Gweedore when he died in 1879, before the Land League commenced its operations there ... bore ample testimony to the success of his efforts.'[77] Clearly, Ward thought it more important to speak up for his father-in-law rather than his brother-in-law. Soon after, Ward stood down as agent and Hill recruited Colonel James Henry Dopping, a former agent to John George Adair and Lord Leitrim, as his replacement.[78] Hill was placing his faith in an old soldier once again.

He was soon called into service. In September 1887, ninety police and the resident magistrate, Ulick Bourke, accompanied Dopping when he served eviction summonses on Hill's Gweedore estate.[79] The large force did not prevent one tenant from assaulting Dopping: he had boiling water (or, more likely, a pan of hot tea) thrown in his face. A woman also threatened to run him through with a pitchfork. As people gathered to jeer at Dopping and throw stones at him, Bourke read the Riot Act and ordered police to baton-charge the crowd. This incident was widely reported in Ireland, England and Scotland.[80] A day later there was 'a sharp encounter' between Hill and McFadden.[81] A couple of weeks later, a Liberal MP, Professor James Stuart, arrived in Gweedore and sought to act on behalf of the tenants, to the extent of offering to pay off rent arrears for those

76 *Hansard*, 27 Aug 1886, par 683.
77 *The Times*, 2 Sept 1886.
78 *Donegal Independent*, 4 Dec 1886.
79 *Freeman's Journal*, 22 Sept 1887.
80 *Freeman's Journal, Northern Whig, London Evening Standard, Dundee Courier*, all 23 Sept 1887.
81 *Morning Post*, 26 Sept 1887.

facing eviction.[82] He also met Hill's brother, Augustus, with the aim of negotiating an overall settlement of the dispute.

In an odd diversion from the main issue, the clash between Dopping and the tenants in Gweedore was translated into a clash between Dopping and the leader of the parliamentary opposition, William Ewart Gladstone. The Liberal party chief, relying on a report from Stuart, declared that during the Gweedore disturbance, Dopping pointed a rifle at a boy.[83] Dopping issued a denial and sued Gladstone for libel.[84] Wisely, given that Stuart's report of the gun-aiming was based on hearsay, Gladstone apologised and agreed to delete the claim from the written copy of his speech. The matter was settled.[85] Hill noted privately that Stuart was 'a busy-body radical' whose intervention smacked of 'cheeky impudence'.[86] He knew by then that Dopping, after sixteen months in the job, had had enough: he resigned.[87]

Not that Hill himself had faith any longer in a Donegal life. Without revealing his intentions in public, he first explored the possibility of selling the estate to his tenants and, when his lawyer thought that a hopeless plan, he considered putting his estate into chancery (allowing the court to administer and dispose of the property). That idea also came to nothing.[88] A couple of months later, his brother, Augustus, amid what Hill called 'Gweedore eviction bothers', tried to help sort out the eviction drama by 'seeing people' in Dublin.[89] That didn't work out. However, a month later, settlement was reached 'to the advantage of the tenants'.[90] Most of the rent arrears and all of the legal costs were wiped out. All the evicted tenants were reinstated. From this point on, if not well before, we must see Hill as a reluctant proprietor. He had come off worst in a struggle with his tenants, yet he couldn't seem to extricate himself from his landlordship.

Just occasionally, there was a measure of sympathy for Hill's plight as he battled with the priest and his flock. According to a *Times* correspondent, the people of Gweedore, aided by McFadden, were masters at gaming the system, frustrating attempts by Hill and his agent to obtain payments of the

---

82 *Pall Mall Gazette*, 7 Oct 1887.
83 *Londonderry Sentinel*, 20 Oct 1887.
84 *Dublin Evening Mail*, 9 Nov 1887.
85 *Dublin Evening Mail*, 23 Nov 1887; *Weekly Irish Times*, 10 Dec 1887.
86 Davis (2020d), 19 Dec 1887.
87 *Dublin Daily Express*, 3 Jan 1888.
88 Davis (2020d), 16 July, 25 Aug, 1887.
89 Ibid, 4 Oct 1887.
90 *Irish Times*, 25 Nov 1887; *Londonderry Sentinel*, 26 Nov 1887.

full rent.[91] This was an isolated example. Most often, while Hill suffered from a poor press, McFadden benefited from the opposite experience. Recognised early on as a charismatic public speaker,[92] he became one of the Land League's most articulate activists and, in his locality, enjoyed 'a reverence and awe scarcely credible'.[93] Over time, he also became a law unto himself. Believing that the legal system did not favour his parishioners, he set up his own courts and appointed local people as justices. Donegal's landlords were outraged; the people thought otherwise, viewing it as a decent way to settle disputes. It is a moot point as to whether McFadden really did boast: 'I am the law of Gweedore'.[94] Supposedly, he was speaking in Irish and may have been inaccurately translated. Then again, given his arrogance, it would not be out of character.

In spite of being a short man, the burly McFadden became known as 'An Sagart Mór' (The Big Priest) and, sometimes, 'the fighting priest of Gweedore'.[95] He saw nothing wrong in throwing his weight around, helped by his brandishing of a blackthorn stick. McFadden was on a collision course with the authorities and the turning point was his advocacy of a tactic known as the Plan of Campaign, a revitalisation of the Land War that involved the withholding of rent and the use of boycotting. It was applied, with McFadden's support, to the 18,000-acre estate centred on Falcarragh owned by Hill's neighbour, and Lord George's long-time friend, the ageing Wybrants Olphert. Although Hill had grudgingly accepted the reduction in rents ordered by the Land Court – hailed as a 'surrender'[96] – Olphert refused to reach a settlement and decided scores of tenants who had withheld their rent under the Plan of Campaign should be evicted.

Hill and Olphert believed McFadden was guilty of instigating the non-payment of rents and, in January 1888, he was arrested on charges of conspiracy and incitement.[97] Michael Logue, having recently been elevated as Archbishop of Armagh, making him the most senior Catholic in Ireland, visited McFadden, his nephew, in prison and offered to put up bail for him. It was refused.[98] The arrest of a priest, any priest, was

91 'Letters from Ireland: Donegal', *The Times*, 2 Nov 1886.
92 *Dublin Weekly Nation*, 5 Feb 1881.
93 Geary (1986): 29.
94 *London Evening Standard*, *Belfast News-Letter*, 30 Jan 1888.
95 Oxford Dictionary of National Biography.
96 *Londonderry Sentinel*, 19 Jan 1888.
97 *Dublin Evening Mail*, 20 Jan 1888.
98 *Dublin Evening Mail*, 20 Jan 1888; *Newry Telegraph*, 24 Jan 1888.

bound to excite interest. Given McFadden's status at a time of heightened political tension, his 'sacrilegious arrest'[99] aroused passion and anger on a scale that frightened the authorities in Donegal and Dublin. Under guidance from the Chief Secretary, Arthur Balfour, there was no suggestion of backing down. McFadden was convicted and sentenced to three months in jail.[100] He lodged an appeal, and the judge responded by doubling his sentence to six months.[101] As a result, Olphert and his family were boycotted and forced to live virtually under siege with police patrolling their house in Falcarragh on a round-the-clock basis.[102] Despite the widespread breakdown of law and order, with many examples of Plan of Campaign confrontations, it was Donegal's celebrated clerical convict who was given huge attention. Editors and journalists ensured that McFadden's case was widely reported.

On his release in October 1888, McFadden was greeted by a large crowd of well-wishers and treated like a hero. He took up where he had left off by encouraging tenant farmers in his parish and those nearby to withhold their rent. It was unsurprising that he would feature in yet more confrontations with the authorities, but no-one could have anticipated the violent and fatal incident in which he was involved. In February 1889, he was leaving the church in Derrybeg after celebrating mass when a party of police arrived, led by Detective Inspector William Martin, to arrest him for inciting people to resist evictions on the Olphert estate. Martin is said to have drawn his sword and the crowd of parishioners, fearing for McFadden's life, leaped on the officer. McFadden was unable to persuade them to stop their assault and Martin was beaten to death with rocks before his police colleagues could intervene.[103] McFadden was arrested along with forty-two local people – thirty-nine men and three women – and charged with murder.[104] The district was subject to a form of martial law. Troops flooded the area, many of whom were stationed at Gweedore Hotel, with the government paying handsomely for the accommodation, both for them and their horses.[105]

At the subsequent trial, the murder charge against McFadden was withdrawn and he pleaded guilty to obstructing the police, agreed to be

---

99 Total Abstinence Society statement, *Dublin Weekly News*, 28 Jan 1888.
100 *Irish Times*, 31 Jan 1888.
101 *Irish Times*, 20 April 1888.
102 *Freeman's Journal*, 16 May 1888.
103 'Dreadful occurrence at Gweedore', *Irish Times*, 4 Feb 1889.
104 Ó Gallchobhair (1975): 112-3.
105 *Belfast News-Letter*, 4 May 1889. McFadden (1889): 22.

bound over and walked free. The court's decision enraged the *Londonderry Sentinel*.[106] His fellow defendants, several of whom pleaded guilty to manslaughter, were less fortunate: four got jail sentences of five to ten years; one got two years; nine were given terms of six to two months; and one woman got three months' hard labour.[107] After his release, McFadden lobbied hard for the release of his jailed parishioners.[108] His campaign was helped by nationalist newspapers which cast the men as political prisoners.[109] The four men who had yet to complete their sentences were finally freed in December 1892.[110]

While they were serving their time McFadden's celebrity continued to grow. People travelled to Donegal from abroad just to meet him. Four women visitors from London who stayed at the Gweedore Hotel complained that it was not close enough to Derrybeg and it therefore meant they had to walk a long way to see McFadden, on whom, they remarked, 'the interest of the district is centred'.[111] Their arrival coincided with the publication of McFadden's pamphlet about 'the agrarian struggle in Gweedore' in which he lambasted Lord George as the 'pioneer' of 'felonious methods of property management'.[112]

He placed himself centre-stage in the fight against rack-renting landlords, happily indulging in illeism (referring to himself in the third person). He viewed Lord George's building works, such as the harbour at Bunbeg, as being 'for his own aggrandisement' rather than for the benefit for his tenants.[113] He lampooned his lordship's book by calling it 'Fictions from Gweedore', which Denis Holland had done more than a quarter of a century before. His main argument was that Lord George's motive for reforming the farming system was profit, although his questionable figures did not provide much, if any, proof. His barrage against the late landlord was extreme and, at times, surreal. At one point, he wrote of Hill having overseen a 'reign of terror'.[114]

McFadden was just as harsh on Olphert, accusing him of 'vindictiveness', of being 'amongst the most heartless and inhuman tyrants of his class',

---

106 *Londonderry Sentinel*, 31 Oct 1889.
107 Ó Gallchobhair (1975): 176. *Newry Telegraph*, 31 Oct 1889.
108 McFadden (2017), chapter 8.
109 *Derry Journal*, 4 Dec 1891.
110 'Release of the Gweedore prisoners', *Northern Whig*, 27 Dec 1892
111 VB 3: Entry signed Misses Lawrence, Glaze, MacDonnell and Irvine, 13 Sept 1889.
112 McFadden (1889): 5.
113 Ibid. 14.
114 Ibid. 48.

and of overseeing 'atrocious deeds' against his tenants.[115] Within weeks of McFadden's diatribes rolling off the *Derry Journal*'s presses, he was doing battle with Olphert over a new set of evictions in Falcarragh in the winter of 1890. McFadden's fame was at its zenith and he managed to arouse huge interest from politicians in London and Dublin for what became known as 'the Olphert clearances'. It resulted in a large party of sympathisers travelling from Dublin to observe an expected 143 evictions.[116] Among them were five MPs, several journalists and the then 23-year-old Maud Gonne, who was at the start of her journey from wealthy socialite to revolutionary.[117] She gave a speech to the crowd and then wrote to newspapers about what she witnessed.[118] McFadden, who also spoke, linked the names of Olphert and Hill as representatives of the evils of Irish landlordism.

Evictions, threats of evictions, and squabbles with McFadden took their toll on Hill and he eventually managed to have the estate placed into the receivership of the Court of Chancery.[119] This transformed non-payment of rent into contempt of court. Hill had washed his hands of his troubled legacy. In effect, Captain Hill – as with many landlords across the country – was evicted by his tenants. With him and his ilk went a political, economic and social system. Ascendancy was defeated. For the people freed from landlordism, however, a new and bitter conflict was about to begin: the struggle that Holland had worked towards throughout his shortened life, the struggle that Hill had never contemplated, the struggle for Irish nationhood.

---

115 Ibid. 85, 96, 99.
116 *Daily News* (London), *Northern Whig*, 12 Nov 1890; *Irish Times*, 13 No 1890
117 Ward (1990): 22-3.
118 *Nuneaton Advertiser*, 15 Nov 1890. Gonne was derided as a 'bird of evil omen' and accused of goading peasant 'dupes' into resisting eviction, *Londonderry Sentinel*, 11, 20 Nov 1890.
119 *Derry Journal*, 2 Oct 1894.

EPILOGUE

PENURY, OBSCURITY, PROSPERITY

Some family trees have beautiful leaves, and some have just a bunch of nuts …it is the nuts that make the tree worth shaking — Unknown

The Peer's descendants

Captain Arthur Hill, desperate for so long to turn his back on Donegal, sold Ballyare House in 1899, soon after the termination of his twenty-year stint as inspector of prisons.[1] He had been trying to sell the house for more than two years.[2] He also left Ireland behind, moving to England, to the village of Hothfield, near Ashford, Kent.[3] During the last years of Arthur's life, with his army pension proving inadequate to fund his lifestyle, he was obliged to borrow from his children.[4] He lived to witness the partial disengagement of Ireland from British rule, dying, aged 86, in 1923. His obituaries noted he was Jane Austen's great nephew.[5] His wife, Helen, was 89 when she died in 1935.

By selling Ballyare, Arthur rendered his unmarried sister, Cassandra, homeless. She had been a companion first to her step-mother, Louisa, and then to her aunt, Marianne. Louisa, who was 72 years old at Lord George's death did not enjoy the best of health, nor was she blessed with much money (although she was able to afford a couple of servants,

---

1 *Dublin Evening Post*, 28 Sept 1898.
2 *Dublin Daily Express*, 21 July 1897.
3 'Captain Hill, late of Ballyarr House, now at The Ashes, Hothfield', *Londonderry Sentinel*, 3 April 1900.
4 Davis (2021a): 59.
5 'A link with Jane Austen', *The Times*, 20 June 1923.

a maid and a cook).[6] For a while, she oversaw the breeding of cattle and pigs on Ballyare's acres, occasionally winning agricultural show prizes.[7] At the end of 1882, she auctioned off her stock and let out the land.[8] Lady George Hill's name regularly appeared in lists of donors to various good causes and as patron of charity bazaars.[9]

In 1884, they were joined at Ballyare by Louisa's sister, Marianne (May), who despite being three years older, had a much stronger constitution which enabled her to travel fairly frequently between Ireland and England. Ahead of one of May's visits to her relatives in Hampshire, Cassandra advertised in the impeccably Protestant *Belfast News-Letter* for a maid – who 'must be a member of Church of Ireland' – prepared to care for 'an elderly invalid' (Louisa).[10] A year later, Louisa died, aged 84, of a cerebral haemorrhage.[11] May lived on for a further six years, dying aged 94.[12] She was buried next to Louisa in Tully graveyard, on a hill overlooking Ballyare House.

Cassandra, much the most interesting of Lord George's children, devoted herself to good works in the community, especially on behalf of the local poor.[13] Due to her 'indefatigable exertions', a convalescent home for working class women and domestic servants was opened at Rathmullan, eliciting praise for her 'philanthropic motives'.[14] Fluent in Irish, she acted as teacher to the children of the tenantry. With little income, she sold eggs from her 'prize-bred chickens' to make ends meet.[15] She also painted. One of her pieces showed a young peasant girl holding an empty bowl. Entitled *No More Breakfast*, it was exhibited by the Irish Fine Art Society in Dublin and was said to be 'a work of much merit'.[16]

---

6 One of them, Nancy Ker, is buried in nearby Tully graveyard: 'For 38 years a faithful servant in Lord George Hill's family at Ballyare House'.

7 *Belfast News-Letter*, 10 Aug, 1881; 17 Aug, 1882.

8 *Derry Journal*, 18 Dec 1882; 9 Jan 1885; 21 Jan 1885.

9 *Derry Journal*, 23 Feb 1880; 5 Sept 1883; 27 August, 1884; 20 July 1885.

10 *Belfast News-Letter*, 5 May 1888.

11 Hillan (2011): 211. Death certificate, 29 July 1889 in death register No 7, 15 Donegal Ancestry, Ramelton. *Donegal Independent*, 10 Aug 1889; *The Times*, 3 Aug 1889. *Londonderry Sentinel*, 6 Aug 1889.

12 *Londonderry Sentinel*, 7 Dec 1895; *The Times*, 13 Dec 1895.

13 According to Gwynn (1909): 47, Cassandra 'laboured strenuously to promote among the peasantry [a] pleasant social life'.

14 *Londonderry Sentinel*, 16 June 1885; *Derry Journal*, 20 July 1885; *Derry Journal*, 21 Oct 1891.

15 *Londonderry Sentinel*, 3 April 1880; *Northern Whig*, 17 Aug 1882; *Derry Journal*, 26 March 1883.

16 *Irish Times*, 1 March 1883. Hillan (2018).

Most intriguing of all, given their political differences, was Cassandra's friendship with Charlotte Grace O'Brien. They were about the same age, both single, and born into a similar landed Protestant background.[17] But Charlotte's father was William Smith O'Brien who, as a Young Irelander, had been convicted of treason for his part in the 1848 rebellion. Although sentenced to death, he was transported instead to Van Diemen's Land. (One of those who sought his release was Denis Holland.)[18] After being pardoned, he returned to Ireland in 1856, taking no more part in politics. Charlotte, his youngest daughter, was a nationalist who supported Home Rule and therefore held views diametrically opposed to those of the unionist Cassandra. Yet, after being introduced by Charlotte's nephew, Stephen Gwynn, son of the rector of Ramelton, the two women became fast friends.[19] Charlotte wanted to overturn the old order; Cassandra wanted to stop the clock.[20] What they shared was a philanthropic commitment to down-trodden women. In Charlotte's case, it was manifested in her setting up a refuge for Irish women emigrants in New York.

So close was their friendship that, in the wake of Marianne's death, when Arthur put Ballyare up for sale, Charlotte offered Cassandra sanctuary in Dublin.[21] For the final years of her life, she lived in Charlotte's house, *Fáilte*, in Foxrock. Her half-brother, George Wandsbeck, joined her in 1900, the year before she died, aged 59, after a short illness.[22] According to her will, her effects were valued at £10,461 5s 6d.[23] George, said to have been a delicate child, studied law at Trinity College, Dublin, and was called to the London bar in 1876, with chambers in Lincoln's Inn.[24] Most of his work concerned the unglamorous duties of equity drafting and conveyancing.[25] He died ten years after his sister, still at Foxrock.[26] He was buried alongside Cassandra in Dublin's Deansgrange cemetery.

---

17 Charlotte converted to Catholicism in 1890: *Midland Tribune*, 26 April 1890; *Freeman's Journal*, 11 March 1891.
18 See Chapter 9.
19 Gwynn (1903 and 1909).
20 Gwynn (1909): 47. Hillan (2011): 225-6.
21 'Clearance sale at Ballyare House', *Derry Journal*, 27 Oct 1899.
22 She died on 16 Aug 1901. Hillan (2011): 227.
23 *National Archives of Ireland*, Calendars of wills 1901: 211.
24 Davis (2021a): 20. Hillan (2011): 227.
25 Men-at-the-Bar (1885) https://en.wikisource.org/wiki/Men-at-the-Bar/Hill,_George_Marcus_Wandsbeck.
26 He left £2,775 6s. *National Archives of Ireland*, Calendars of Wills, 1911: 262

Their brother, Augustus, was a civil servant who evidently prospered because, in retirement, he lived in London's Hanover Square, where his grandfather had spent much of his childhood.[27] He was also rich enough to be a director and investor in a Canadian mining company along with a distant cousin, George Edwyn Hill-Trevor.[28] Augustus joined the Artist Volunteer Corps, was a member of the Travellers' Club, and his hobby was said to have been collecting manuscripts.[29] His death was a tragic accident. In 1908, he was knocked down by a London taxi and died from his injuries, aged 69, at the Kent home of his brother, Arthur.[30]

Cassandra, George and Augustus were unmarried and childless. Their elder sister, Norah, had three children with Somerset Ward, whose activities as agent for his brother-in-law ended, as we have seen, in acrimony. He went on to act as land agent for Lord Clanmorris and also his own brothers, the fourth and fifth Viscounts Bangor, dying in 1912.[31]

The Wards lived in some style in Isle O'Valla House in Strangford, County Down. Norah died there in 1920, aged 84. Her eldest son, George Augustus Crosbie Ward, became a Royal Navy commander who was decorated for his service in the first world war. Their daughter, Norah Louisa Fanny, married the second Baron Dunleath (Eton, Oxford, major in the Royal Irish Rifles, and magistrate for County Down). Their second son, Charles Crosbie Ward, acted as executor for various members of the Hill family.

Arthur and his wife had seven children, four girls and three boys. The sons took a similar career path to their father and grandfather. The eldest, Arthur Fitzgerald Sandys Hill, joined the Royal Engineers, serving in India, Burma, Jordan and in France during the first world war. By his retirement, he was a lieutenant-colonel.[32] He inherited the Sandys title, making him the sixth baron, and with it came his great grandmother's impressive country house, Ombersley Court in Worcestershire.[33] At 47, he married his wealthy third cousin, 26-year-old Cynthia Trench-Gascoigne.

The second son, Sir Richard Augustus Sandys Hill, joined the Royal Navy and rose to the rank of vice-admiral. He fought in both the first

27 Registered at 89 Hanover Square, 1891 Census.
28 *London Evening Standard*, 29 May 1899.
29 Hillan (2011): 227.
30 *The Globe*, 18 Dec 1908; *Faversham Times & Mercury*, 26 Dec 1908.
31 *The Times*, 27 Dec 1912; *Newry Reporter*, 28 Dec 1912.
32 *Military List* 1941: officers on retired pay, 1390.
33 'Sandys of Ombersley: fragments of nine lives, no. 8', Davis (2021a).

and second world wars, briefly acting as an aide-de-camp to King George V. He did not marry.[34] The third, George Chenevix Hill, was an officer in the Duke of Edinburgh's Wiltshire Regiment and, later, the King's African Rifles, retiring, like his elder brother, as a lieutenant-colonel.[35] George married Patricia Wilmot Tufton, granddaughter of a baron and niece of an earl. He died, aged 76, in 1963.[36] One of Arthur's four daughters, Cicely, married into the same family: her husband was the Hon Sackville Philip Tufton. Madeline remained close to her Downshire ancestors by marrying Edward Sclater, agent for the sixth marquess's Hillsborough estate.[37] And the couple lived in grand style in Kilwarlin House. Mary married a Sussex landowner and gentleman farmer, Edgar Chippindale.[38] Dorothy did not marry.

So, it is fair to say that Lord George Hill's descendants took paths expected of them, paths that he would doubtless have admired.

The Press Man's descendants

Denis Holland's abandonment of his family and sad decline was, to an extent, mirrored in the obscurity of the generations that followed him. Nothing is known of his eldest son, possibly Eugene or Eugenius, born in 1859.[39] Nor, indeed, do we know the fate of his wife, Ellen. Holland's estrangement from her after 1863 meant that he had no discernible input into his sons' lives. It is certain that he could never have envisaged the trajectory taken by his second son, Gerald Edward, who was born three years before his father decamped to London.[40]

Gerald went on to enjoy an illustrious career as a senior British soldier, originally in the Royal Indian Marines. He also married into Dublin's high society. In 1896, the 'tall, good-looking' Commander Holland wed the 'beautiful and much admired' Mary Gray, daughter of Edmund Dwyer Gray, Parnellite MP and owner of the nationalist newspaper, the *Freeman's Journal*.[41] Holland would, at least, have liked that nationalistic, journalistic link.

---

34 Davis (20121a): 54-5. *The Times*, 8 July 1954.

35 *Warminster & Westbury Journal*, 1 Sept 1906; *The Sketch*, 21 Dec 1921; *The Times*, 16 Oct 1963. *Military List* 1941: officers on retired pay,1390.

36 *The Times*, 16 Oct 1963.

37 *Northern Whig*, 13 June 1917; *Belfast News-Letter*, 13 June 1917.

38 *The Times*, 2 Dec 1909. Emails from Jean Chippindale, 15, 16 March 2022.

39 *Freeman's Journal*, 10 May 1859; *Belfast News-Letter*, 12 May 1859; *The Irishman*, 14 May 1859.

40 *Freeman's Journal*, 22 Oct 1860; *The Irishman*, 27 Oct.

41 *Freeman's Journal*, 30 July 1896; *Derry Journal*, 28 Aug 1896.

Following his discharge from the marines, Gerald settled with his wife and three children in Holyhead, Wales, holding the post of marine superintendent for the London and North West railway.[42] Recalled by the army in the first world war, he was promoted to brigadier-general of the Royal Engineers, overseeing the movement of supplies in France, and was decorated on three occasions for his efforts.[43] In 1917, he was taken ill while working near the front line, repatriated, and died soon after in a Sussex hospital, aged 57.

All three of Gerald's children, Holland's grandchildren, were childless. The son, Bertram, followed his father into the army and was commissioned as a lieutenant in the Royal Engineers. He fought in France from 1914, got promoted to captain and was mentioned in dispatches.[44] But his wartime experiences contributed to psychological problems, and he died in 1942, aged 44, after a prolonged stay in a Northampton mental hospital. He did not marry. The eldest daughter, Lillian, married an actor, was divorced and did not remarry before her death in 1958.[45] Her sister, Evelyn, married a man convicted of embezzlement who later became a Royal Flying Corps officer. She died in 1977.[46] And that, sadly, was the termination of Denis Holland's direct line.

But we know just a little of Holland's journalist brother, known as John Callanan Holland. During his career, he worked for the *Limerick & Clare Examiner* and *Clonmel Chronicle*, and edited the *Drogheda Argus and Leinster Journal*.[47] Sometimes confused with Denis, on one occasion, many years after his brother's death, he wrote to a paper to correct the error.[48] His last years were spent in Clonmel, Tipperary where he died, aged 89, in 1921.[49]

The Priests' fate

Lord George's 'obnoxious' clerical opponent, the Rev John Doherty, maintained a close interest in Gweedore, and in Hill's affairs, following his reassignment in 1856 to Carrigart. There, he resolved to build a chapel and, unable to collect sufficient money locally, he was allowed to a take a fund-

42 https://holyheadstoriesofaport.com/2021/01/27/brigadier-general-gerald-edward-holland-cb-cmg-cie-dso-royal-engineers-1860-1917/.
43 Phillips (2016 and 2020).
44 *Western Mail*, 27 Jan 1915; *Irish Independent*, 27 June 1917.
45 *The Bystander,* 20 April 1927.
46 *Norwood News*, 31 March 1933, 7 April.
47 *Argus and Leinster Journal*, 18 Sept 1915; *Cork Daily Herald*, 2 March 1891.
48 *The Globe*, 21 June 1880.
49 *Daily News*, 24 Dec 1921.

raising trip to America, which lasted three years. On his return, he became parish priest in Donegal town, staying there until his death, aged 62, in 1881.

A supporter of the Land League, he was widely admired across the county for his letters to newspapers in which he was harshly critical of landlordism and of specific landlords. He was often billed as Father Doherty 'of Gweedore notoriety', or 'the guiding star of Donegal', and even 'the Parnell of the priesthood'.[50] His funeral was attended by a reputed four thousand people, including a host of fellow priests, among whom was James McFadden. Doherty had always been very supportive of his Gweedore successor.[51]

Like Doherty, but many years after him, James McFadden spent time in America on fund-raising duties. His mission was to collect money for the building of Letterkenny Cathedral. After his return, he was made parish priest of Inniskeel in south-west Donegal, where he spent seventeen largely uncontroversial years. He remained committed to nationalist politics, favouring Home Rule, and was passionate about the need to retain the Irish language.

A lengthy obituary in the *Derry Journal* recalled his 'wonderful fight against landlordism' on behalf of the people of Gweedore and Falcarragh.[52] 'No priest in Ireland has been so hated by the Ascendancy party', said an accompanying tribute. His authoritarianism was entirely overlooked, as has tended to be the case ever since. Canon McFadden died, aged 74, in April 1917.

Gweedore's transformation

Then, of course, there is Gweedore. After the eviction of the landlords came the turmoil of the Easter Rising, the Tan War (aka the War of Independence), the civil war and partition, which cut Donegal off from its neighbouring Ulster counties. It also effectively isolated Donegal from the other twenty-five counties. Following the formation of the Free State, there was only a slight improvement in circumstances for its residents. The local economy, based around knitting, produced little income. Hundreds of men, year after year, emigrated, most to Scotland, but also to England and America. One positive factor was the district's designation as part of the Gaeltacht due to the continuing prevalence of the Irish language. It attracted some investment which led to the creation of several factories,

---

50 *Derry Journal*, 26 March 1875; 22, 25 Nov 1881.

51 *Derry Journal*, 7 Feb 1881.

52 *Derry Journal*, 20 April 1917.

producing carpets, textiles, rubber, electronics, and cleaning agents. But they didn't last.[53] The development of Carrickfinn airport, offering 35-minute flights to Dublin, had only a marginal effect.

Even so, as I noted during my first visit to Bunbeg in 1990, the area was in the process of undergoing a dramatic transformation. Large modern houses and bungalows were springing up, largely funded by the repatriated earnings of people who had emigrated to Scotland and England. Many of them were delighted to return. In spite of its economic problems, Gweedore was exhibiting a pride in itself. It was also in the process of securing a reputation as the home of Irish culture, through its firm retention of the Irish language, its GAA sports success, and because of the popularity of traditional music, in which Gweedore bands such as Clannad and Altan, excelled. Now, there is not the slightest sign of destitution and, although his harbour and church survive, it is clear that Lord George would not recognise modern Gweedore.

As for his hotel, that fell into ruins. It was eventually replaced with a building now known as An Chúirt (and wrongly marketed as the restoration of a 'classical 18th century house'). It opened in 2001 and its owner for many years, the Doherty family, made much of its connection to Lord George.[54] Its current owners do not.

Ballyarr House

Finally, Ballyare (or Ballyarr) House. In 1899, Captain Hill sold it, for £4,000, to William Russell, a Presbyterian miller, who had been leasing the adjacent mill for seventeen years beforehand.[55] In the late 1960s, he and his family apparently abandoned the house to move into a cottage on the estate. The house was sold in 1974, along with the accompanying mill, to a former British soldier, Ian Smith, who was much decorated for his world war two exploits in the Balkans. He demolished one large wing and dispensed with several portions of land before selling the house and a few acres to a bank manager, Andy O'Loghlin, in 1981. It was eight years later that my wife and I bought it … only then to discover the previous existence of a landlord called Lord George Hill. Hence, this book.

---

53 *Irish Independent*, 4 Aug, 29 Sept, 19 Nov 2001.
54 *Sunday Tribune*, 15 July 2001.
55 *Derry Journal*, 3 Nov 1899.

Bibliography

Aalen, Frederick H.A. and Brody, Hugh, *Gola: Life and Last Days of an Island Community* (Cork: Mercier Press, 1969)

Almack, Edward, *The History of the 2nd Dragoons Royal Scots Greys* (2015 ebook https://www.gutenberg.org/files/49488/49488-h/49488-h.htm)

Anderson, J, 'The decay and breakup of the rundale system in the barony of Tyrhugh', *Donegal Annual*, vi, No 1 (1964) pp.1-43

Andrews, Ann, *Newspapers and Newsmakers: The Dublin Nationalist Press in the Mid-nineteenth Century* (Liverpool University Press, 2014)

Bardon, Jonathan, *A History of Ulster* (Belfast: Blackstaff Press, 1992)

Barry, John, *Hillsborough: a parish in the Ulster plantation* (Belfast: William Mullan & Son, 1965)

Bayne, Samuel G., *Derricks of Destiny* (id est Media, 2016)

Beattie, Seán, *Ireland in Old Photographs: Donegal* (The History Press, 2004)

Beckett, J. C., *The making of Modern Ireland 1603-1923* (London, 1966)

Bell, Thomas, 'The Reverend David Bell', *Clogher Record*, Vol. 6, No. 2 (1967 https://www.jstor.org/stable/27695597

Bennett, William, *Narrative of a Recent Journey of Six Weeks in Ireland in Connexion with the Subject of Supplying Small Seed to Some of the Remoter Districts* (London: Hatchard & Son, 1847)

Bigelow, Gordon, 'Ireland and the Colonial Critique of Political Economy,' in *Fiction, Famine, and the Rise of Economics in Victorian Britain and Ireland* (Cambridge, 2003)

Blaney, Roger, *Presbyterians and the Irish Language* (Ulster Historical Foundation, 1996)

Bowen, Lucey, 'James M'Carthy, Teacher, Publisher and Politician', *The Old Limerick Journal*, Vols. 46, Winter 2012, and 47, Winter 2013 http://www.limerickcity.ie/media/olj%202012%20p039%20to%20044.pdf and http://www.limerickcity.ie/media/olj%202013%20p011%20to%20016.pdf

Boyd, Andrew, *Holy War In Belfast* (Dublin: Anvil Books, 1969)

Brady, Ciaran, O'Dowd, Mary and Walker, Brian, eds. *Ulster: An Illustrated History* (London: Batsford, 1989)

Campbell, Patrick, *The Famine Years in North West Donegal*, 1845-1850 (Self-published, 2015)

Carlyle Society (2010), Occasional Papers No 23, University of Edinburgh, 2010-11 https://www.ed.ac.uk/files/atoms/files/carlyle_papers_no._23.pdf

Carlyle, Thomas, *Reminiscences of my Irish journey in 1849* (London, Sampson Low, Marston, Searle & Rivington, 1882) https://archive.org/details/reminiscencesofm82carl/page/248/mode/2up

Casey, Brian, 'The Decline and Fall of the Clancarty Estate, 1891-1923', *Journal of the Galway Archaeological and Historical Society*, Vol. 67, 2015

Clarke, Joseph Ignatius Constantine, 'An Interesting Letter', *The Pilot*, Vol 36/2, 11 Jan 1873

Clarke, Joseph Ignatius Constantine, *My Life and Memories* (New York: Dodd, Mead, 1925)

Comerford, R.V., *The Fenians in Context: Irish Politics and Society, 1848-82* (Dublin: Wolfhound Press, 1985)

Coogan, Tim Pat, *The Famine Plot: England's Role in Ireland's Greatest Tragedy* (London: Palgrave Macmillan, 2013)

Cooke-Trench, Thomas RF, *A Memoir of the Trench Family* (London: Spottiswoode 1897)

Cooper, Pamela, *A Cloud of Forgetting* (London: Quartet, 1993)

Coulter, Henry, *The West of Ireland: Its Existing Condition and Prospects* (Dublin: Hodges & Smith, 1862)

Cousens, S.H., 'Regional death rates in Ireland during the great famine, 1846-51', *Population Studies*, xiv, No 1, July 1960

Craik, Dinah Mulock (The Author of *John Halifax, Gentleman*) *An Unknown Country* (London: Macmillan, 1887)

Creevey, Thomas, *The Creevey Papers: A Selection from the Correspondence Diaries of the Late Thomas Creevey MP* (Forgotten Books, 2018)

Cregan, Donal F, 'An Irish Cavalier: Daniel O'Neill', *Studia Hibernica*, No. 3, 1963

Croker, John Wilson, *The Croker papers 1808-1857*, ed., Bernard Pool (London: Batsford, 1967)

Cross, Ira Brown (1931) *Frank Roney, Irish rebel and California Labor Leader: an autobiography* (California University Press, 1931) https://babel.hathitrust.org/cgi/pt?id=mdp.39015005788990

Crowley, John, Smyth, William J, and Murphy, Mike, eds, *Atlas of the Great Irish Famine* (Cork: Atrium Books, 2012)

Davis, Martin, *Arthur Marcus Cecil Hill, 3rd Baron Sandys, 1798-1863* (Ombersley Archive, June 2020a)

Davis, Martin, *Mary Marchioness of Downshire & Baroness Sandys, 1764-1836* (Ombersley Archive: July 2020b)

Davis, Martin, *Arthur Moyses William Hill, 2nd Baron Sandys of the 2nd creation, 1792-1860* (Ombersley Archive, Aug 2020c)

Davis, Martin (2020d), 'Capt ABGSH: Annotated journal entries', Private communication to author, 14 July 2020

Davis, Martin, *Arthur Fitzgerald Sandys Hill, 6th Baron Sandys* (Ombersley Archive, Feb 2021a)

Davis, Martin, *Augustus Frederick Arthur, 4th Baron Sandys of the 2nd creation, 1840-1904* (Ombersley Archive, April 2021b)

Davis, Martin, *Letters to Mary Marchioness of Downshire & Baroness Sandys, from the third Marquess of Downshire and Sir Philip Francis KCB* (Ombersley Archive, nd)

Davis, Richard, *The Young Ireland Movement* (Dublin: Gill & Macmillan, 1987)

De Beaumont, Gustave, *Ireland: Social, Political and Religious* (Harvard University Press, 2006)

Bourke, Marcus, *John O'Leary – A Study in Irish Separatism* (Tralee: Anvil Books: 1967)

De Burca, Marcus, 'Denis Holland 1826-1872', *Our Games, 1968 Annual of the GAA*

De Burca, Marcus, *The GAA - A History* (Dublin: 1980)

De Nie, Michael, Untitled review, *New Hibernia Review*, Summer 2008, Vol. 12, No. 2

Donovan, Dick, *Crime of the Century: Being the Life Story of Richard Pigott* (London: John Young, 1904)

Dorian, Hugh, *The Outer Edge of Ulster: A Memoir of Social Life in Nineteenth-Century Donegal*, ed. Breandán Mac Suibhne and David Dickson (Dublin, 2001)

Evans, Estyn, *Irish Folk Ways* (London: Routledge and Kegan Paul, 1957)

Farrell, Sean, *Rituals and Riots: Sectarian Violence and Political Culture in Ulster, 1784-1886* (Kentucky: University Press, 2000)

Farrell, Stephen, 'Hill, Lord George Augusta (1801 1879)', *The History of Parliament*, nd https://www.historyofparliamentonline.org/volume/1820-1832/member/hill-lord-george-1801-1879

Dun, Finlay, *Landlords and Tenants in Ireland* (London: Longmans Green, 1881)

Fitzpatrick, Rory, *God's Frontiersmen: The Scots-Irish Epic* (London: Weidenfeld and Nicolson, 1989)

Flood, Henry, *The speech and proposition pf the Right Hon. Henry Flood, in the House of Commons of Great Britain, Thursday March 4th, 1790, on a reform of the representation in Parliament* (HardPress, 2018, reprint of 1790 original)

Foster, R.F. (ed), *The Oxford Illustrated History of Ireland* (Oxford University Press, 1989)

Foster, R.F., *Modern Ireland, 1600-1972* (Allen Lane, 1988)

Foster, Thomas Campbell, *Letters on the Condition of the People of Ireland* (London: Chapman & Hall, 1846)

Foulkes, Nick, *Dancing into Battle* (London: Weidenfeld & Nicolson, 2006)

Fox, Robin, *The Tory Islanders: A People of the Celtic Fringe* (University of Notre Dame Press, 1995)

Freeman, T.W., *Ireland: A General and Regional Geography* (London: Methuen, 2nd edn, 1959)

Freeman, TW., *Pre-Famine Ireland: A Study in Historical Geography* (Manchester University Press, 1957)

Frost, Ginger S., *Living in Sin: Cohabiting as Husband and Wife in Nineteenth-Century England*, (Manchester University Press, 2008)

Gallagher, Thomas, *Paddy's Lament, Ireland 1846-1847: Prelude to Hatred* (US: Harcourt Brace Jovanovich, 1982)

Geary, Laurence M., *Plan of Campaign, 1886–1891* (Cork University Press, 1986)

Gibbons, Stephen Randolph., *Captain Rock, Night Errant: The Threatening Letters of Pre-famine Ireland, 1801-45* (Dublin: Four Courts Press, 2004)

Glenbervie, Sylvester Douglas, *The Diaries of Sylvester Douglas (Lord Glenbervie)* Vols. 1 & 2, ed., Francis Bickley (Boston: Houghton Mifflin, 1928)

Green, E.R.R., 'A Catalogue of the Estate Maps, etc., in the Downshire Office, Hillsborough, Co. Down *Ulster Journal of Archaeology*, 1949, Third Series, Vol. 12

Greer, Roy H., *Con O'Neill, Last Gaelic Lord of Upper Clannaboy* (Belfast: White Row: 2019)

Greville, Charles C. F., *The Greville Memoirs: A Journal of the Reigns of King George IV and King William IV*, Vol 1, ed, Henry Reeve (London: Longmans Green, 1874) http://www.gutenberg.org/files/25700/25700-h/25700-h.htm

Grousset, Paschal, *Ireland's Disease: The English in Ireland 1887* (Belfast: Blackstaff Press, 1986)

Gwynn, Stephen, *Highways and Byways in Donegal and Antrim* (London: Macmillan, 1903) https://archive.org/stream/highwaysandbyway00gwyniala/highwaysandbyway00gwyniala_djvu.txt

Gwynn, Stephen, *Charlotte Grace O'Brien* (Dublin: Maunsel, 1909)

Hamilton, John, *Sixty Years' Experience as an Irish Landlord: Memoirs of John Hamilton, D. L. Of St. Ernan's, Donegal* (London: reprint by Forgotten Books, 2017)

Hart, E., *Cottage industries: and what they can do for Ireland. Being a verbatim report of an address given by Mrs Ernest Hart at the Club House, Bedford Park*, 30 May, 1885 (London: Smith, Elder)

Herity, Michael, 'John O'Donovan's Last Illness', *The Journal of the Royal Society of Antiquaries of Ireland* Vol. 137, 2007

Hibbert, Christopher, *George IV: Regent and King* (London: Penguin, 1975)

Hill, Charlotte and Mary, *Journal of Two Goseys*, Vols 1-4, ed: Martin Davis (Ombersley Archive, nd)

Hill, Lord George Augusta, *Facts from Gweedore*

1st edition (1845) Dublin: Philip Dixon Hardy & Sons

2nd edition (1846) Dublin: Philip Dixon Hardy & Sons

3rd edition (1854) Dublin: Philip Dixon Hardy & Sons; London: Hatchards https://www.jstor.org/stable/pdf/community.29822515.pdf

4th edition (1868) Dublin: Hodges, Smith & Foster www.jstor.org/stable/10.2307/60217315

5th edition (1887) London: Hatchards. Facsimile reprint, Queen's University of Belfast, 1971 www.jstor.org/stable/pdf/60217301.pdf

Hillan, Sophia, *May, Lou & Cass: Jane Austen's nieces in Ireland* (Belfast: Blackstaff Press, 2011)

Hillan, Sophia, 'Daughter of the house: Cassandra Hill, Jane Austen's Irish great-niece,' *Irish Times*, 19 December 2018 https://www.irishtimes.com/culture/books/daughter-of-the-house-cassandra-hill-jane-austen-s-irish-great-niece-1.3735343

Hillard, George S, ed., *Life, letters and journals of George Ticknor* (London: Sampson Low, Marston, Searle, & Rivington, 1876)

Hobsbawm, Eric, 'Peasants and politics', *Journal of Peasant Studies*, 1, No 1 (1973) pp 3-22

Holan, Mark, Irish-American Blog (2018), https://www.markholan.org/archives/tag/lord-george-hill

Holland, Denis, *The Landlord in Donegal: pictures from the wilds.* (Belfast, 1856–1863) 2nd ed Printed at the *Ulsterman* Office, nd [c1858]

Holmes, Janice, 'The Role of Open-Air Preaching in the Belfast Riots of 1857', *Proceedings of the Royal Irish Academy: Archaeology, Culture, History, Literature*, Vol. 102C, No. 3 (2002)

Hurlbert, William Henry, *Ireland Under Coercion: The Diary of an American* (1888, reprint HardPress, 2016)

Hyde, H.M., *The Rise of Castlereagh* (London: Macmillan, 1933)

James, Kevin J., 'The Little Big House at Gweedore: inscribing sociality and space in north-west Ireland, 1842–1859', *Irish Geography*, 2012, Vol.45/3

Joule, Benjamin St John Baptist, *A Letter to Mr James H. Tuke: An Answer to the Statements made by him in his Pamphlet, Irish Distress and its Remedies* (London: Simpkin Marshall, 1881) Cf. https://www-jstor-org.ezproxy2.londonlibrary.co.uk/stable/pdf/60226790.pdf

Jupp, Peter J, 'County Down elections, 1783–1831', *Irish Historical Studies*, Vol. 18 (September 1972)

Kelly, Matthew, 'Irish nationalist opinion and the British empire in the 1850s and 1860s', *Past & Present*, No. 204 (Oxford University Press, 2009)

Kennedy, Brian A, 'Tenant Right before 1870', in Moody, T.W. and Beckett, J.C. eds., *Ulster since 1800: a political and economic survey* (London: BBC, 1955)

Kennedy, David, 'A Plan for Irish Agriculture', *Irish Ecclesiastical Record*, November 1944

Kennedy, Liam, and Ollerenshaw, Philip, (eds), *An Economic History of Ulster, 1820-1939* (Manchester University Press, 1985)

Kinealy, Christine, *This Great Calamity: The Irish Famine 1845-52* (Dublin: Gill and Macmillan, 1994)

Kinealy, Christine, *A Death-Dealing Famine: The Great Hunger in Ireland* (London: Pluto Press, 1997)

Kinealy, Christine, and Trevor Parkhill, *The Famine in Ulster: The Regional Impact* (Belfast: Ulster Historical Foundation, 1997)

Kinealy, Christine, 'Private Donations to Ireland during An Gorta Mór', *Journal of the Armagh Diocesan Historical Society*, Vol. 17/ 2, 1998

Kinealy, Christine, *Charity and the Great Hunger in Ireland: The Kindness of Strangers* (London: Bloomsbury, 2013)

Kingon, Suzanne T, 'Ulster opposition to Catholic emancipation, 1828–1829', *Irish Historical Studies*, Vol. 34, No 134, November 2004

Lavelle, Patrick, *The Irish Landlord since the Revolution* (Dublin: W.B. Kelly, 1870)

Le Faye, Deirdre, (1986) 'Fanny Knight's Diaries: Jane Austen through her niece's eyes', *Journal of the Jane Austen Society of North America*, Persuasions Occasional Papers No2, 1986 http://www.jasna.org/persuasions/printed/opno2/le-faye.pdf

Legg, Marie-Louise, (1999) *Newspapers and nationalism: the Irish provincial press 1850–1892* (Dublin: Four Courts Press, 1999)

Light, Alexander Whalley, *A Plan for the Amelioration of the Condition of the Poor of the United Kingdom (more particularly Ireland)* (London: John Brooks, 1830)

Lloyd, David, 'The Indigent Sublime: Spectres of Irish Hunger', California: *Representations*, Vol. 92, No. 1, Fall 2005

Lloyd, David, 'The Clachan, and the Chartists: Irish Models for Feargus O'Connor's Land Plan', *The Irish Review*, No 47, Winter 2013 (Cork University Press)

Lynch, Patrick, and Vaizey, John, *Guinness's Brewery in the Irish Economy, 1759-1876* (Cambridge University Press, 1960)

Maguire, Edward, *A History of the Diocese of Raphoe* Vol. 1 (Dublin: Browne & Nolan, 1920)

Maguire, W.A., *The Downshire Estates in Ireland, 1801-1845: the management of Irish landed estates in the early nineteenth century* (Oxford: Clarendon Press. 1972)

Maguire, W.A., (ed.). *Letters of a Great Irish Landlord: a Selection from the Estate Correspondence of the Third Marquess of Downshire, 1809-1845*. (Belfast: H.M.S.O. 1974). pp.189

MacArthur, C.W.P., 'Authorship of Facts from Gweedore', *Donegal Annual*, 2001

McCall, Hugh, *The house of Downshire: A Sketch of its History from 1600 to 1868* (Belfast: Archer & Sons, 1881)

Mac Cnáimhsí, Breandán, 'North-West Donegal after the Great Famine', *Donegal Annual*, No 2 (1970)

Mac Cnáimhsí, Breandán, 'Arranmore in the Irish famine 1846-48', *Donegal Annual*, x, No 3 (1973)

McCourt, Desmond, 'The Rundale System in Donegal: Its Distribution and Decline', *Donegal Annual*, 1954-55

McCourt, Desmond, 'Infield and Outfield in Ireland', *The Economic History Review*, Vol. 7, No. 3 (1955)

MacDonagh, J.C.T., 'Shore Dwellers and Sandhill Settlements of Co. Donegal', *Donegal Annual*, 1950

McFadden, James, *The Present and the Past of the Agrarian Struggle in Gweedore: with Letters on Railway Extension in Donegal* (Derry Journal: 1889) https://www.jstor.org/stable/60245482

McFadden, Martin, *Canon James McFadden: The Patriot Priest of Gweedore* (Self-published, 2017)

McGeady, Paul, *A Short History of Gaoth Dobhair* (Self-published, 1998)

MacKnight, James, *The Ulster Tenant Right: An Original Grant from the English Crown* (Dublin: James McGlashan, 1848)

McLaughlin, Gerry, *Cloughaneely: Myth and Fact* (Dublin: Johnswood Press, 2002)

McLaughlin, Jim and Beattie, Seán, eds., *An Historical, Environmental and Cultural Atlas of County Donegal* (Cork University Press, 2013)

MacLoingsigh, Peadar, 'Rural Villages and the Rundale System', *Donegal Annual*, 1948

McNicholas, Cornelius Anthony, 'Faith, Fatherland and the Politics of Exile: The Irish Press in Mid-Victorian England', PhD thesis, University of Westminster, December 2000

McNicholas, Anthony, *Politics, Religion and the Press: Irish Journalism in Mid-Victorian England* (New York: Peter Lang, 2007a)

McNicholas, Anthony, 'Rebels at Heart: The National Brotherhood of St Patrick and the Irish Liberator', *Media History*, Vol 13/1, (2007b)

Mac Suibhne, Breandán, *The End of Outrage: Post-Famine Adjustment in Rural Ireland* (Oxford University Press, 2017)

Mac Suibhne, Breandán, 'Agrarian improvement and social unrest: Lord George Hill and the Gaoth Dobhair Sheep War, 1856-1860', in Nolan, Ronayne etc, 1995

Mac Suibhne, Breandán, 'Bastard Ribbonism: The Molly Maguires, the Uneven Failure of Entitlement and the Politics of Post-Famine Adjustment', in Delaney, Enda and Mac Suibhne, Breandan, eds, *Ireland's Great Famine and Popular Politics* (London: Routledge, 2015)

Mac Suibhne, Breandán and Martin, Amy, 'Fenians in the Frame: Photographing Irish Political Prisoners, 1865-68', *Field Day Review*, Vol. 1 (2005)

Malcomson, A.P.W., 'Absenteeism in eighteenth century Ireland', *Irish Economic and Social History*, vol. 1 (1974) (Belfast: Ulster Historical Foundation, 2006)

Malcomson, A.P.W., 'The Gentle Leviathan', in McCracken, J.L. and Roebuck, Peter, *Plantation to Partition* (Blackstaff Press, 1981)

Malcomson, A.P.W., *The pursuit of the heiress: aristocratic marriage in Ireland, 1750–1820* (Belfast: Ulster Historical Foundation, 1982)

Malcomson, A.P.W., *Virtues of a Wicked Earl: The Life and Legend of William Sydney Clements, 3rd Earl of Leitrim* (Dublin: Four Courts Press, 2008)

Malcomson, A.P.W., 'The Clements Archive', Irish Manuscripts Commission, 2010 https://www.irishmanuscripts.ie/product/the-clements-archive/

Massingham, H.W., *The Gweedore Hunt: A Story of English Justice in Ireland* (London: Fisher Unwin, 1889) https://www-jstor-org.ezproxy2.londonlibrary.co.uk/stable/pdf/60214295.pdf

Massingham, H.W., *A selection from writings of HWM Massingham* (London: Jonathan Cape, 1925)

Maume, Patrick, entry on Denis Holland, *Dictionary of Irish Biography* (2009)

Mokyr, J., *Why Ireland Starved: A Quantitative and Analytical History of the Irish Economy, 1800-1850* (London: Allen & Unwin, 1983)

Morris, R.J., 'Reading the riot commission: Belfast, 1857', *Irish Historical Studies*, Vol 43, No 164 (Cambridge: November 2019)

Morrow, John, Carlyle, 'Thomas, "Young Ireland" and the "Condition of Ireland Question"', *The Historical Journal*, Vol. 51, No. 3 Cambridge University Press, September 2008

Mortimer, Ian, *The Time Traveller's Guide to Regency Britain* (London: Random House, 2020)

Murphy, Desmond, *Derry, Donegal and Modern Ulster 1790-1921* (Londonderry: Aileach Press, 1981)

Nicholls, George, *Poor Laws Ireland: Three Reports* (London: Clowes & Sons, 1838)

Nicholson, Asenath, *Annals of the Famine in Ireland in 1847, 1848 and 1849* (New York: E. French, 1851. Reprint, Belfast: Books Ulster, 2017)

Nicholson, Asenath, *Lights & Shades of Ireland* (London: Charles Gilpin, 1850)

Nolan, William, Ronayne, Liam, Dunlevy, Máiread, eds, *Donegal History & Society: Interdisciplinary essays on the History of an Irish County* (Geography Publications, 1995)

O'Boyle, Edward J, 'Classical economics and the Great Irish Famine: A study in limits", in *Forum for Social Economics* (September 2006)

O'Brien, Richard Barry, *The Life of Lord Russell of Killowen* (London: Smith, Elder, 1902)

O'Brien, W.P., *The Great Famine in Ireland* (London: Downey, 1896)

O'Connor, James, *Recollections of Richard Pigott* (Dublin: MH Gill, 1889)

O'Donoghue, D. H., *The poets of Ireland; a biographical and bibliographical dictionary of Irish writers of English verse* (Dublin: Hodges, Figgis, 1912)

O'Donoghue, Patrick, 'Opposition to the Tithe Payments', *Studia Hibernica*, No 6 (1966)

Ó Gallchobhair, Proinnsias, *History of Landlordism in Donegal* (Ballyshannon: Donegal Democrat, reissue 1975)

O'Hagan, John (Slieve Gullion), 'Ulster in the Summer of 1845', *The Irish Monthly*, Vol. 41/No. 481 (July 1913)

Oldfield, T.H.B., *The representative history of Great Britain and Ireland*, vol. 6 (1816)

O'Leary, John, *Recollections of Fenians and Fenianism* (2 Vols, London: Downey, 1896)

O'Sullivan, Thomas Francis, *The Young Irelanders* (Tralee: The Kerryman, 1944)

O'Sullivan, Tim, Names extracted from Commons Select Committee 'Report on Destitution alleged to exist in the Gweedore and Cloughaneely District in the County of Donegal', 2 July 1858 (House of Commons Sessional papers, 1857-58, Vol. XIII) http://donegalgenealogy.com/minute1.htm

Pares, Richard, *King George III and the Politicians* (Oxford: Clarendon Press, 1953)

Percival, John, *The Great Famine: Ireland's Potato Famine 1845-51* (BBC Books, 1995)

Perraud, Adolphe, *Ireland in 1862* (Dublin: James Duffy, 1863)

Phillips, Christopher, 'Logistics and the BEF', *British Journal for Military History*, 2016

Phillips, Christopher, *Civilian Specialists at War: Britain's Transport Experts and the First World War* (University of London Press, 2020)

Pichot, Amédée, *L'Irlande et le pays de Galles: esquisses de voyages, d'économie, Vol 1*, chapter 21, "Un episode d'économie politique et de civilisation agricole: Lord George Hill à Gweedore." (Paris, 1850)

Pigott, Richard, *Personal Recollections of an Irish National Journalist* (Dublin: Hodges, Figgis, 1882)

Pitt Kennedy, John, *Instruct; Employ; Don't Hang Them: or Ireland Tranquilized without Soldiers and Enriched without English Capital* (first published 1835; reprint Monana: Kessinger Publishing, 2010)

Pitt Kennedy, John, 'Digest of evidence taken before Her Majesty's Commissioners of inquiry into the state of the law and practice in respect to the occupation of land in Ireland', (Dublin: Alexander Thom, 1847)

Reilly, Ciarán J, *Edenderry 1820-1920: Popular Politics and Downshire Rule* (THP Ireland, 2007)

Rummel, Dale F, 'Research into Gallagher family', unpublished. North Dakota, November 2013. Courtesy of Michael McClafferty

Rush, Richard, *Memoranda of a Residence at the Court in London* (London: Hamilton, Adams, 1872)

Scott, James C, *Weapons of the Weak: Everyday Forms of Peasant Resistance* (Yale University Press, 1987)

Shaw Lefevre, George, *Peel and O'Connell: A Review of the Irish Policy of Parliament from the Act of Union to the Death of Sir Robert Peel* (London: Kegan Paul Trench, 1887)

Sitwell, Osbert, and Barton, Margaret, *Brighton* (Faber & Faber, 1938)

Smith, E.A., *George IV* (Yale University Press, 1999)

Society of Friends, *Transactions of the Central Famine Relief Committee of the Society of Friends during the famine in Ireland in 1846 and 1947* (Dublin, 1852)

Somerville-Large, Peter, *The Irish Country House: A Social History* (London: Sinclair-Stevenson, 1995)

Southey, Robert, *Letters from England* (London: Longman, Hurst, Rees and Orme, 1807)

Sullivan, T.F., *The Young Irelanders* (Tralee: Kerryman, 1944)

Symes, Edmond P., 'Sir James Dombrain and the Coastguard', *Dublin Historical Record*, Vol. 56, No. 1 (Spring, 2003)

Thompson, FML, 'Review of W. A. Maguire, *Letters of a Great Irish Landlord: a Selection from the Estate Correspondence of the Third Marquess of Downshire, 1809-1845*', *Irish Economic and Social History*, Vol. 2 (Sage, 1975)

Tillyard, Stella, *Citizen Lord: Edward Fitzgerald, 1763-1798* (London: Chatto & Windus, 1997)

Trevelyan, Charles, *The Irish Crisis* (London: Longman, Brown, Green and Longmans, 1848)

Tuke, James Hack, 'Society of Friends Report on the Famine in Co Donegal: Extracts from James H Tuke's report in December 1846', *Donegal Annual*, 1973

Tuke, James Hack, *Narrative of 2nd, 3rd and 4th Weeks of W. Forster's Journey journey in the distressed districts of Ireland* (York, 1847)

Tuke, James Hack and Fry, Edward, *James Hack Tuke: A Memoir* (Ulan Press, 2012)

Tuke, James Hack, *Irish Distress and its Remedies: A Visit to Donegal and Connaught in the Spring of 1880* (London: W. Ridgway, 1880)

Vaughan, W.E., *Landlords and Tenants in Ireland 1848-1904* (Dundalk: Dundalgan Press, revised ed., 1994)

Vaughan, W.E., *Sin, Sheep and Scotsmen: John George Adair and the Derryveagh evictions, 1861* (Belfast: Appletree Press, 1983)

Vaughan, W.E., *A New History of Ireland: Volume V: Ireland under the Union, I: 1801-1870* (Oxford: Clarendon Press, 1990)

Vaughan, W.E., *Landlords and Tenants in mid-Victorian Ireland 1836-1914* (Oxford: Clarendon Press, 1994)

Von Raumer, Friedrich, *England in 1835; being a series of letters written to friends in Germany during a residence in London and excursions into the provinces* (London: John Murray, 1836)

Wall, Maureen, 'County Donegal in 1845: Excerpts from the journal of John O'Hagan, giving an account of a tour in Ulster in the summer of 1845', *Donegal Annual,* 1970

Ward, Margaret, *Maud Gonne: A Life* (London: Pandora, 1990)

Wilson, Deborah, *Women, marriage and property in wealthy landed families in Ireland* (Manchester University Press, 2005)

Woodham-Smith, Cecil, *The Great Hunger* (US: Old Town Books, 1962)

Woods, C.J., 'Samuel Turner's information on the United Irishmen, 1797-8', Woods, C.J., *Analecta Hibernica*, No. 42, 2011

Miscellaneous other publications/sources

Correspondence Relating to the Measures for Relief of Distress in Ireland (Commissariat Series, Second Part, January-March 1847) http://sarkoups.free.fr/relief1847.pdf

Destitution: House of Commons Select Committee, 'Report on Destitution alleged to exist in the Gweedore and Cloughaneely District in the County of Donegal', 2 July 1858 (House of Commons Sessional papers, 1857-58) https://archive.org/stream/op1247997-1001/op1247997-1001_djvu.txt

Famine Relief Commission Papers 1845-47, RLFC3/2/7/12 National Archives of Ireland Gweedore Hotel visitors' book, 1 (1842-59) https://www.donegalcoco.ie/media/donegal-countyc/archives/pdfs/P46_1_Gweedore_Hotel_Visitors_Books_optimised.pdf

Gweedore Hotel visitors' book, 2 (1856-74) https://www.donegalcoco.ie/media/donegal-countyc/archives/pdfs/Gweedore%20hotel%20book%202.pdf

[These books are held by Donegal County Council. A third book is held by a former owner of An Chúirt, Patricia Doherty.]

LGH's Memorandum Book (dated 1859) PRONI D3054/3/1/2

Famine Relief Commission Papers 1845-47, RLFC3/2/7/12 National Archives of Ireland

Report of the Commissioners of Inquiry into the origin and character of the riots in Belfast in July and September 1857 (HM Stationery Office, 1 Jan 1858)

RTÉ documentary, "His Life and Fortune to Civilize Gweedore", first broadcast 4 May 1975, repeated 27 May 2014 https://www.rte.ie/radio1/doconone/2014/0527/647659-radio-documentary-gweedore-george-hill-donegal/*Marriage*: First Report of the Commission Appointed to Inquire into the State and Operation of the Law of Marriage as Relating to the Prohibited Degrees of Affinity, and to Marriages Solemnized Abroad or in the British Colonies. (London: Clowes, 1848. Shannon: Irish UP, 1969)

Index